Dynamics of Consciousness

Dynamics of Consciousness

The Trichotomy of Mind, Body and Consciousness

Shivendra Vikram Singh

PRINTWORLD
Publishers of Indian Traditions

Cataloging in Publication Data — DK
[Courtesy: D.K. Agencies (P) Ltd. <docinfo@dkagencies.com>]

Singh, Shivendra Vikram, 1994- **author.**
Dynamics of consciousness : the trichotomy of mind, body and consciousness / Shivendra Vikram Singh.
pages cm
Includes bibliographical references and index.
ISBN 9788124612828 (HB)

1. Dualism. 2. Consciousness. 3. Mind and body. 4. Hindu philosophy. I. Title.

LCC B812.S56 2025 | DDC 147.4 23

ISBN 978-81-246-1282-8
First published in India in 2025

Printed and published by:
D.K. Printworld (P) Ltd.
Regd. Office: "Vedaśrī", F-395, Sudarshan Park
ESI Hospital Metro Station, New Delhi - 110015
Phones: (011) 4172 2626, 98713 94815
e-mail: indology@dkprintworld.com
Website: www.dkprintworld.com

Dedicated to

Dr Grace Darling
Dr Alok Bajpai
and
Professor Devendra Nath Tiwari

Foreword

What is consciousness? Ask any motley group of neuroscientists, cognitive scientists or physicists to define consciousness and we will have a lot of patchy definitions. Any attempt to elaborate it creates further confusion. Six decades of research has focused on placing various processes and parts of consciousness in the human brain. A few theories have tried to integrate them, while others have placed consciousness outside the biological substrate.

This quest is not new though. Ancient thought from Upaniṣads to Greeks, the Buddha to medieval poetry, West to East philosophy has kept consciousness as its leitmotif. Consciousness became the thread to unite and explore life, death and the meaning of human existence from the physical to the cosmic. Spiritual practices talk about raising consciousness but what does it mean? It remains an experiential subjective state rather than an objective state.

The attempts to understand the enigma called life mind and brain inadvertently bring in this incomplete cloud called consciousness that wraps all explanations.

This attempt to delve into the dynamics of consciousness is both bold and unique, in approach and scope. Dr Shivendra has built the story of consciousness from first principles, philosophy to neuroscience and integrated it well.

This book should serve as a guiding light for future research and understanding the complexity called consciousness.

Alok Bajpai
Psychiatrist

Preface

THIS book is a culmination of my attempt to understand myself. I was plagued by mental health issues for quite some time. Various problems arose repeating significant distress. I was then introduced to Dr Alok Bajpai whom I now consider as my *guru*. He gave my malady a different direction. I was fascinated by the fact that how certain medication could alter my way of thinking. Dr Alok guided me towards a research statement. This led me to explore the "hard problem of Consciousness". I then took his lectures on the brain and how brain creates the mind. I was so captivated by the problem that I left my IAS coaching and joined research at Banaras Hindu University. The institute is a pillar of education in all fields of knowledge. There I met my guide and my mentor Dr Grace Darling. She was such a pillar of support in my life and my research that I can never repay the debt all through my entire life. Professor Devendranath Tiwari, who always gave suggestions to improve my thesis, showered his love *immensely* on me.

This book is a culmination of my struggle with my mental health issues and a desire to understand myself better. In philosophy, the mind-body problem is a fundamental dilemma. The stems from the concept that there are two distinct domains or basic categories of substance which stand metaphysically separate. The problem of dualism main issue is divided into two camps: substance dualism and property dualism. Both dualism and monism may be accurate, necessitating a philosophical examination. The ontological mind-body problem is initially addressed in Sāṁkhya philosophy, which resolves the issue through *prakr̥ti* (matter) and *puruṣa* (energy) (consciousness).

According to dualism, the mind is irreducible to a simple physical entity like the brain. An alternative set of solutions comes in the form of specific philosophical commitments that may be classified as monism with two subcategories: physicalism and anti-physicalism. Physicalists hold that the mind is not a distinct entity from the rest of the physical universe — for many, it is simply the brain. The brilliance of Indian, specifically orthodox Indian philosophical thinking, is that it is on a par with modern understanding regardless of its age. Many of our tradition's cognitive and psychological issues have paved the way for new concepts and theories. The Advaita Vedānta school of Indian philosophy advocates a three-dimensional unity of consciousness: absolute, empirical and illusory. Existing quantum theories, particularly those proposed by Buddhism and Advaita Vedānta, are addressing old metaphysical disputes.

Consciousness, the intangible part of human experience, has replaced the human soul. Neurobiological processes in the brain, higher-level brain features, are responsible for all of our "mental life". In spite of our progress in understanding human experience, the problem remains unresolved, and we face new challenges daily. We still do not know how the brain generates awareness, and the mystery will persist until we find a scientific explanation. One of the most evident realities is the presence of consciousness, although it appears to be buried in secret. The aim is to see consciousness as a biological phenomenon, similar to breathing or photosynthesis. However, we all have this inner subjective qualitative feeling behind the veil of physical phenomenon. This is the essence of the enigma. The present debate on consciousness is diverse, comprising contributions from philosophy, psychology, computer science, physics and medical sciences. Some criticize René Descartes, claiming that we now know more about the brain, but one truth cannot be denied: consciousness exists.

Given the multidisciplinary nature of the research and the wide range of questions involved, it is critical to acknowledge relevant research questions, which the book trics to address. In addition, the thesis recognizes the imperative for a more comprehensive overview of the problem. Therefore, it uses critical analysis of various philosophical and scientific models of consciousness and the historical method for literature review. It also attempts to fuse the commonalities of different theories by mapping the common points of agreement.

The book seeks to investigate the case for an integrated approach to consciousness by mapping philosophical understandings of consciousness with several famous scientific theories while laying the groundwork for a psycho-philosophical model capable of predicting real-life scenarios. It also analyses how different consciousness theories attempt to fill gaps in explanations and explore the first-person subjective experience, commonly known as qualia. The emphasis here is not on third-person scientific objectivity but first person introspection because objectivity was never the intention in Indian models. Finally, this book investigates a comparative account of modern understanding of the mind-body problem, by focusing on the ontological question of the emergence of phenomenal consciousness.

Contents

Acknowledgements

I HAVE no words to express my gratitude for Dr Alok Bajpai's invaluable assistance (Neuroscientist and Consultant Psychiatrist, IIT-Kanpur). He has served as a confidante, philosopher, mentor and psychiatrist in the fragmented diaspora which I call life. He has been a cornerstone in my life and this research. I cannot thank him enough for his faith in me and engaging me in numerous topics and activities that I enjoy, such as poetry, film and music, apart from core academics. Furthermore, I cannot thank him enough for being so passionate about my life and career growth while still serving as my mirror and, most importantly, standing by my side amid my mental health struggles.

I am deeply grateful to the Indian Council of Philosophical Research (ICPR) for granting me a Junior Research Fellowship. Without the fellowship, completing this book would have been really difficult, and self-education in neuroscience, psychiatry, and psychology, both Indian and Western, would not have been possible with a clear head and total enthusiasm. I am particularly grateful to Dr Grace Darling for acting as my supervisor and to all of my Philosophy and Religion Department colleagues who helped create a friendly and exciting environment for philosophical study and conversation.

Professors D.N. Tiwari, S.P. Pandey, M.R. Mehta, Ananda Mishra, Sachchidanand Mishra, Dr Baleshwar Prasad Yadav from my department, and Dr Nirmalya Guha, IIT-BHU and Dr Arvind Jaiswal were instrumental in the development of my research. I would also like to thank Professors Galen Strawson, David Chalmers and Sthaneshwar Timalsina for their kind interaction. In addition, I am grateful to Professors Braj Bhushan Sharma (IIT-KANPUR) and V. Srinivasa Chakravarthy for their outstanding online courses on the SWAYAM-NPTEL platform. Finally, I would like to express my gratitude to the department for organizing the departmental lecture series and acknowledge my indebtedness to all my respected professors and the enduring legacy of this department.

I consider myself extraordinarily fortunate to work in an era with online libraries accessible from anywhere and freely available Internet resources (e.g. Internet Archive, Shodhganga, books.google.co.in, and https://plato.stanford.edu, Vidya-Mitra, Swayam Prabha) and other resources. I would especially mention my humble thanks to SWAYAM-NPTEL for the wonderful courses that helped me understand the issue's complexity. Also, they reimbursed the fee for two online courses. Subscriptions to online content from the University Central Library, such as Journal Storage (JSTOR), proved immensely beneficial. Citation management software such as Google Scholar and Zotero has simplified the process of recording and presenting the final form. Academia, ResearchGate, PhilPapers and other academic networking and research showcasing and sharing sites helped me find the most recent studies worldwide. I owe the department librarian a debt of gratitude for the large borrowing limit. In addition, the department office has been conducive throughout the process.

I would like to thank my friend Navneet Nagar, my family and my *guru* Dr Bajpai, who has been my anchor during my most challenging phases. I also acknowledge the unconditional help from my fellow scholars Ark Mukhoty and Ankit Jaiswal at the department.

Lastly, I would also like to thank Susheel Mittal of D.K. Printworld, New Delhi for showing his faith in me and giving me an opportunity to publish this book. He has been very cooperative and helpful and has guided me through the whole process of publishing.

Introduction

How do you perceive the world? How do you know that you are reading this book in your hand? You know it, because it has a parallelogram shape, it has a cover that is soft and has plastic on it. At the same time, the inner pages are white sheets with black ink, displaying letters in a language you have known since childhood. Imagine, you had been asleep for thousands of years, and a mutant who had been put to rest. But how can you be sure of that too? Nick Bostrom, in his paper, "Are You Living in a Simulation?" opines that our lives may be a simulation in the computer of a highly advanced species. Similarly, claiming to have answered the question of life is to pertinently answer these related questions with all the complexities that start with the basic question "What is life?". Even our minuscule thought on these questions will tell us that we do not have answers to them. Instead, what we have are just theories.

An honest observation of the fairly stringent conception will make us have a look at our loose definitions of life and hope that a loose grasp of the questions will dissolve the problem. The functional capacity of biological operations such as reproduction and respiration is what defines life. The question we must ask ourselves is: do these functional capacities define life? Saying so would mean that all that we know about these capacities is what life is, and there is no need to endeavour to understand it any further. To limit life only to its functional capacity is like tying a whale to an aquarium. In real life, we cannot tie the whale to the aquarium; we just buy a caricature of the whale. Similarly, to say that we understand a problem as complex as life would be an attempt to drop the magnitude of the problem to a caricature version of the resolution.

This is how sciences are meant to operate. The correlations are deemed to be marks of causation or in many places causation itself. The evolution (or signs of the growth of functional capacities) is what is deemed to be life. We let go of the whole inner world of subjectivity, the feelings of curiosity and perplexion which made us question life itself to answer the question, "What is life?". The point here is not to merely object to the advance of sciences but to remind ourselves of the fact that we do not have answers to "the questions" of life, for we do not know what the nature of the questions is. We limit the ways a question can manifest itself and then seek what is left and think of that as the answer. Philosophy too has not fared any better.

Philosophy, on the other hand, covers a wide range of theoretical mechanisms that lead to the final human experience. In a systematic philosophical argument, we begin by questioning the cosmos, the subject of metaphysics, and work our way to the human level and their knowledge of this world, the realm of epistemology. Herein the possibility of knowing about the nature of existence ontology and experience is discussed. Finally, by combining various cognitive mechanisms into a single coherent whole, the study of the nature and knowledge thereof is brought to consciousness. This study of the foundational basis of all human experiences and the knowledge associated with them is then brought into the realm of the philosophy of mind as a holistic matter of inquiry.

The present topic of discussion in the book is the "mind-body problem" and the related questions of consciousness, which are perennial conundrums in the domain of philosophy. The conundrum pertains to the ontological dichotomy of mind and matter. Though the precise problem can be stated in a single line about this dichotomy, what it holds within itself is a bunch of interlinked questions arising from the same statement. Does the mind prevail over matter or does matter prevail over the mind, or are both fundamentally synonymous? These similar-sounding questions may look similar and may make one feel that they are the same questions but they have perplexed philosophers and scientists alike for centuries.

In a discussion over such a problem which seemingly has no direct answers; the direct right answer may seem futile and an exercise in vain. So why does it matter at all? Questions such as these may sound as magnanimous and as life-threatening as the sound of the last nail in the coffin of the person left in a box of endless questions, that is the world. These questions and the entire domain of philosophy are a reverberating vastitude of similar-sounding questions trying to question the world itself. As for philosophy as an abstraction, it is a reflection on these questions and the nature of life and its inextricable paradoxical nature. What may seem obvious and so mundanely familiar with the typical everyday usage of the various terms aforementioned, may hold in its bosom an intricately meshed weaving of human knowledge and the conception of what it means to be thereof. It is precisely for this reason that we philosophize and in our case return to the "mind-body problem" to tussle with the conceptions of our human knowledge and add to the mesh the discoveries of our hitherto present and make sense of it all in a new narrative.

The history of philosophy can very well be deemed as a history of understanding the mind-body problem itself. The fact that in philosophy we question these questions is tantamount not just to our ignorance, but the hope of finding an answer as well. This, however, is not meant to diminish the human quest for questioning and curiosity but to remind us of the true nature of enquiry. The true nature of an enquiry is humble and starts with the acceptance of ignorance, then moves on to curiosity seeking an answer to the true nature of the question such as why life exists rather than no life. The true nature of humble curiosity is to accept that the answer can be something one already knew. The inevitability of hoping for a definite answer is the biggest illusion and the only disdain to be refrained from.

It is a paradigm issue in the philosophy of mind. Most ontological viewpoints and schools in various philosophies can be traced in some way or other as a response to the problem. Before we move forward, we must consider how we got engulfed into the problem. The main difficulty at the conceptual level is pertinently how can these two be distinct. The earliest attitudes to the problem were dualist, those which believed in the existence of two primary ontological realities, i.e. the mind and matter. René Descartes is credited with a modern conceptual understanding of the problem. Mind is *res cogitans*, the thinking substance which is devoid of extension, and the matter is the *res extensa*, the substance with spatial extension. How something with an extension can interact with something that has no extension is a pertinent and valid point of contention. All the while, we know that they do interact. If I think of sipping water, I shall go to the refrigerator to get water. How this interaction comes to be is then the question. This, as we shall delve further, is known as "subtance dualism". Another variety of dualism prescribes saying that there are not two substances but just one substance with two different kinds of properties. Such an enormous exertion would be justified if a widely agreed answer could be even scientifically found, if not philosophically. This would ultimately elucidate the meaning of our existence amidst the cosmos.

The other solution seems to be monism. Let us consider physical monism first. The viewpoint that everything is matter and the mind too can ultimately be reduced to matter. The question is: how can the mind be reduced to matter as the mind and matter appear to be distinct with different properties as mentioned earlier. The body is a physical entity with mass. It occupies space and moves across it with velocity and momentum, and contains chemical constituents. It is tangible like trees. The body, if it is purely matter, is built according to the rules of physics and its components would then follow the well-known principles of physiology and ultimately physics. The mind, on the other hand, works by very different mechanics. If one has seen the Leaning Tower of Pisa, then one can perhaps see it while one is sitting in Delhi. Now where one knows that the Leaning Tower of Pisa is in Italy, then how can it be in Delhi? Similarly, one can imagine flying unicorns, but one knows that there are no actual flying unicorns. The attempt then by the physical monist, i.e. the physicalist, is to reduce the mind into various neurons, neurochemicals and the interactions thereof.

In the current philosophy of mind, the most sought-after explanation of the workings of the mind is monism wherein an inexhaustible age-old attempt is being to reduce the mind to matter or to show that they are somehow two sides of the same coin. That coin might be information or some deep understanding of matter that we do not know. While we start with obvious dualism, the other set of solutions comes in the form of philosophical commitments that may be classified as monism with two subcategories: physicalism and anti-physicalism. The reason for this is that physical substances pale in comparison to the mind. We can observe one's brain (with neuro-scientific instruments), but not the mind. For, the mind is impenetrable to a third-person perspective in a way that one's brain does not. For many physicalists, the mind is simply the brain — we may not fully understand how it works, but all phenomena can be described in terms of the brain. Occam's razor propels the physicalists: the notion that all else being equal, the simplest explanation is the best explanation. A hypothesis that includes both the brain and another *sui generis* entity, the mind, with its mental properties, violates this principle since it includes two types of entities: brains and minds when only one is required to explain the other. We may not yet comprehend how the mind operates since it comprises physical complexities which can only be explained by further development of the sciences as a physicalist would argue.

The other viewpoint is anti-physicalism comprising three distinct sets of philosophical commitments, namely idealism, solipsism and panpsychism. They in some form hold the primacy of the mental substance. The idealist holds the primacy of the mind by adhering to the claim that the physical substance is dependent on the mind. This may constitute the viewpoint that nothing can be known without the mind or that everything is mind. A solipsist would claim that the mind is all there is. Finally, panpsychism holds that the mind is all there is, or that all that there is, has a mind-like aspect attached to it.

The initial mention of the problem is stated in the Sāṁkhya philosophy, the originator of which is thought to be Sage Kapila.[1] The school addresses the problem by using the concept of *puruṣa* and *prakṛti*. According to the Sāṁkhyans, the cosmos comprises of two fundamental entities as mentioned above: one is the principle of consciousness and the other is matter. According to them, the mind is also considered matter. However, individual consciousness is linked with the mind, which is matter. The cognitive functions and physical bodily actions work through the interaction of these two fundamental principles. There are also Indian schools of monism like the emergentist school of Cārvāka which believe that consciousness is an emergent property of the body. Other schools of thought like the Advaita Vedānta which emphasizes the absolute nature of consciousness. Although many scholars try to attach a monist position to the schools due to its emphasis on the primacy of consciousness, the position that the school subscribes to is the rejection of duality, i.e. non-dualism. Similarly, various multifarious views, found in Western philosophy, can also be found in Indian philosophy. It has discussed various philosophical viewpoints in minute detail. The brilliance of Indian thought lies in its far-reaching impact beyond the aegis of time and space. Relevant insights into various pertinent issues like quantum theories, which

---

1 This is prior to Plato's *Phaedo,* wherein we find classical accounts of the Western concept of dualism.

are a major point of contention among philosophers and even scientists, lead to the belief that consciousness is anti-physical. This is a testimony to its brilliance. Concepts of nothingness in Buddhism and the absence, even of the absence in hymns like the Nāsadīya Sūkta, address questions at the forefront of quantum research and even allied research in the domain of philosophy of mind (Sreekantan and Roy 2020).

To live is to question and questioning the paradigm of life itself is the very nature of philosophy. When the question of mind, body and consciousness is raised, the oft-quoted statement from the side of empirical sciences is that it is just a matter of time. With new data from the sciences and a better understanding thereof, the problem will dissolve and the seeming dichotomy will fade. The so-called dualist problem of interaction will be resolved as was the question of life itself. The frustration and the anxiety over the unsolvability of the problem of "life" had blinded the scientific temper so much that they overlooked the evidence that calls for a resounding problem. The problem is: how can a concoction of chemicals, which are "non-life" in nature, give rise to life? How does it emerge from a substratum where it was not? How can something come out of nothing? Just as life cannot come out of nothing, the mind too cannot come out of nothing. This is where Indian philosophy merges the question of mind and life.

The question that one might ask now is, if so much has been said and written on the issue, why should one come back to the issue at hand? Even with all the scientific advancements, the problem still confronts scientists and philosophers alike, and it is open to further and more refined interpretations, which is an arduous task in itself, i.e. reducing the mind to matter. The idea of reducing consciousness to a biological phenomenon, just like respiration or photosynthesis, is in many ways a distant dream. Although the existence of consciousness is one of the most obvious facts in the world, it appears to be shrouded in mystery. We all have this inner subjective qualitative experience behind the curtains of the physical phenomenon responsible for it, which is the brain. The reason to think so is the vast amount of research from the side of empirical sciences. Yet we do not understand how this comes to be. This is what the mystery is all about, known as the "hard problem of consciousness". The biggest reason is that we have a conception of reality derived from the progress of sciences since the Renaissance which gives primacy to matter, leading us to a delusion that reality and ultimately consciousness must be something physical.

Consciousness is one aspect of humans that is the closest to them which makes them aware of themselves yet, it eludes their understanding. Descartes said we could doubt the existence of anything in the world, but we cannot doubt the act of doubting itself and hence we cannot doubt that there is a mind/consciousness. This calls for prepondering over the subjective, conscious experience of qualia. Some philosophers argue that consciousness is an illusion and does not exist. There has been tremendous scientific advancement in the field of philosophy of mind which deserves attention. An attempt to comprehensively understand the problem is more than needed when we see the primacy of the mind growing in some form or other. Even those, who argue that the mind is nothing but the connections in the brain, try to mimic the brain by building various cognitive models. The question of whether the mind is physical or not, remains unsettled, but the primacy of the question of mind persists. Hence, we shall try to look at the same from various perspectives in the chapters that follow.

The book is an attempt to remind us that we have a large amount of information about the conundrum, but that it does not mean that we have "the answer". Wittgenstein says that the task of philosophy is to organize the known in a series of coherent-sounding resolutions. The book seeks to observe the known positions about the conundrum and examines them under the known formulations to see where each of the viewpoints stands. There are several books which have addressed this task much more brilliantly. What then is new about this book?

The newness lies not in the conglomeration of the already stated viewpoints but in showing how they can be complementary to each other. Most earlier attempts to better understand the mind-body problem hold only a part of the solution in terms of putting the philosophical or the scientific side on a higher pedestal. This book, however, puts them on an equal footing, and rather than claiming to have "the answer", it tries to analyse the problem thoroughly in terms of the advances the sciences have made and amalgamates them with the philosophical understanding to simply show what is known, what is questionable and what is still dubitable in the "known order of things". In this sense, the book does not claim to be a new answer or a work of new-thought invention but an attempt to systematize what is already known more coherently. The book, in these terms 'serves more as a compendium for the most part and is an attempt at large to weave a narrative of advances and deficits.

This attempt will proceed by looking at consciousness from three perspectives, i.e. Indian thought, Western philosophical thought and scientific thought. This book aims to examine a comparative account of the contemporary understanding of the mind-body problem, with the current iteration being the ontological question of phenomenal consciousness. To do so, it answers some fundamental questions like whether is consciousness fundamental and, if not, how the mind and the body interact such that they generate what we call the phenomenal consciousness. To do this, I shall examine various philosophical viewpoints and compare them with the scientific understanding and show how an Advaitin model of consciousness fares better than other models of consciousness and also show why it needs to be developed more in our contemporary understanding of the problem. Lastly, I shall also point out some lacunae of the model in terms of our contemporary understanding of the problem.

I think philosophy is one of the humblest of endeavours, yet many a time philosophers dealing in pure philosophy are rightly deemed as armchair thinkers. Philosophy is the mother of all sciences. Many times, sciences accuse philosophy of laziness and since the turn of the Industrial Revolution, this has been the case. In my opinion, the disciplines should work in tandem. Every new advancement in sciences is an older question of philosophy like a beloved to be met at each turn. Neither philosophy nor the sciences are but lovers choosing to stick to one lover. Yet, when they meet at crossroads, it is the comfort of armchair talks that one remembers and the hot-headed disagreements that one relinquishes. The job of philosophy or for that matter of the sciences is not just to engage in redundant questioning but to contribute to the other. Philosophy in that case has the power to not just question the sciences but offer consolation, reaffirmation and positive solutions like eternal love. The job of sciences is just to be vigilant in questioning and understanding, accepting and moving on to meet the beloved, philosophy at another crossroads to sit silently and have a chat again.

1

Orthodox Indian Thought

Introduction

"Who am I? (*ko 'ham?*)" and "What is my place in the universe?" (Wikisource 2021). These questions form the foundational basis of all inquiries in Indian philosophical thought. Later, systemic accounts of philosophical traditions can be traced back to these questions, which, in turn, have their first written mention in the Vedas. Knowing thyself entails knowing everything. What is this "I", which is so immediate to any human that makas him feel intrinsic to his existence?

> *parāñci khāni vyatṛṇat svayaṁbhūs tasmāt parāṅ paśyati nāntarātman* ।
> *kaś cid dhīraḥ pratyag-ātmānam aikṣad āvṛtta-cakṣur amṛtatvam icchan* ॥ — Radhakrishnan 2019: *KaṭhaUp* 2.1.1

This *śloka* from the *Kaṭha Upaniṣad* tells us more philosophically about the process of cognition. One starts by looking outside since the senses are extroverted. He wishes to return from the external world when his search is excruciatingly deepened in the later phase. This *śloka* remarks a lot about the process of philosophy, spiritual growth and even cognition as we shall see later.

The initial thoughts of the human were related to the external world seeking his place in the cosmos. One's senses were in awe of the complexities of the world which was simple yet intricate like a clock with only three needles moving around a dial hiding a bunch of mechanisms behind it. Similarly, the senses of humans being extroverted were out to catch a glimpse of the vastness of the world around them. With this extroversion, humans mastered the secrets of the repetitive patterns in nature like seasons, days and nights, and in many ways the planet by the cyclical motions of the stars. The knowledge of the inner workings of the world then led to affect his life in many ways. Now, when humans were settled and comfortable, they began an inward journey towards the inner workings of the self. This is just similar to inquisitive mind of a child who is first taught to keep track of time using a clock. Once he learns it, he wants to learn about the mechanism that goes into making the clock itself. Once that journey begins, one is inexpressibly awed towards the inner self that one is, the life and the mind bestowed upon him by the grace of God and the universe itself.

In this chapter, we shall ponder upon similar questions as mentioned above, particularly the nature of the mind-body complex and consciousness. Almost all schools of Indian philosophy owe their allegiance to the Vedas, which shall be referred to here as pre-systematic thought.[1] Then we shall move on to the structured philosophical thoughts in both orthodox and heterodox systems of Indian philosophy. We shall delve into the theories they present and discuss them as elaborately as possible. In the end, we shall have a brief look at a psycho-philosophical model of consciousness based on the Advaitin framework of mind-body complex and consciousness.

I

Consciousness in the Vedas

The Vedas have been referred to as pre-systemic thought by Saksena (1944: 18). To begin with, in the second stanza of the Gāyatrī *mantra* of the *Ṛgveda* (III.62.10), it is said:

> *tat savitur vareṇyaṁ bhargo devasya dhīmahi* ।
> *dhiyo yo naḥ pracodayāt* ॥

[1] By pre-systemic thought I mean the Vedas whose discourse on these questions pave the way for later systemic inquiry. I owe this terminology to Shri Krishna Saksena (1944) whose book has been a seminal source for my work herein.

Radhakrishnan (2019), in his translation, uses the words understanding and intelligence as the translations of the word *dhī*. This is fully expressed in the following word *buddhi*, which means intellect tasked with discrimination. This word has been later used by the Upaniṣads and various other systems of philosophy. In the venerated Nāsadīya Sūkta of the *R̥gveda* (X.129.3), we find the term *manaso retaḥ*[2], which means germs of the mind which in the context of the *śloka* means that desire (*kāma*) is a product of the mind. Radhakrishnan commenting on the same, writes, "Desire (*kāma*) is the sign of self-consciousness" (Radhakrishnan 2008: 74).

In the initial verse of the *sūkta*, it says:

nāsadāsīnno sadāsīttadānīṁ nāsīdrajo no vyomā paro yat ।

— *R̥V* X.129.1

What this means is that in the beginning, there was neither *sat* (being) nor *asat* (non-being). They do not go beyond this. It is unclear whether this primal reality is conscious or unconscious. On the other hand, it also suggests another viewpoint of the sages pertinently that phenomenal *sat* is a subset of the absolute *sat*. They are distinct in the sense that one is bounded by conditioning laced with desires while the other is unbounded and free from any conditioning whatsoever. *Asat* does not mean non-reality or absolute non-existence. It just refers to conditioned existence, which is the opposite of the term *sat*. *Brahman*, prior to the birth of the world, has only been addressed as *asat* in this secondary sense. The power of absolute existence, devoid of any *lakṣaṇa* (characteristic mark), is incapable of being thought of in any way other than "negation", which is equivalent to non-existence (of the conditioned *sat*). *Asat* is not an absolute non-existence but only something that has not yet manifested, i.e. it holds the seed for future transformation. It resembles the latter Buddhist notion of Samvriti and Paramarth, or the Para and Apara *Brahman* of Vedānta and the *avyakta* of Sāṁkhya philosophies. Its reality is not only formless but also perfect and

---

2 *kāmastadagre samavartatādhi manaso retaḥ prathamaṁ yadāsīt* ।

complete. *Sat* here means conditioned embodiment, as opposed to the idea of the formless and the possibility of forms in the concept of unconditioned *asat*.

What is the meaning of *sat* being rooted in *asat*? The conditioned being emerges from the formless, unlimited being and although they may appear distinct, they are not so. Once the conditioning of the self is removed, the distinctions fade and they become one in the state of *mokṣa* (*prāptasya prāpti*). The roots of *sat* are embedded in *asat*, just as *māyā* has its roots in *Brahman*. It is a unique characteristic of Indian philosophical schools to place the multiplicity of the world of objects of experience as conditioned and to show that they have their basis in this primal substance in which they ultimately merge. This primordial reality is defined by emptiness and absolute wholeness. *Asat* in this sense is unexpressed and uncreated, a sign of the power of creation. In *Yogasūtra* II.23,[3] the same fact is expressed as the condition where both the seer and the seen exist only as potentialities, before contact, and not as the actuality of either the seer or the seen.

Asat is higher than *sat* because non-being in a specific form means existence as a possibility, which essentially forbids the attempt to constrain *asat* into any finite characteristic. This is why the sages called the origin of *sat* opposing names. The Supreme Truth, which is eternal, cannot be defined by names such as the *kāma*, *manas*, *sat* or *asat*. To call it *sat* is to deem it limited and definite. Moreover, to speak of him as non-being in terms of absolute negation is to deny it, which is not genuinely possible. The absolute reality, which lies in the background of the whole world, cannot be designated by us as either existent or non-existent for the distinction is not of existence or non-existence but of potency and actuality, which is a manifestation of the potency itself. For this reason, it can neither be rejected ultimately nor can it be accepted empirically. The only knowledge we have about it is that it is devoid of limitations of the form.

3 *svasvāmiśaktyoḥ svarūpopalabdhihetuḥ saṁyogaḥ* ।

Our next question is: where can the ultimate and the fundamental truth be discovered? Where can we find it? It is mentioned that the sages discovered it in their own inner being. The fact that the sages had to seek it not in the external world, but in their being gives the explicit instruction that the Ultimate Reality is the inner being or that the mind or consciousness is fundamental. In the Upaniṣads, the soul has been declared as the light of the heart; as pure consciousness (*citta*), as *Brahman* in Vedānta and *puruṣa* in Sāṁkhya-Yoga. The Ultimate Reality that has been considered the primordial root in the Vedas was embedded in the seed of the mind, which later became differentiated. It also indicates that this Ultimate Reality is the beginning of phenomenal consciousness[4] since there must have been some form from which it cannot be separated; even though it cannot be equated with it. Hence, in the Vedas, we find the ultimate culmination of the absolute principle of the Upaniṣads, which has been developed as a gradual exploration of a universal and inner principle, at the core of the fundamental reality.

Kāma in the above context of the Nāsadīya Sūkta is translated by Radhakrishnan (2008) as desire, but there are later translations, particularly in the Vedānta system, which state it as will or volition, i.e. *saṅkalpa.*[5] Another important comment that it makes is *arvāgdevā asya visarjanenāthā ko veda yata ābabhūva* ॥ (*R̥V* X.129.6). Herein we find a claim which is different from many other systems of thought that even gods are later than creation, i.e. in the primordial state of negation of both being and non-being, there were no gods and hence it even created the gods.[6] Here in this *sūkta*, we get a spontaneous taste of the philosophy of mind with all the philosophy

---

4 There is a distinction between the Self, which is pure consciousness, and the phenomenal consciousness which is experiential consciousness as is discussed further.

5 For a detailed discussion, see Bhatt (2002), Maurer (1975) and Saksena (1944: 18).

6 In Advaita Vedānta *Brahman* laces with *māyā* is *Īśvara.*

of the Upaniṣads in one piece.[7] Nothing about the ontology of the Vedas and later thought lies beyond this *sūkta*. The meaning of *kāma* (desire) has certainly not been taken here in the ordinary empirical sense. In its place, its reference is more about the doctrine of a cosmic, central and unitary creative force that is neither mind nor non-mind. Instead, there is only the fulfilment of an indeterminate spontaneity, which vibrates to become particular and limited, and is eager to express itself in the way of mind or consciousness. It is, in essence, a worldly impulse to express itself.

In the Śiva-Saṅkalpa Sūkta of the *Vājasaneyī Saṁhitā* of the *Yajurveda*, we find terms like *manas* (mind), *saṅkalpa* (resolve), *prajñānaṁ* (intelligence), *cetāḥ* (conscious agent), *dhṛti* (determination) and the concept of seven sacrificers. These terms can be translated to mind, resolve agent, intelligence, consciousness, determination and the seven sacrificers are the five cognitive senses and the two breaths of inhalation and exhalation. Mind in the first *śloka* is described as that which goes afar (*dūraṅgam*), and it is the illuminator of the five senses (*jyotiṣāṁ jyotirekam*). Further, it is said that the mind is accompanied or comprised by consciousness and determination, without which no action is possible, be comprised of right determination.[8] These are some tremendous insights considering the texts as ancient as these. What we find here is that the mind is theorized as having consciousness and that it travels afar, and it is this mind that draws forth resolve and ordains the sensory input towards some action. Unity of thought, will, action, and even the cognitive faculties and their relation with breath are postulated here.

One more point deserves our attention here, and perhaps this is among the most crucial insights, is the concept of *ṛta*.

---

7 The desire mentioned here is the initial pronouncement of a later Upaniṣadic thought, *māyā*, which is the seed of all the world.

8 *yatprajñānamuta cetō dhṛtiśca yajjyōtirantaramṛtaṁ prajāsu* ।
yasmānna ṛte kiñcana karma kriyate tanme manaḥ śivasaṅkalpamastu ॥
— Tejomayananda 2018

Radhakrishnan (2008: 53), commenting on the same, calls it the "order of the world which existed before the manifestation of all phenomena". The principle of every ordered thing in the universe is *ṛta*, located behind the entire phenomenon of nature as the primary governing principle. It is superior to God Varuṇa himself because it is more intrinsic and essential due to the internal energy in the world. The principle *ṛta* obligates every living being and non-living being to follow the law of existence. It orders the winds to move, water to flow, and man to gain knowledge. It is the root of consciousness and regulates the extraordinary actions of all nature and is, therefore, the cornerstone of the process of human knowledge. Human brains execute their functions based on the power of *ṛta*. Man comes to know about the power of *ṛta* by the same underlying driving force that ignites the fire and causes the rivers to flow. Just as all other entities have to complete the tasks allotted in their parts, similarly, humans also have to fulfil their unique function of conscious knowing (*saṁvit*), in both the figurative and literal sense of the word, i.e. knowing all the relative knowledge (multiple facets of an animate or inanimate object as in Jaina philosophy) concerning the universal manifestations of *ṛta*. Even gods cannot bypass *ṛta*. This means for our present concern that even the faculties of individual consciousness come under the purview of *ṛta* (Brown 1961: 373; Kak 2000; Werner 1977: 233).

To sum up the discussion on the Vedic underpinnings of consciousness, I would like to point out two more *sūkta*s from the *Ṛgveda* to reiterate some crucial metaphysical insights: *ekaṁ sat viprā bahudhā vadanti* (I.164.46) and the story of the two parrots in *dvā suparṇā ...* (I.164.20) (Wikisource 2021). One truth manifests itself as many in I.164.46, and the concept of two beings is postulated in I.164.20, one being the individual soul and the other being the transcendental one that does not get involved in the action.[9]

---

9 For a detailed discussion, see Norelius (2016). The same story of two birds is invoked in the *Muṇḍaka Upaniṣad* and *Śvetāśvatara Upaniṣad* (Radhakrishnan 2019).

Systematization in the Upaniṣads

In the recorded history of humankind, it is for the first time that we find at least an attempt towards a systematic discussion of the problem of consciousness, mind and body. The language of elucidation is unique (some may say peculiar in approach) considering the current academic debates, formulations and understandings of the issue. It must be pointed out that the original number of the Upaniṣadic texts is either ten or eleven. Ten of them have been commented upon by Śaṅkarācārya (Hacker 1995: 30-31). So for our present concern, we shall try to see what insights are found therein. The Upaniṣads, considered as the latter part of the Vedas, further, elucidate the concepts and lay out a more structured account of the same issues. For this reason, the import of these texts is referred to as *ātma-vidyā*. This is highlighted in the four famous *mahāvākyas*.[10] So what is this *ātman* and what is its nature according to the different texts?

In the *Chāndogya Upaniṣad*'s dialogue between Indra, Vairocana and Prajāpati, a discussion on the concept of the self is found. Prajāpati negates the self as one who wakes and wanders the world. Neither is it one who dreams nor the one who sleeps. It is beyond these three ordinary states of being. Hence four states of being are propounded, i.e. *jāgrat* (waking), *svapna* (dreaming), *suṣupti* (deep sleep) and the final stage *turīya* (beyond thought). The true untainted self is beyond the four normal states of everyday transition (Radhakrishnan 2019: 501-10). The self is the basis of these states and yet transcends them all. Another crucial point of error is very rightly enunciated. During the waking state, we identify the self with the body. In the dreaming state, we identify the self with our internal psychic being, while in sleep, there is no identification

---

10 Referring to the four *mahāvākyas* of the Upaniṣads:
- *prajñānam brahma* — *Aitareya Upaniṣad* 3.1.3
- *ayam ātmā brahma* — *Māṇḍūkya Upaniṣad* 2
- *tat-tvam-asi* — *Chāndogya Upaniṣad* 6.8.7
- *aham brahmāsmi* — *Bṛhadāraṇyaka Upaniṣad* 1.4.10

since there is nothing to identify with. Examining these three states reveals that the true self is neither identified with the body nor with the one who travels through the world of dreams. It is also not the abstraction of the non-transactional.[11] The true self can never be an object, albeit it sees the object, including the objects of dreams and even objectless sleep. It is beyond all actions and fruits thereof and hence lies untainted.

> *... ya ātmāpahatapāpmā vijaro vimṛtyurviśoko vijighatso-'pipāsaḥ satyakāmaḥ satyasaṅkalpaḥ so 'nveṣṭavyaḥ sa vijijñāsitavyaḥ sa sarvāṁśca lokānāpnoti sarvāṁśca kāmānyastamātmānamanuvidya vijānātīti ... ha prajāpatiruvāca ...* — Radhakrishnan 2019: 50

Similarly, in the dialogue between Sanatkumāra and Nārada, it is said that speech prevails over the name for it makes the name known. Mind prevails over speech and engulfs them both. A man learns what his mind intends. *Saṅkalpa* (will) is greater than the mind, for it is the will that dictates the mind towards speech and behaviour. Higher than will is cogitation (*citta*). The cogitation situates one's concern on an object based on the time, space and situational cause (*deśakāla-nimitti*). One can only will when there is thought. Without thought, there is no will. *Dhyāna* is further up the ladder. *Dhyāna* is what can be called attention,[12] i.e. restraint of one's thoughts on one subject (Radhakrishnan 2019: 474), understanding (*vijñāna*) is higher than all. Here we find a clear overview of all the processes that lead to the phenomenal consciousness and how it churns out into the final verbal report.

Kaṭha Upaniṣad 1.3.3-4 invokes the parable of the chariot (Radhakrishnan 2019: 623-24), which I would like to cite here. It says:

> *ātmānaṁ rathitaṁ viddhi śarīraṁ rathameva tu* ।
> *buddhiṁ tu sārathiṁ viddhi manaḥ pragrahameva ca* ॥

---

[11] Non-transactional in the sense of knowledge transaction from the world and its processing thereof.

[12] Here I do not agree with Radhakrishnan's translation of *dhyāna* as contemplation and have sticked to the term attention.

indriyāṇi hayānāhurviṣayāṁsteṣu gocarān ।
ātmendriyamanoyuktaṁ bhoktetyāhurmanīṣiṇaḥ ॥

The Self, which is consciousness, is equated with the master of the charioteer. The body is the chariot, the *buddhi* is the charioteer and the mind is the reins. The senses are the horses that ride over the roads of the sense objects. The self gets associated with the body and commands the *buddhi* to use the mind to control the senses and enjoy the sense objects. This is a brilliant insight and a significant leap in understanding the functions of the different concepts involved. The insight is twofold: the mind is not the self or consciousness, and the mind controls the senses, not the self or consciousness. Otherwise, it will become an object, and we shall fall into infinite regress.

A similar analysis is articulated in the *Māṇḍūkya Upaniṣad*, which is the shortest of all Upaniṣads. Here another[13] crucial insight is found, which is present in almost all religions of the world, i.e. the unity of the microcosm and the macrocosm. The second *śloka* itself says, all this is, verily, *Brahman*. This self is *Brahman*. This same self has four quarters (Radhakrishnan 2019: 695).[14] The connection of man to the universe is very explicitly stated here. It resonates with the biblical dictum "As in heaven, so on earth".[15] This is crucial because the current understanding of the subject matter (the mind-body problem) remains unresolved in the modern context and there

---

13 The first insight is the mention of four quarters or the states of self as mentioned in the dialogue between Indra, Vairocana and Prajāpati.

14 *sarvaṁ hyetad brahmāyamātmā brahma so 'yamātmā catuṣpāt* ।
— *MāUp* 2

15 *Quod est superius est sicut quod inferius, et quod inferius est sicut quod est superius.* Emarald Tablet — an Arabian artefact of occult traditions. Its markings are variedly found. That which is above is like to that which is below and that which is below is like that which is above us. In Sanskrit यत्र पिण्डे, तत्र ब्रह्माण्डे ।

is a desperate need for a unified theory of consciousness that takes into account phenomena at the quantum scale, the mesoscopic human scale and the macroscale of the universe (Bajpai 2018: 27-31).

The text describes the self as having four quarters, as stated above. In the waking state, the collective consciousness of all beings is the Vaiśvānara,[16] wherein man wills and acts. His bodily needs and conditioning impel these decisions. The second quarter is *tejas*, which cognizes the inner world built upon desires, imagination and memories. The third quarter is that of *prajñā*, wherein duality is dissolved, but it is the final *turīya* state wherein no duality exists. This state cannot be put into thought and words.

For the Upaniṣadic writer, consciousness is not an abstraction, but a feature of reality that is imbued with consciousness. This is the primary import of the Upaniṣadic *mahāvākyas*. Consciousness is not a product of evolution, and neither is it a manifestation in itself. However, it may manifest itself through beings and things based on their structural make-up. A holistic approach in every phase of thought, debate and deliberation is a characteristic feature of Indian thought. It does not divide reality into rigid divisions based only on factual analysis. According to this vision of reality, each object is a part and parcel of the whole. Reality is unitary and devoid of the distinctions of internal and external. From the absolute comes the absolute:

> *ānando brahmeti vyajānāt* । *ānandādhyeva khalvimāni bhūtāni jāyante* । *ānandena jātāni jīvanti* । *ānandaṁ prayantyabhisaṁviśantīti* ।
> — *TaittUp* 2.6.1 in Radhakrishnan 2019: 557

As the idea developed, naive wonder was replaced by discussion and conceptualization; in the same way, the attention of human beings began to move away from mere inquiry of external facts and the visual world. The world of cosmic stars, the celestial and the visible world, is not outside the human being because where everything is

[16] *viśveṣām narāṇāma anekadhā nayanāda vaiśvānaraḥ* ।
yad vā viśvaś cāsau naraś ceti viśvānaraḥ viśvānara eva vaiśvānaraḥ ।।
— *Śāṅkara Bhāṣya on MāṇḍUp* 3; Radhakrishnan 1994: 695

universal and every moment is complete, there can be no difference between external and internal. After all, humans are also a part of the whole. When attentively concentrated upon, each object can reveal the whole because that too is a metaphorical microcosm of the whole.[17] This is why it is said that no land is entirely new in human progress and the development of knowledge. There is no place to reach that is entirely unfamiliar. All exploration, revelation and wisdom are only incidents of human re-exploration and rediscovery present from eternity.

> *pūrṇamadaḥ pūrṇamidaṁ pūrṇātpūrṇamudacyate* ।
> *pūrṇasya pūrṇamādāya pūrṇamevāvaśiṣyate* ॥
> — *BṛUp*, *śāntipāṭha*, in Radhakrishnan 2019: 289

To conclude this section, we must ask what crucial insights we see in the Vedas and the Upaniṣads on the present issue. We see here a layman's foundation of the basic terms, which with little or no modifications by the later philosophies of the Indian tradition. The elementary ideology of the Vedas is the unification of both the internal and the universal reality, i.e. pure consciousness without form. The later notion of transcendental consciousness and self-consciousness as it manifests at the level of worldly existence is one of the imports of the Vedic and the Upaniṣadic discourses. Also, gods are not the progenitors of consciousness. There was an entity, before, whenceforth arose consciousness. The law of *ṛta* governs even the gods and faculties of individual consciousness; there is an order even in the immaterial realm rather than absolute chaos. The truth, which is absolute consciousne ss, is beyond our categorical understanding of being and non-being and manifests as the four states of being. It is guided by the mind which mediates the sense organs and is imbued with consciousness. Hence, consciousness is both immanent in the mind and yet transcends it.

---

17 This idea can be seen as humans being formed of the same elements as the stars formed by the Big Bang. So, in this sense, we are stardust on a tiny speck of dust in the grand scheme of the cosmos.

II

Consciousness in the Indian Philosophy

What is consciousness? It is difficult to respond to this question since consciousness is, for most schools, the ultimate inquiry. However, we must reconsider it in phenomenal terms and attempt to classify it in the broad categories of thought, either under the categories of *dravya* (substance), *guṇa* (quality), *karma* (action) or other conceivable categories. The contemplation of supreme consciousness is depicted in Indian philosophical thought in various ways. *Dravya*, *guṇa* and *karma* are ways that consciousness is portrayed. It is referred to as eternal and unchangeable or changeable and transient depending on the school under consideration. It can also be considered as the vital force that creates a distinction between subject and object. Consciousness in these terms can be defined as the relation between subject and object.

These various perspectives can be classified into two categories: realism and idealism. The realist believes that consciousness starts from a combination of specific conditions and then fades away when the combination is no longer there. Therefore, it is not always present and is affected by circumstances. The realists' viewpoint can be further divided into two categories. There are two types of realists: materialists and spiritualists.[18] The Cārvāka philosophy, which represents materialistic realism, regards consciousness as a mere coincidence — a by-product of material substances. In contrast, the Nyāya-Vaiśeṣika philosophy, which represents spiritual realism, believes in the existence of a spiritual substance known as the soul (*ātman*), which is distinct from material substances, viz. the body. Phenomenal consciousness, according to Nyāya-Vaiśeṣika, arises from the interaction of the mind (*manas*), senses (*indriya*) and external objects, as well as the *ātman*. It is important to emphasize that consciousness only lives inside the

18 Those who believe consciousness to be immaterial.

spiritual substance, the soul, and is merely a quality. However, even the *ātman* does not maintain consciousness indefinitely. The quality of consciousness is listed among the qualities of the soul caused by its interaction with the mind (*manas*), senses (*indriya*) and external objects.

The difference between materialist Cārvākas and Nyāya-Vaiśeṣika realists appears to be rooted solely in their non-belief in an immaterial substance, i.e. the soul. Absolute consciousness, they both believe, is non-existent apart from a set of precise conditions and is just an inadvertent property of substance; this is also known as *āgantuka-dharma*. The idealist such as the *yogācārin*, on the other hand, expresses his belief in a fundamental consciousness that exists eternally as a pure unrestricted and formless mind, existing as mere knowledge (*vijñaptimātra*). It cannot be generated or destroyed. It is perpetually there in its own right, without the aid of any other substance. Some theorists, such as Rāmānuja, believe that consciousness is a distinguishing attribute (*dharma*) of the *ātman*, whereas others, such as Śaṅkara, feel that consciousness is the primal substance itself. Advaita Vedānta is congruent with Sāṁkhya-Yoga. According to this view, consciousness is eternal and inseparable from the *puruṣa*. They also view the soul as *sui generis*, Svayambhū, a separate reality from all objects. Pure consciousness, in which there is no sensation of "I" or "That", is contentless existence. As a result, the following perspectives on the nature and existence of consciousness are obtained:

- It is just a case of material substances colliding. It does not exist on its own. Material substances, on the other hand, exist independently. This is the Cārvāka philosophy's vision.
- Consciousness is formed as a synthesis of diverse objects, as per the Nyāya-Vaiśeṣika's realist viewpoint. However, it also happens to be a spiritual substance, as the categorical relation of *samavāya* inheres in it (the spiritual substance, the existence of consciousness). This is a unique differentiation.

It goes through three stages of existence: being born and generated, nourishing and destroyed.

- Consciousness is a pure and indestructible reality, which is also a non-discrete, unobjectified reality under which there is no distinction between "ego" and "non-ego". Individual self-consciousness is a continual and conscious component of an all-existing eternal consciousness.
- Its existence is self-sustaining and independent. Śaṅkara's Advaita Vedānta and Sāṁkhya-Yoga both envision this transcendental and fundamental consciousness.

MATERIALISM AND THE CĀRVĀKA THOUGHT

Consciousness is considered non-negatable in its unprecedented and foundational nature, as well as due to its epistemological precedence. It might, however, be argued against. As a result, Indian materialism in its purest form considers consciousness merely a representational and subjective epiphenomenon. Consciousness, they believe, arises from the mixing of material constituents, much like alcoholic inebriation arises from the combining of fermented wheat. This corollary should be remembered and acknowledged since neither wheat nor the yeast that acts on it possesses the attribute of inebriation. The Cārvāka school of materialism is said to have been founded by Ācārya Bṛhaspati. It attempts to explain the birth of consciousness in the same manner that a combination of beetle leaf, lime and some nuts, or sugar syrup acted upon by fermentation respectively leads to a new colour and molasses inebriation.

Cārvāka's philosophy is a proponent of materialism and accidentalism, also known as Yadṛcchāvāda. It is a philosophical position in which an unintentional combination of events or substances results in the production or emergence of a new phenomenon. There is no specific cause of anything in the world for the Cārvāka. It is all hit-or-miss in the world, with unexpected circumstances leading to a phenomenon to which no straight lineage can be traced back to the pre-emergent cause or phenomenon. The development of a phenomenon results from a series of unrelated events occurring at the same time. It is all the result of natural emergence.

> *kālaḥ svabhāvō niyatiryadr̥cchā bhūtāni yōniḥ puruṣa iti cintyā* ।
>
> — Radhakrishnan 2019: 709

Both the concept of naturalism and the concept of accidentalism are discussed in the *Śvetāśvatara Upaniṣad*. These principles, naturalism and accidentalism, are mentioned as causes in *śloka*s 13-15. It has non-existence in the form of the emergent property before the phenomena and a subsequent emergence at any time and without cause. It is seen as unintentional and hence might be referred to as uncaused. Nature (*svabhāva*) is sometimes the source of all things. It is the inherent power and potency of each substance that is triggered and generates a specific effect due to some occurrence. Here is another example of a beetle leaf, nut and lime combination. There is no consequence until it is triggered by the cause, which in this case is chewing. A trigger is required to bring in the mixture's red hue produced by chewing; this is referred to as the act of causation. Because of their intrinsic nature, fire burns and water flows downhill. Their fundamental nature accounts for the entire disparity in their qualities. As a result, the ontological experiential aspect of consciousness results from the consciousness' inherent nature.

In the Cārvāka philosophy, nothing is everlasting. They do not believe in an eternal creator or a soul that lives forever. They do, however, believe in things that have an animated character. Consider it, the body of a person who can comprehend experience through consciousness. It has a non-eternal character. Why one would wonder, do they respond that it is an intrinsic natural trait of theirs. Why does the body become aware of its surroundings? It is caused by the inherent accidental quality of the body's amalgamation of components or individual parts. Causation is not general in their case. It is all a ruse — a creative imagination. Only the antecedence of one event and the consequence of another event are perceived. For them, perception is confined to specific situations. Unlike the *puruṣa* or *Brahman*, it cannot hold the linear consciousness of past, present and future all at once, as the idealist notion does. The Cārvāka does not believe in a necessary and invariable relationship from an epistemic standpoint. This is correct on both a causal level and an epistemic level (their stance on inference). It is possible that the correct combination of events and substances for them will not result in a definitive cause. In this regard, the position is similar to that of David Hume.

According to the Cārvāka school of thought, consciousness results from the perfect combination of material bodily entities. The elements of water, fire, air and earth work together to bring consciousness into being. When such a basic physical set-up is disrupted and ceases to exist, the phenomenon of consciousness is also destroyed and ceases to exist. For them, the entire corporeal set-up is made up of elements, and consciousness, which is a by-product of their apprehension, vanishes when its antecedent vanishes. Many Western philosophers who identify as materialists or physicalists have this viewpoint. They solely believe in the existence of material or physical substances and forces. Furthermore, the union of these two forces gives life to consciousness.

THE NYĀYA-VAIŚEṢIKA THOUGHT

The Nyāya-Vaiśeṣika are allied schools of philosophy and share much of the conception regarding the philosophy of mind and shall be discussed as such. Both of these schools profess a dualist stance (Chakrabarti 2001: 19-29). In terms of the concept of consciousness, spiritual realism can best be described as a thought in the light of materialism. Consciousness, unlike the Cārvāka, is not fundamentally of the origin of matter, according to Nyāya-Vaiśeṣika philosophy. It is not a property of any natural entity and is not a coincidence either. He tries to show this by using the *ad residuum* method of elimination. In his text *Nyāya-Mañjarī*, Jayanta Bhaṭṭa concludes that consciousness is linked to the soul. Based on *anumāna* (inference), the ontological soul has its epistemological consideration in *pariśeṣānumāna* (ibid.: 225).

This conclusion assumes that a substance or a quality is associated with a particular substance since it is not related to any other substance or event *ad residuum*. The characteristics are precisely as real as the substances in Nyāya-Vaiśeṣika ontology. "That which has substance for its substratum" is a quality (Praśastapādācārya 1982). Nyāya-Vaiśeṣika scholars identify consciousness as something related to the soul because it cannot be attributed to one of the corporeal elements, such as the *manas* (senses), nor the collective body as a whole (ibid.). Śrīdhara (Praśastapādācārya 1982: 152-98) uses identical arguments to Jayanta Bhaṭṭa to arrive at the same conclusion about establishing consciousness as an entity. He asks why, since the *ātman* is unconscious, consciousness cannot be established in any combination of *manas* and its *viṣayas*. Why do they believe that consciousness is established in the *ātman* (self)? He then goes on to say that this is due to natural law. Although consciousness comes from all four sources: the mind, the senses, the *viṣayas* and the *ātman*; it is only the self that has ontological inherence. The self, mind and senses, all of which are involved in the process of cognition, are substances, according to Nyāya. Substances or attributes of substances are the perceptual objects.

To illustrate, he uses the famous example of the relationship between threads and spindle. This example is unique to this school and has appeared in all of the school's epistemological and ontological literature. The thread and the spindle give birth to the cloth, but the locus of the cloth is in the threads, not the spindle. Although the soul does not have the nature of consciousness, it is nonetheless the locus of consciousness in this fashion (Praśastapādācārya 1982: 198-208). For this reason, knowledge is a quality originating in the soul and is based on it the combination of the mind, senses and *viṣayas* (Gautama 1939: 41-42, 351-78).

The spiritual substance, *ātman*, is *nitya* and can have many manifestations. Its size is atomic. The *ātman*'s distinctiveness is derived from its interaction with the *manas*. The *kartā* and the *bhoktā* are *vibhu parimāṇa* (all-pervasive). The ultimate agency initiates contact with other senses and is aided by the *manas* as the penultimate agency. The *manas* can be classified as a sense organ, a crucial distinction. It is not the mind that can comprehend. It is non-local, unstable (*asthira*) and eternal (*nitya*). This Nyāya-Vaiśeṣika realism theory is founded on the extreme dualism of matter and quality premise. As a result, the scenario is not unlike that of materialists, but there is a distinction due to the conception of consciousness, which is a product here.[19] This phenomenon is dependent on a specific set of circumstances. Furthermore, according to the Nyāya-Vaiśeṣika, there is no inseparable tie between consciousness and the *ātman*. According to Kaṇāda, consciousness emerges in the same way as red colour emerges from contact with fire within a pot.[20]

The mind and the self are inextricably linked. Every *ātman*, according to the Nyāya-Vaiśeṣika viewpoint, has its *manas* (mind). After the death of the physical body, the mind remains with *ātman* and does not cease to exist. All psychological processes such as consciousness, emotion, and volition do not belong to the self or the mind but only appear when both are present. While there can be no consciousness without the self (*ātman*), consciousness is not the self's essence; instead, it is a property of *ātman* that arises from its interaction with the mind. Nyāya-Vaiśeṣika thinkers talk about the self and how it relates to the mind. Every *ātman*, according to the Nyāya-Vaiśeṣika viewpoint, has its *manas*. The *manas* feels pain, pleasure and the universals in this situation. It brings the inputs from the other five senses together and directs them towards action. The self, mind and senses, all of which are involved in the process of cognition, are substances, according to Nyāya. Substances or

19 *indriyārthaḥ sannikarṣottapannaṁ jñānaṁ* । — Gautama 1939: 18-25

20 *agnighaṭa saṁyogaja rohitādi guṇavata* । — Śaṅkarācārya 2000

attributes of substances are the perceptual objects. The mind is the theoretical instrument that aids the *ātman* in gaining knowledge of the exterior world and interior conditions, and the vivid picture generated therein via initiating contact.

Nyāya-Vaiśeṣika thinkers consider the mind to be corporeal. Indeed, one could argue that the mind is neither physical in the way that the body is nor non-physical in that consciousness is and that it falls into a third category. The wholly non-physical self is fundamentally different from physical substance. It is the foundation of consciousness, just as matter is the foundation of all attributes manifested in physical objects. Consciousness is a self-quality that manifests when the self is in contact with the mind. Consciousness is "sustained" by a non-physical substance called the self. In Nyāya, "consciousness" refers to empirical consciousness that unfolds as intentional consciousness. On the other hand, pure consciousness is devoid of any empirical qualities, which are incidental and arise in association with the physical mind. Self is consciousness as-it-is or pure consciousness when not associated with the mind (Kuppuswamy 1993: 101-02, 104-06).

Mokṣa, the key to personal freedom, is to overcome the mind-body complexes' grip on the self. *Mokṣa* is the state of the self (*ātman*) when it is free of the mind's entanglements. The physical body, after death, remains with *ātman* and does not cease to exist. The self separates from the body after death, but it maintains contact with the mind. The mind connects the self and carries the accumulated *karma*, resulting in reincarnation and the *saṁsāra cakra*. To achieve *mokṣa*, one must cultivate the spirit of detachment. The system recommends a three-stage method. The first level entails conquering selfish wants and hedonistic impulses via the cultivation of moral deeds (*dharma*). The second level entails realizing the ultimate truth about oneself through inquiry and thought. Finally, the third level concerns itself with detachment.

In this sense, neither the Cārvāka materialists nor Nyāya-Vaiśeṣika spiritual realism claim that knowledge or thought is fundamentally everlasting. It is just an unplanned output and a reliant quality for them. Nevertheless, the following considerations must be noticed regarding the nature and notion of consciousness in the Nyāya-Vaiśeṣika school:

- Consciousness depends on something else. It is, by definition, a coincidental and mechanical result of a series of occurrences. Hence, it is called *anitya*.
- The states of consciousness, among other topics, are not distinctive except that they express and illumine other substances. However, their form is not self-illuminated or self-established in Nyāya-Vaiśeṣika.
- It is neither self-illuminated nor self-proven (*svataḥprakāśa* and *svataḥsiddha*).
- The mind is the theoretical instrument that aids the *ātman* in gaining knowledge of the exterior world and interior conditions.
- The mind and the self are inextricably linked.

THE SĀṀKHYA-YOGA THOUGHT

Sāṁkhya and Yoga are two philosophical systems classified as Ṣaḍ-Darśana (six orthodox Indian thought systems). Sāṁkhya is the oldest among them. Sāṁkhya and Yoga, as conventional systems, owe their loyalty to and acknowledge the authority of the Vedas (Dasgupta 2018). *Puruṣa* and *prakṛti*, according to Sāṁkhya and Yoga, are the two primary principles of reality that govern our being. *Puruṣa* is immaterial pure consciousness and *prakṛti* is the origin of all material manifestations, including the mind (Rao and Paranjape 2017). They are thus the universe's "spirit and substance" (Dasgupta 2018), and our subjectivity and objectivity. *Prakṛti* gave rise to the manifest world of objects. Following the Cartesian mind–matter dichotomy, the rejection of such a perspective has put us in the insoluble "mind-body problem", a problem Western philosophy has been unable to escape.

Puruṣa manifests pure consciousness, experienced in the fourth state, rather than mental events encountered in the states of wakefulness and dreaming, which distinguishes Sāṁkhyan dualism from Cartesian dualism (Larson 2011: 75). Consequently, the *puruṣa* of Sāṁkhya is the only conscious element. It is a substance that exists. It is not the source of any action or the cause of any activity. Nevertheless, it is genuine in its own right. It is not a phantom concept or a flimsy attempt to model cognition. It has no shape and it is transcendental (Misra 1995). It is infinitely powerful like an unchangeable principle of omnipresence, with no possibility of modification, action or progress:

> *atha yo vededaṁ manvānīti sātmā mano 'sya daivaṁ cakṣuḥ sa*
> *vā eṣa etena daivena cakṣuṣā manasāitāṅkāmānpaśyanramate*
> *ya ete brahmaloke* ॥ — Radhakrishnan 2019: 509

Puruṣa's exact involvement in the evolutionary process is unknown, but it is considered that the process would not have begun or continued without it. *Prakṛti* is in perfect harmony and equilibrium in its primordial stage, with its three constituents — *sattva*, *rajas* and *tamas*. This equilibrium was disturbed due to vibration in the *rajas* element and evolution occurred. When the equilibrium is disrupted, each *guṇa* competes for domination with the others, resulting in an evolutionary process and the manifest world of one's experience.

Mahat, which means "great one", was the first to emerge from the primeval *prakṛti*. If *prakṛti* is the foundation, *mahat* is the first evolute to appear. It is, in and of itself, a little hazy and undifferentiated. *Mahat* is a cosmic intellect that serves as the foundation for all knowledge. By reflecting *puruṣa* it acts as a bridge between consciousness and the world of physical objects by generating subjective consciousness of the items. As a result of *puruṣa*'s reflections, the *buddhi* undergoes a qualitative transformation. This causes the phenomenal self to emerge, which is *puruṣa*'s image reflected in the *buddhi*. Behind all manifest experiences, this "reflected image" is the person's essence (Whicher

2000: 135-42). The *buddhi* as a whole emerges, as a concatenation of all individual *buddhis*. It plays a special and unique role in that it is responsible for establishing a link between *puruṣa* and the objective world of *prakṛti*, which are otherwise entirely separate and mutually exclusive. The *buddhi* is largely sāttvic and permeable, allowing it to catch *puruṣa*'s reflections. The quality of consciousness is bestowed on one's experience by the reflection of *puruṣa* in the *buddhi*. Furthermore, introspection fosters a feeling of self and establishes the empirical self as the person's essential condition, allowing him to have subjective experiences. The ego (*ahaṅkāra*) is born out of this process.

As an individual with an ego, the undifferentiated and indeterminate *buddhi* becomes structured and definite. The rājasic element dominates the sāttvic in the ego, and the person is more likely to crave, desire, engage in action, and enjoy or suffer the consequences. According to Sāṁkhya, the ego, on the other hand, is not a person but a process. In conjunction with the body, *ahaṅkāra* initiates the identity-development process and gives identity to the person's psychophysical framework. The evolution of *ahaṅkāra* ends with *manas* and *indriyas*. The central processor is the *manas*. The sensory-motor apparatus is known as the *indriya*. The *manas*, which processes sensory inputs, connects the ego and the sensory functions. The *buddhi*, *ahaṅkāra* and *manas* combine to form the *citta* or *antaḥkaraṇa*, as it is known in Sāṁkhya-Yoga. The interior instrument, *antaḥkaraṇa*, relates to what we may call the mind. The person comprises the *citta*, the senses and the physical structures that make up the body. The person is a fully functional, differentiated human who is involved in knowing, experiencing and responding.

The Sāṁkhya system offers a naturalistic perspective on evolution. Sāṁkhya implies a succession of transformations that purportedly resulted in the creation of countless atoms from which things are constructed, consistent with the Vedic idea of something "One" at the beginning of the cosmos manifesting into a multitude of things. The five primary sorts of atoms termed *tanmātras* in the Sāṁkhya system correspond to the five senses, such as auditory and visual *tanmātras*. In other words, the atomic constituents of nature are regarded to have both a conscious and a physical aspect. The objective here is not to find proof of the *tanmātras*' existence but to acknowledge that the physical and mental are seen as integrated components of nature in the Sāṁkhya world view.

Puruṣa is the source of consciousness in Yoga. *Puruṣa* is consciousness in and of itself, and there are many of them. It has a self-manifesting and self-luminous quality. It does not have any content, and it does not have any discernible object. It is intuitively understood. In principle, it cannot be reduced to any form or manifestation of matter. *Citta* in Yoga is the operating name for the mind. It comprises cognitive and ego processes, innate tendencies inherited from the past, and the repercussions of past deeds in this life (*vāsanās* and *saṁskāras*). They tend to tint one's perceptions and predispose them to act in particular ways. It also exhibits volitional activity, allowing it to pay attention to some objects while ignoring others. Finally, it possesses latent power (*śakti*), which can be harnessed to oversee and control its path.

Citta is the source of one's consciousness, volition, emotions and actions. The consciousness of the world that we gain through sensory mediation is not consciousness in the traditional sense. Instead, it is adulterated by the senses, frequently imperfect and blemished. It is lit by consciousness reflected in the mind, which is muddled for various reasons. Ordinary consciousness is mediated by the mind and so is indirect and cognitive, but transcendent consciousness is direct and unmediated (Whicher 2000: 78-85). The *citta* is divided into three stages of functioning: *buddhi*, *ahaṅkāra* (ego function) and *manas*. The *manas* is the core processor that selectively reflects sensory input and defines its character through assimilation and discrimination. The *ahaṅkāra* appropriates what the *manas* offers as one's own and considers the perceiving person the object of perception. The *buddhi* then responds appropriately to the information presented. The *citta*'s functions or processes are to ensure that everyone who comes into contact with an object first intuits it, then reflects on it, then appropriates it, then resolves "this is to be done by me" and then acts.

It should be noted that in Yoga, the *buddhi*, *ahaṅkāra* and *manas* are not considered separate entities or faculties. They are simply *citta*'s operational aspects. These three functions of the *citta* are referred to collectively as the internal organ (*antaḥkaraṇa*), as opposed to the senses, which are regarded as external organs. The senses serve as portals to knowledge and the *citta* serves as the gatekeeper. As the internal organ, the mind is the interconnecting instrument that helps to connect the conscious *puruṣa* with the unconscious objects. *Puruṣa*'s mind is both like and dislike to the mind. It differs from *puruṣa* in several ways. For instance, it fluctuates and changes. Second, the mind is said to exist just for *puruṣa*. Third, the mind participates in the world of objects by taking on their forms, whereas *puruṣa* is merely a witness to the items and does not engage with them. *Puruṣa*'s reflections in the *buddhi* culminate in the mind's erroneous identification with *puruṣa*, which operates as the empirical self with its ego. These reflections give rise to the erroneous belief that the *buddhi* states belong to *puruṣa*. Another Sāṁkhya commentator, Vijñānabhikṣu, believes that *puruṣa*'s reflections on the *buddhi* reflect on *puruṣa* and that this mutual reflection is the reason why *puruṣa*'s *buddhi* experiences are misattributed (Whicher 2000).

The fact that there is no contact between consciousness (*puruṣa*) and the material world of *prakṛti* in Sāṁkhya-Yoga is vital to remember. They have a relationship that is based on closeness. It is commonly misunderstood that *puruṣa* is bound to *prakṛti* and that emancipation (*kaivalya*) entails releasing *puruṣa* from this enslavement. The concept of a multiplicity of *puruṣa* is interpreted as endorsing this viewpoint. *Prakṛti* is what is bound and released.

Even though *puruṣa* and *prakṛti* are continually close, they never interact. The Cartesian trap of mind-body interaction is avoided in this concept.

On the other hand, such an interpretation is goes against to the spirit of Sāṁkhya-Yoga dualism. Even though there is no causal relationship between the two, *puruṣa*'s proximity to *prakṛti* has a significant impact. Due to its close vicinity, *prakṛti* may benefit from *puruṣa*'s reflected light. Subjectivity is bestowed by these reflections, which develop knowledge and consciousness of one's feelings and actions. Īśvarakṛṣṇa and the other commentators on the Kārikās do not cite or discuss the genesis of the relationship between *puruṣa* and *prakṛti*, which is fascinating. Instead, it is said that the association has existed since its inception. Similarly, the consciousness attributed to the mind is an illusion that will dissolve with the dawn of discriminative knowledge. This interpretation is essentially a reaction to the "Cartesian trap", as it is known (Larson 2011).

THE ADVAITA VEDĀNTA THOUGHT

As illustrated earlier, the discussions regarding the issue of consciousness date back to the times of the Vedas and the last part of the Vedas, i.e. the Upaniṣads. Hence, we also had a brief encounter with the kind of terminology and the level of discourse found therein. The Vedānta tradition of Indian philosophy, particularly Advaita Vedānta is the final culmination of the entire discourse.[21] It is the most uncompromising and systematic philosophical discourse that deals exclusively with the problem of consciousness. Hence, we shall now discuss their standpoint regarding the same over here.

According to Śaṅkara, the core argument of Advaita Vedānta is that *Brahman/Ātman* is the fundamental reality. In its most abstract form, *Brahman* is the Absolute Consciousness. It is the intelligent

---

21 The original discourse of the Vedānta tradition owes its allegiance to the *prasthānatrayī* texts which include the Upaniṣads, *Bhagavadgītā* and *Brahmasūtra*.

and unifying principle that underpins all of the world's dynamic manifestations. It is a self-manifesting and self-illuminating consciousness that is non-intentional and non-relational. It does not have a form and does not rest in anything else. It exists outside of space and time. It serves as both a subject and an object. It is information in its purest form, unequalled and entirely subjective. As a result, it is ineffable and impossible to categorize. Knowing what it is not, instead of what it is, is the ideal approach to comprehending it. The difficulties of comprehending consciousness in its undifferentiated form are well acknowledged. We are, in some ways, cognitively blind to it. The closest approximation to a portrayal of *Brahman* is *Sat-Cit-Ānanda.*

To begin with, *Brahman* denotes existence (*sat*). It does not distinguish between knowing and being. Second, it is consciousness in totality (*cit*). There is no distinction between knower, known, and knowing at the *Brahman* level. Absolute bliss (*ānanda*) is also a concept associated with *Brahman.* As a corollary, *Brahman* is the source of all existence (*sat*), knowledge (*cit*) and bliss (*ānanda*). What is the connection between *Brahman* and the individual (*jīva*)? The relationship is exemplified in the *Chāndogya Upaniṣad*'s *mahāvākya: tat-tvam-asi* (Thou Art That). All existence, including one's own, is rooted in *Brahman*. The integrity of the relationship is obscured by the existential conditioning of ignorance and *prapañca*, i.e. *māyā.* It is the Advaitic concept of cosmic illusion or veiling power. The empirical disguise of the true Self on the stage, i.e. *saṁsāra*, through the act of *māyā*,[22] is the individual's identity. The transcendental subject "I" is *ātman*, whereas the empirical subject "me" is *jīva*. It is genuine in every way. The empirical "me" is transitorily real, similar to how a dream experience is legitimate while dreaming, but not when awakened.

Before we delve deeper into the metaphysical background of the discussion, let us address the current domain of discussion; the

---

22 Kabīr succinctly puts it in his *dohā* verses: *māyā mahāṭhaganī hama jānī* ।

Advaita conception of the mind, so that we can, in the end, knit an integrated fabric of the discourse. Even though Śaṅkara is one of the most ardent critics of Sāṁkhya philosophy, Advaita's notion of the mind is almost identical to that of Sāṁkhya-Yoga. Here the mind is the instrument of knowledge, passion and intention, distinguished from consciousness. For both systems, the mind travels to objects to have perceptual experiences. In Advaita, the mind is alluded to as *antaḥkaraṇa*. It is the psychological mechanism that allows one to understand, feel and act. The mind encompasses all mental states and the processes that give rise to them. Yoga and Advaita Vedānta both regard the mind to be physical. In terms of the mind, one fundamental distinction between Sāṁkhya-Yoga and Advaita Vedānta is that in Advaita, consciousness is the only thing that exists, whereas, in Sāṁkhya-Yoga, the mind is not ultimately existent. Its reality is limited to the phenomenal illusory world (*vyāvahārika sattā*). Both consciousness and mind are genuine in Sāṁkhya. However, as earlier said, a person seeking liberation intends to empty the mind of its content to establish a condition of mind control. Anything that exhibits such changes, according to Advaitic philosophy, is not ultimately genuine. As a result, the difference between the two systems is mainly in their conception of reality, which is not significant from a psychological standpoint (Kuppuswamy 2001; Rao 1962).

In Advaita, the mind (*antaḥkaraṇa*) is an internal organ (Rao 1960: 21). It is the result of combining consciousness and response systems. It can be functionally split into (1) *buddhi*, (2) *ahaṅkāra*, and (3) *manas* (which is sometimes further subdivided into *manas* and *citta* in Advaita) related to the sensory-motor system (*jñāna-karma indriyas*), much as it is in Yoga. The mind (*antaḥkaraṇa* in its *buddhi* function) goes out to the object via sensory channels in the perceptual process. The *buddhi* comes into contact with the object through the sensory channels during perception. This causes changes in the *buddhi* and the emergence of *vṛttis* in mind.

Vṛttis are processed by the *manas*, which use selective attention to analyse, assimilate and discriminate *vṛttis*. As a result, *vṛttis* become determinate and definitive, and the subject–predicate interaction is dissolved. This is the method of apprehending items reflectively. When the *ahaṅkāra*, the self-referencing system, appropriates *vṛttis* in the following stage, they become associated with the person. Then there is the object's self-apprehension. *Vṛttis* return to the *buddhi* with all the manifested modifications owing to the *ahaṅkāra*'s self-referencing and the *manas*'s determinate form. Advaita differentiates between (a) perceiving an object, and (b) perceiving an object as an object. The first is concerned with distinguishing between cognitive (*pramā*) and object consciousness (*viṣaya caitanya*). In the perception of an object as an object, there is an identification with the person who has that perception and the identification of the thing. For example, the intimate experience that the rose is red, but he also acknowledges that he is aware of the rose's redness. The *jīva* refers to and appropriates the *vṛtti* in this case (the empirical self) (Advarindra Dharmarāja 1983: 58-59).

In Advaita, perception entails the mind "reaching out" to the object through the senses and taking on the object's shape. This stance on the perceptual process may seem peculiar because the globally acknowledged belief is that the stimulus object commences the perceptual process. Electromagnetic waves are emitted by the stimuli, impinging on the sensory component of the nervous system and generating a sensation in the brain. The person then has the object's perceptual experience. In other words, the flow is through the sensory system from the object to the brain. In Advaita, the situation is precisely the opposite. The mind, in a way, pours out to the object of perception through the senses. What exactly does that mean, the mind flows out to the object? Does it make sense to believe that the mind initiates the perceptual process? It is illogical to believe that the mind leaves the body and travels to the object. In this regard, I shall like to bring forward two approaches by two eminent (posthumous) Indian psychologists of India, K. Rama Rao and S.K.R. Rao respectively.[23]

Koneru Ramakrishna Rao, in *Handbook of Indian Psychology*, states that the mind's flowing out function entails nothing more than the assertion that the person, not the object of perception, is paramount in the perceptual process. It refers to a person's ability to choose his perceptual object. Objects devoid of functional minds cannot choose a subject with whom to interact. A subject with a functional mind, on the other hand, has the option of entering or exiting a relationship with an object. The claim that the mind takes on the object's shape through the senses can only mean that the mind, or a part of it, goes through a sensory metamorphosis that represents the object of perception. Unlike a gross item confined to a locale, flowing out does not indicate movement because the mind is physically subtle and non-local. As a result, flowing out entails forming a perceptual relationship through which the mind is transformed, and perceptual experience results from that transformation. In other words, perception is similar to how a radar works in that it is a continuous activity. The perceptual process is more like a searchlight that draws attention to a specific object, emphasizing the attention required to focus on the object rather than the intensity of the stimulus (Rao and Paranjape 2017: 103).

It would be prudent to refer to S.K.R. Rao's discussion of the same problem, and hence I would like to quote him as such:

> What role does the mind play in cognition? Śaṅkara responds: The physical object, as a presentational detail of the outer world, impinges on a sense organ that apprehends the stimulation — then deposited in mind, which, due to the predominance of *rajas*, is always active except in deep sleep. The mind is now said to "flow out" through the sense avenue, taking on the form of

---

23 This problem forms a point of further academic discussion which shall be posed as such in the concluding section. I would like to thank Devendra Nath Tiwari for providing me with crucial insights into the issue.

> the object presented. The form thus assumed by the mind (or the modality of mind) is termed a *vṛtti*. Śaṅkara's position is stated thus: The object is not mental, for it is a presentation to the subject. It is private; others cannot attest to its existence ... (it is) built by the individual and belongs to him alone. Three entities are thus required in a cognition instance: the object (*viṣaya*), the subject (*pramātṛ*), and the subjective modification (*vṛtti*). The object stimulates the sense organ and thus creates disturbances in the subject, or more properly in mind; mind by its very constitution is dynamic and is increasingly active in receiving the forms of objects. — Rao 1960: 27-28

In the Advaita school, the *manas* is concerned primarily with determination and ambivalence (*saṅkalpa vikalpātmikā manaḥ*). The crucial phrases *saṅkalpa* and *vikalpa* are derived from the root verb *klip*. *Saṅkalpa* refers to bringing thoughts together, synthesizing or integrating them, whereas *vikalpa* refers to the process of distinguishing between competing conceptions. In modern psychological terms, the mind involves the two most important cognitive processes: differentiation and integration. As a result, the mind's core purpose is to cognitively construct a given scenario in various alternative ways, which leads to decision making. Given the mind's inherently processing nature, *antaḥkaraṇa vṛtti* is a common term in the tradition, as the root verb, *vṛt*, means "to turn, move, or go on", signifying continuous movement. The Advaitic phrase *antaḥkaraṇa vṛtti* is synonymous with the Yogic term *citta-vṛtti* and both are equally significant and foundational notions in the psychology of Sāṁkhya-Yoga and Advaita systems, respectively.[24] Past impressions influence the *vṛtti*, which undergoes more modifications before manifesting as a kind of *buddhi*. *Brahman*'s light always surrounds the *buddhi*. As a result, the consciousness of the nature of light reflects on the *buddhi* in its *vṛtti* form, causing the conscious perception of the object. The *buddhi* can then choose to react accordingly by commencing action through its *karmendriya*'s

[24] To ponder upon the differences between *manovṛtti*, *antaḥkaraṇa-vṛtti* and *citta-vṛtti* one can refer to Bilimoria (1985).

feedback mechanism. The *buddhi* reflects consciousness, revealing the corresponding *vṛtti*. When the *buddhi* is altered by a touch with sense objects, it takes the *vṛtti* form.

The *jīva-sākṣī* is a term used to describe human consciousness. It aids in the relationship between immutable and inactive consciousnesses that illuminate the mind and dynamic matter. *Sākṣī* is also helpful in comprehending how *Brahman/ātman*, the one and indivisible consciousness, emerges as many *ātmans* in a plurality of people without undergoing any modifications. *Sākṣī* is the witnessing consciousness, whereas *jīva* is the embodied consciousness. The mind's link with the *jīva*'s consciousness limits, qualifies and modifies it. The *sākṣī*, on the other hand, remains detached from the mind and is unaffected by it. Consciousness is defined as what is mirrored in the mind in the *jīva*. It is consciousness as such in the *sākṣī*. Consciousness is immanent in the mind in *jīva*; it transcends the mind and exists independently as the *sākṣī*. This never-ending self-luminosity offers the impression of a continuous stream of consciousness. Pure conscious experience is conceivable for the *jīva*, the embodied consciousness that imparts illusory knowledge cloaked in subject–object duality. The *Sākṣī*, which is none other than consciousness as-such, *Brahman* manifesting at the level of a person, is the *jīva* without the baggage of the mind (Śaṅkara 1931: 26-43).

Phenomenal consciousness is the empirical mode of consciousness and is described as follows. It is the existential state of human cognition and action. Advaitins believe that as one awakens with the dawn of pure conscious experience, the limiting nature of such consciousness and its illusory nature becomes evident. When consciousness reaches the level of pure consciousness, one's relationship with reality changes dramatically. The subject–object duality is then no longer present. Knowledge loses its representational nature. As a result, consciousness becomes contentless. "Contentless" refers to the ineffability of experience as a whole. This is a condition of transcendence in which knowing and being merge, differences and distinctions fade away, and utter subjectivity and objectless consciousness are experienced. This consciousness which is the nature of the soul (*ātman*), is neither a distinct attribute of it nor of the nature of the activity (*karma*). We relate it as subject knowledge based exclusively on the constraints of language, as we describe it in terms of the state of the bright sun. But it is not authentic to portray consciousness in this way, even though it is vital and indispensable. It cannot be described as a false representation resulting from critical thinking and reflective constraints. its nature resembles a figurative statue that instructs towards transcendental consciousness, and inside which there is no distinction of any type. It has become essential to embrace this way due to the inadequacy of thought and language to explain the nature of ultimate consciousness. All because that which is known is known by the *buddhi*, i.e. the intellect itself, which can only consider in terms of divisions and differences. As a result, the following essential points about the idealist perspective towards consciousness emerge:

- The consciousness (*cetanā*) is all-knowing. It is the presumption of the cognitive triangle's distinction of knowledge: the knowing recipient of knowledge (*grāhaka*), the knowledge: attribute (*grahaṇa*) and the known object (*grāhya*). The cognition triangle is seen here. It is devoid of distinctions and is a single thing.
- Consciousness is neither a property nor a feature of the *ātman*. There is nothing that the *ātman* has assimilated. It is the *ātman* in its purest form of consciousness.
- The knowledge of the matter, quality or action has no bearing on ultimate consciousness. It is the fundamental reality of everything.
- That consciousness is unlike anything else on the planet. It is one-of-a-kind and non-dual. It is not the result of any combination, chance of circumstances, or material.

- It is eternal, uncaused and unproduced, and it is not the result of any combination, coincidence of conditions or material. It is also unlimited or without limits. It is irreducible and cannot be reduced to a single item or a mixture of components.
- The distinction between consciousness and its object has an inner nature. Where the object is specific and subject to change, consciousness is universal and eternal.

A CRITICAL REVIEW OF ONTOLOGY

Now that we have had an overview of the standpoint of primary orthodox Indian philosophical schools, it shall be prudent to look at their points of difference. After we have looked at the points of differences, we shall try to find a common framework under which we can unify these distinct and varying orders of thought and try to sum up this section with a bird's-eye view of the overall unifying framework. Consciousness, according to Śaṅkarācārya and the Sāṁkhya-Yoga scholars, is a permanent and everlasting light of being. The true nature of the *ātman* in Advaita Vedānta and *puruṣa* in Sāṁkhya-Yoga is this eternal luminous consciousness. It is an independent entity in and of itself, not an attribute or an action of the soul. Consciousness is regarded as a soul's attribute in Nyāya-Vaiśeṣika. Nyāya's position on consciousness is that it is a mechanical property emerging from the interaction of various variables inherent in a substance separate from itself. This is the least acceptable from an ontological standpoint. It has no foundation, neither in terms of thought's independent existence nor its self-conscious nature.

This viewpoint, that matter is distinct from its properties and functions, is philosophically untenable. This makes the soul a material, but it also makes it impossible to explain the cognitive process and experience cognition. At the inception of its idea of *puruṣa*, Sāṁkhya philosophy acknowledges the independent principle of consciousness, but it unfortunately totally bifurcates the form of knowledge from its subject matter. This transcendental principle of *puruṣa* is so distinct from the knowledge substance that it becomes an enigma; how the pure element of knowledge takes on a completely different identity from that which is not its own.

In Sāṁkhya epistemology and metaphysics, this problem has proven to be the most complex. We cannot deduce consciousness from a collection of physical substances (*saṅghāta*) as Nyāya-Vaiśeṣika does. It is also worth remembering that consciousness is always expressed empirically through its material substance (*sāmagrī*). The Sāṁkhya philosophy gets in trouble by failing to acknowledge the fundamental link between these two principles of knowledge, formal and material. Śaṅkara's Advaita Vedānta provided a specific expression to consciousness 'autonomous and eternal existence, which illuminates everything with its light. He declared that the preconceived notion of omniscience is the fundamental fact of pure consciousness.

The subject and the object of knowledge are not distinct and independent in and of themselves but solely in terms of enumeration. They are not that distinct from the realm of experience. Only under unified and universal consciousness are they distinguished. This self-contained existence of consciousness has both transcendental and empirical aspects of reality. It should be deemed non-dual, ubiquitous, immutable, quasi and non-discriminatory under the first. At the same time, it should be regarded as specific, dynamic, functional and full of variations under the latter. This pure consciousness is both within and beyond these distinctions. It is immanent as well as transcendent.

Now I think it would be prudent to discuss the standard framework and points of agreement therein:

- To begin with, the mind and consciousness are regarded as fundamentally different.
- The form perceived is different from the sense perceiving it. The mind is different from the senses it perceives. The

witnessing consciousness yet perceives the mind and its modifications.[25]

- There is a broad consensus that the mind is physical, unlike consciousness, which is viewed as a non-physical reality.
- The mind is considered as the interface and conduit between consciousness and the physical world on the one hand and the physical world on the other.
- Non-agreement with Cartesian dualism and considering the distinction between mind and consciousness while considering the mind as the interacting buffer between pure consciousness and the world, we have a model wherein there is no interaction in the Western sense of the term.
- Mind is a subtle matter and, hence, this buffer bridges the interaction problem quite enough.

TOWARDS A UNIFIED MODEL

- The mind-body complex is the vehicle by which one's qualia, or first-person subjective experience, is expressed. Consciousness is not the same as the mind.
- The mind, unlike consciousness, is made up of subtle matter that obeys physical principles.
- The mind does not generate consciousness; instead, it is reflected by it.
- The mind is also distinct from the brain and, as such, it is non-local in that it can function outside the typical restrictions of space and time. The mind is conditioned, limited and, driven by physical principles in conjunction with the body.
- The mind, on its whole, is an interface that connects the brain and bodily functions of the person with whom it is associated on the one hand.

---

25 *rūpaṁ dr̥śyaṁ locanaṁ dr̥k taddr̥śyaṁ dr̥k tu mānasaṁ* ।
dr̥śya dhīvr̥ttyassākṣi dr̥geva na tu dr̥śyate ॥ — Śaṅkara 1931: 2

- On the other hand, the mind is ready to receive the illuminating light of consciousness.
- The mind makes the body its instrument. Watching the mind-body complex is the *sākṣī* which illumines intentionality but is untainted.
- The ego is the most visible manifestation of the conditioned mind, and it serves as a bridge between the external subjective perception of the world while eluding the true nature of ultimate consciousness.
- Again, the mind has two functions: as an internal receptor and as a link between external sensory inputs and consciousness. Internal states are also something we are conscious of.
- The five external receptors, i.e. the five *jñānendriyas*, which work on their respective modalities, cannot accomplish this.
- The senses register and reflect the energy patterns that emanate from the world of objects on the *manas*.
- As a result, we require another instrument to serve as an internal receptor, allowing us to become aware of our interior states. Only in the existence of the conscious principle, the *sākṣī* is subjective consciousness conceivable.
- The *manas* and mind are not the same. The *manas* is a component of the mind that in the Advaita system is labelled as the *antaḥkaraṇa*.
- The *citta*, *buddhi*, *ahaṅkāra* and *manas* are the four components of the *antaḥkaraṇa* (mind).
- The *buddhi*, which is commonly translated as intellect in its purity, has the power to reflect consciousness. It is a tool for discrimination.
- The ego-sense is manifested through *ahaṅkāra*. It takes the form of the "I", i.e. individual identity, its defining feature. It is the source of the difference between the self and others. The *ahaṅkāra* element of the mind appropriates sensorially

processed data, disrupts the inherent link between knowing and being, and intentionally separates them.

- The *manas* functions like a central processing unit. Its distinguishing characteristic is attention; its other functions include filtering and analysis. It serves as an internal sense organ as well. The *manas* processes the sensory inputs.
- The *manas* serves two purposes: (a) it analyses sensory data, and (b) it serves as a sixth sense, receiving inputs from interior states.
- On the other hand, the *manas* is what starts and prompts the cognitive process.
- In other words, the flow of information in the perceptual process is from the mind to the object rather than from the stimulus to the person. This gives the idea that the mind is directing itself towards the thing. However, because the mind is nuanced and nonlocal, such a "journey" may not be required.
- The mind is the source of one's cognition contents and the repository of past acts and their consequences.
- Consciousness in the mind is always laced with emotions that are dependent on prior memories and desires (*saṁskāra*s and *vāsanā*s).
- The mind is in a perpetual state of flux and instability, always trying to predict the future, and hence it is prone to prejudice, distortion and misinterpretation. As a result, the individual misinterprets the ego as the self. Here comes the scope of training the mind.
- To achieve mastery over *indriya*s, one must first understand their nature and function. Proper management of the *indriya* function helps achieve cognitive excellence and attain altered states of consciousness.

III

Metaphysical Underpinnings

THE PROBLEM OF TRANSCENDENTALISM

The dilemma of self-consciousness leads us to an exaggerated conception of an ultimate and eternal consciousness that is devoid of the conception of the self and transcendent, something that could only be the prerequisite of our comprehensive knowledge. We have seen that every satisfying meta-theory of knowledge probably involves room for two varieties of consciousness, or two distinct theories of consciousness, one of which undergoes modification while the other remains unaltered and immutable. The former conception can be labelled as the *antaḥkaraṇa* (mind), *citta* (memory) and *buddhi* (intellect). In contrast, the latter is known as the *cit* or pure awareness. When left to themselves, the mental transformation and *vr̥tti*s (modifications) of the *antaḥkaraṇa* do not comprise true knowledge because they are imbued with phenomenal consciousness (*sacetana*) and form. Knowledge of an object arises when the light of consciousness (*cit*), which is other than the modes of the *antaḥkaraṇa*, collects and illuminates both the object and the *vr̥tti* (modification). The distinction between the *antaḥkaraṇa* and *cit*, the unconscious changing principle and conscious non-changing principle, is so essential that no metaphysics of consciousness can ignore it. This distinction is so vital that it can be called an essential part of any metaphysics related to the problem of consciousness.

The commentary on the *Yogasūtra* by Vyāsa, also called *Yoga-Bhāṣya*, presents three reasons for accepting this distinction between the mind and the soul, as is elucidated in *Yogasūtra* II.20:

> *draṣṭā dr̥śimātraḥ śuddho 'pi pratyayānupaśyaḥ* ।
>
> — Sutton 2019: 69

The mind differs from the soul in that, it is principally, the former transforms into its *vr̥tti*s. Second, the mind serves the function of the *cit* for which it is an object, but the transcendental soul (*puruṣa*) is elusive in daily life. Furthermore, the mind takes on the properties of *sattva*, *rajas* and *tamas*, whereas the *ātman* is free and does not embody any of these primary constituent elements' traits on its own.

> *tadartha eva dr̥śyasyātmā* । — Ibid.: 71

The existential *sākṣī, kevala* or *akartā* is the experiencer of the absolute transcendental consciousness. It is distinct from its counterpart, the *buddhi*, in that it does not engage in alterations or modifications (*vr̥ttis*). Instead, its existence is that of a pure subject, the all-experiencer who can undergo various mental alterations (*citta-vr̥ttis*). As a result, because he is also the knower of these knowledge events, the true (*sat*) existent soul is distinguished from practical knowledge events in this way:

> *tasmāt-ca viparyāsāt siddhaṁ sākṣitvam-asya puruṣasya* ।
> *kaivalyaṁ mādhyastyaṁ draṣṭr̥tvam-akartr̥bhāvaḥ ca* ॥
> — Misra 1995: 61-62

The split of consciousness into two forms, the former being unchanging and the latter changing according to its contextual content and mental modifications, has been the source of many misconceptions and fruitless disputes, perplexing the philosophizing community. Realists such as Kaṇāda, Śrīdhara and Jayanta Bhaṭṭa begin with the stable footing of daily experience and explore a transformative and rapidly sequential consciousness, full of different contents, which is itself a result of contiguous circumstances played out linearly, with an inevitable reference to both object and subject, imitating as the only visible nature of consciousness. To generate a consistent stream of experience, the realist must accept a constant and unchanging theory to explain remembrance and personal identity. The realist must embrace a theory that is always present and immutable. He is unable to perceive beyond the empirically observable realities of transformational consciousness. As a result, the realist is forced to dismiss the "core" of ultimate transcendental consciousness.

However, for the Upaniṣads, Advaita Vedāntins and idealist Sāṁkhya-Yoga philosophers, this experience — absolute consciousness — is the backbone and foundation of the entire experiential cognition, without which no knowledge, even partial knowledge, is possible. Therefore, it is critical to understand the fundamental principles of absolute or transcendental consciousness experience and what and how much meaning this idea applies in this situation. This is one more significant component of studying the transcendental nature of consciousness, and that is the particular focus that Hindu thinking and ideology have placed on our life and experience of existence in its purest form. As a result, research on it is becoming increasingly popular. Furthermore, this concept of absolute consciousness has been developed further in Indian thinking, leading to the concept of transcendental consciousness, which is separate from the total experience as the sole actual reality.

ON THE NATURE OF TRANSCENDENCE

Eternity and Omnipresence

Transcendental consciousness is a state of consciousness that is unperturbed by time — immutable, eternal — and exists outside of temporal perception. It is not temporally limited because time is encompassed inside it. Because no sort of time can be envisaged without consciousness, creating the category of *kāla* (time) is owing to self-consciousness. There has never been a time when its existence came to an end, and there will never be a time when it does. The presence of the eternal non-intentional consciousness' preceding or retrospective existence or effect cannot be demonstrated by silently admitting the presence of that consciousness itself, which is being denied at any point in time.

> *svapnāntaṁ jāgaṟtāntaṁ cobhau yenānupaśyati* ।
> *mahāntaṁ vibhumātmānaṁ matvā dhīro na śocati* ॥
>
> — *KaṭhaUp* 1.2.22

It is absolute divinity because it is a witness to all modifications. It is eternal and the notion of eternity means that it remains present in all the three divisions of time (*sarvakāla vartamānam*):

> *sadājñātāścittavṛttayastatprabhoḥ puruṣasyāpariṇāmitvāt* ।
>
> — Sutton 2019: 120-22

On Causality

Transcendental consciousness is both reasonless and causeless because there is nothing in the world that could be its forerunner. It has nothing in front of it or beyond it. For this reason, it is known as *aja*. Because nothing else exists, it is not only an uncaused cause but also delves into inaction. It is free of all timeframes, space and cause–effect constraints. It is not only free of these constraints but it also transcends time, space and cause–effect causation. The same point is elucidated in the discussion between Yājñavalkya and Gārgī in *Bṛhadāraṇyaka Upaniṣad* 3.8.7, and I quote:

> *sa hovāca, yadūrdhvaṁ gārgi divo, yadavāk pṛthivyāḥ, yadantarā dyāvāpṛthivī ime, yadbhūtaṁ ca bhavacca bhaviṣyaccetyācakṣata, ākāśa eva tadotaṁ ca protaṁ ceti, kasminnu khalvākāśa otaśca protaśceti* ।

In response to this, it is later said:

> *ekadhaivānudraṣṭavyametadapramayaṁ dhruvam* ।
> *virajaḥ para ākāśādaja ātmā mahāndhruvaḥ* ॥
>
> — Radhakrishnan 2008: 231-32, 278

Brahman has no reason or function; thus, it can never be the action, effect or cause of anything. The temporal category of cognition of cause and effect cannot be used to describe the *ātman* since there is no background for an account of its origin as an ontological phenomenon or activity from the perspective of ultimate existence. As a result, the debate is pointless in this context. Perhaps the only truth is an utterly unquestionable non-origin (eternity). If the Ultimate Truth is complete and self-fulfilling, content in its being, complete in itself, then no form of logic can deduce the action of creation. The universe does not exist from a supreme experience or transcendental standpoint, but we appear to see it because our self-created phenomenological view is limited and unenlightened. From the standpoint of absolute being, everything, which is an illusion (in connection) from an empirical standpoint, does not exist.

The entire world's conceptual hypothesis is an explanation given to and for itself. There is no duality. There is no bifurcation of ontology at any level. This entire hypothesis, according to Vedāntins, is a loosely translated dilemma for those who have not yet tasted the heavenly nectar of knowledge, the Ultimate Truth, which is above and beyond all ontic subjectivity. According to Ācārya Gauḍapāda, a fundamental non-dualist Advaita Vedāntin of his day and Śaṅkarācārya's supreme *guru*, there is no occurrence of any substance other than the soul and itself (*ātman*) in his *Māṇḍūkya Upaniṣad Kārikā*. The doctrine states no evolution, becoming, origin or end (Gauḍapāda 1949: 91-144). Any attempt to explain the ontological bifurcation based on desire (*bhoga*) or play (*līlā* or *krīḍā*) is useless and unforgiving in all considerations and perspectives. Other than in the categorical concept of illusion, the origin of creation cannot be clearly defined or understood (*bhrama*). Absolute and all-encompassing consciousness exists outside the chain of cause–effect causation and causality.

Non-Duality

There are no external relations or internal distinctions in absolute consciousness. There is nothing beyond it in the world, whether homogeneous (*sajātīya*) or heterogeneous (*vijātīya*). Its nature is to have no internal differentiation (*svagata-bheda*). A tree's leaves have a homologous relationship, but other substances, such as stone and snow, have a heterogeneous relationship. On the other hand, absolute consciousness has no similar or dissimilar material or object. It does not have any internal distinction or differentiation. It is *nirāśraya* (without any locus) and *nirviṣaya* (without an object of desire). As a result, it has no discernible features and is indistinguishable. All variations and differentiations of consciousness are linked to its practical and relative representation and are dependent on the variations and conditions that define it. The *ātman*, on the other hand, is self-contained and exists outside of them.

In everyday language, there is a consciousness "of" something and "for" something. However, when we talk about absolute consciousness, such a distinction is impossible to make. Because it is a part of that indistinct consciousness, and knowledge of ego-consciousness or ego-cognition does not exist. However, it is of the nature of consciousness, self-illumined, of the nature of knowing, rather than a passive and material consciousness. All apparent divisions and differentiations in absolute consciousness are attributable to the existence of the ego concept (*ahaṅkāra*). According to the ego condition, total consciousness, for example, moves through the stages of profound sleep, dream and awakening. Ego-consciousness is in the dream and awakening states, while pure consciousness is sleeping. There is no conscious sensation of difference in numerous stages of deep sleep since, in that condition, half or complete distinctions exist according to the ego's full or partial functioning:

> *ahaṅkāralaye suptau bhaveddeho apyacetanaḥ* ।
> *ahaṅkāra vikāsārdhaḥ svapnaḥ sarvāstu jāgaraḥ* ॥
>
> — Śaṅkara 1931

The mind's functioning is the only reason for dualism, which has been posited as an eternal property of consciousness.[26] The non-dual mind is not differentiated in Advaita. It does not have any inherent differentiation. Furthermore, whoever perceives distinctions in it is doomed to wander from death to death (Radhakrishnan 2019: 277-78).

---

[26] *prakāśādivaccāvaiśeṣyaṁ prakāśaśca karmaṇi, abhyāsāt* ।
— Śaṅkarācārya 2000: 3.2.25

Beyond Good and Evil

Pure consciousness is untouched by happy and sad experiences. It exists outside the realms of good and evil, and auspiciousness, or its inverse, does not exist in its environment. How can this happen, one might wonder? If the soul is of the nature of consciousness, and consciousness is what cognizes these categories, how is it beyond them if they are meaningless and out of context without it? According to the idealist, its existence is that of a distinct seer, not the bearer of experience (distinct from the one who enjoys it, *bhogārthī*). Desires for pleasure, happiness and grief cannot touch it because they are not a part of it.

The defects and misfortunes, maladies and predicaments that follow from them are linked to the level of limitation and finitude, which is the level of *jīva*, rather than absolute consciousness. Absolute or pure consciousness is untouched by the possibilities of happiness or misery, yet it imposes physical and mental limitations on itself. It perceives itself as happy or sad after this imposition. It is virtually unaffected by the intellect's (*buddhi*'s) limiting adjectives, without which it cannot be an experiencer, enjoyer or doer of any *karma* (Sutton 2019: 47-48). It has nothing to do with any physical, emotional or mental object. This has nothing to do with other adjuncts (Radhakrishnan 2019: 186, 242). Impurity is caused by bonding, mixing or contagion. In an absolute sense, transcendent consciousness is pure on all levels.

The Upaniṣads say that the *puruṣa* is unrelated or unconnected. *Asaṅgo hy ayaṁ puruṣaḥ* (Radhakrishnan 2019: 260) is the doctrine. Although the *kevalī puruṣa* is pure and everlasting in himself, due to contact with outer attachments, he becomes tarnished, soiled and sorrowfully deformed with faults, much like holy water becomes impure due to its contact with other exterior substances. The nature of *Brahman*, according to Vedānta, is entirely irreconcilable. This form of consciousness is the only substance with a fundamental foundation, and its existence, i.e. *sattā*, is regarded as *pāramārthika*.

In contrast to transcendental consciousness, there is empirical consciousness, also known as *vyāvahārika*, whose formal nature is based on differences, differentiation, interrelations and changes. This empirical *vyāvahārika* consciousness's *sattā*, or being, is contingent and relative. The presence of *vyāvahārika sattā* is neither totally rejected nor completely undermined, which appears to be the most remarkable element of this line of thought. All that has been contested is that empirical consciousness exists in a relative sense and is due to the fundamental reality of absolute transcendental consciousness, which is not dependent on or contingent on other circumstances. It is essential to remember that there is a distinction between realist and idealist perspectives on these two levels of consciousness and the reality (*sattā*) that comes with them. The idealist opposes the totality of empirical consciousness, whereas the realist denies transcendental and absolute consciousness. Nevertheless, empirical consciousness is never entirely rejected or despised by idealists.

It is not surprising that the actuality of "reality of truth" or "truth of truth" (*satyasya satyam*) is frequently disputed outright because it does not adhere to the ordinary norms of knowledge and proof. The sole evidence for the presence of transcendental consciousness, on the other hand, can only be based on the development of preconceptions in empirical consciousness. The legitimacy and efficacy of this indirect proof technique appears to have been undervalued. Even if it can never be directly proven, anything that pre-exists in the existence of reality is as inevitable a reality as that which presupposes it. For this reason, to believe in the transcendental nature of consciousness, other than directly perceiving it in supra-intellectual vision *samādhi* or *brahma-jñāna*, is a logico-epistemological attempt. Hence, the pieces of evidence to be put forward for such an approach should follow a line of a priori deduction. An analysis of the possibility of a knowledge event follows a seemingly axiomatic theory of present and permanent consciousness, whose concomitant refusal can inevitably lead to two undesirable alternatives of materialism and agnosticism. Neither of them is knowingly considered the solution to the problem of consciousness.

Knowing the Absolute through Intellect

As previously discussed, our logical mind and any of our rational categories of thought cannot fully comprehend the experience of absolute, transcendental consciousness. In this sense, it transcends words, speeches and even literal connotations. We have also proposed that what remains outside our intellect and reasoning is not necessarily undetected, much like infinite space is not unknown, even if it is not fully grasped in solitary spatial perception. However, it is unknown only in a logical sense. Therefore, it cannot be deduced by logical methods in the same way that an ontological entity can be deduced by logical calculation or relativistically because absolute consciousness is neither logical nor relativistic. Thus, all our attempts to comprehend it will inevitably fail. As a result, the best description can only be offered negatively by rejecting any adjectives typically used for other objects.

This negation-based paradigm has a long history in Christian ideology. Christian theologians name it "Via Remotionis" or "Negativa". This approach is referred to as *neti-neti*. We can see "What he is not" more clearly than "What he is" (Braine 1998). Also, it cannot be attained in any other way except by negation (Spencer 2022: 32). The ultimate subject cannot be exhausted in our individual or collective foresight. There are no adjectives in our language that can adequately describe it. As a result, its negative descriptions should be confined to symbols and metaphors. It is also worth remembering that we can have a clear vision of the things that these symbols and metaphors observe from the world of objects, making complete and absolute consciousness entirely acceptable to the intellect.

At this point in our investigation, one might wonder how a philosophy of transcendental consciousness could be feasible in such a setting. In answer, we can only emphasize that, even though the undifferentiated absolute lacks logical qualification by definition, its power is highly positive, and we can learn about it by means other than definition and description. It is also fitting that we cannot have definitive knowledge of *Brahman* because definitive knowledge can only be had of objects that can be distinguished from one another. Pots and flowers, for example, can be regarded as limited and fixed items that can be isolated from other objects and are associated with objects other than themselves (Radhakrishnan 2019: 193). However, its knowledge is inextricably linked to other things because it is not well-defined. It is only entirely unknown in this sense (the pure, transcendental absolute). The sole objective of his negative description is to reject the entire platter of categories created with objects in mind. This negative description does not eliminate every object's force and potency, but it rejects everything but *Brahman*. Not because of the delusion that it is not, but because every item and subject that may be subject to perception is also the subject of one who perceives, the perceiver of all that is perceived.

System of Adhyāropa

However, if transcendental consciousness exists, it must be adjusted and reconciled with the demands of critical thinking, and Advaita Vedānta solves this problem by the concept of *adhyāropa* (imposition) also known as *mithyāropa* (false imposition). This theory states that, even though pure consciousness is ineffable, it may be identified by the *adhyāropa* system with well-defined objects such as body, soul, mind and ego-consciousness, and then each of these can be denied as "not-this" in turn. It is not valid as long as this process does not allow critical intelligence to go beyond its bounds and explain it, unlike any empirical item we are familiar with. The state of *Brahman*'s relationship is the same as when the royal army is visible. The parasols, banners and other royal symbols indicate the king's presence, but the spectators begin to say that the king is present, even though he is not visible, even though the spectators see only signs of his presence.

This system of *adhyāropa* (rhetorical imposition) is the only way to point towards perfection, which is inimitable to relative intelligence in its perfection, and to which the closest access is found in a condition of deep sleep. Hans Vaihinger stated in *Die Philosophie des Als Ob* (*Philosophy of As-if*) that human beings can never truly grasp the world's fundamental reality and that, as a result, we develop systems of thought and then presume that this fits reality: we act "as if" the world matches our models. He used examples from the physical sciences, such as protons, electrons and electromagnetic waves, to illustrate his points. Although none of these events have been explicitly observed, science claims they do and uses observations based on these assumptions to develop new and better constructs (Vaihinger 1924/1935). As stated above, the method of *adhyāropa* resembles Vaihinger's concept of "as if". This method has already been used in *Bṛhadāraṇyaka Upaniṣad* 4.3.7 as

> *katama ātmeti; yo 'yaṁ vijñānamayaḥ prāṇeṣu hṛdyantarjyotiḥ puruṣaḥ; sa samānaḥ sannubhau lokāvanusañcarati, dhyāyatīva lelāyatīva; sa hi svapno bhūtvemaṁ lokamatikrāmati mṛtyo rūpāṇi* ||
>
> — Radhakrishnan 2019: 256

The imputed intellect describes *Brahman* by using names, forms and actions, and assigning it to joy and ecstasy. When we want to think about consciousness's independent and objective nature, however, the various disparities originating from restricting adjectives obstruct our efforts. Then, after much introspection and other mental rigour, it is seen that these adjectives cannot be tied to pure consciousness. So, the only way to know and learn it in this scenario is to exclude all possible descriptors. There is just one way to characterize him effectively: he is not this (*neti-neti*) (Radhakrishnan 2019: 193-94, 200, 243-44).

PROBLEMS IN CONSCIOUSNESS STUDIES

The Problem of Language

The grammatical forms of language in which we communicate our ideas have often influenced our experiential analysis. Therefore, the fundamental form of existence is interpreted and advocated in analogy to the forms of language when no such analogy exists. As a result, we must be aware of this *vikalpa-vṛtti* of language. The critical understanding, referred to by various titles such as the *buddhi* (intellect), *antaḥkaraṇa* (understanding) and *vijñāna* (concept), provides us with merely a descriptive and explanatory self (soul). We must remember that the soul we receive in this manner is merely a reflection of the true soul, not the true soul itself.

The form in which the pure self exists is not the one in which expressive language exists. The linguistic shape or force of words (*śabda-māhātmya*) that causes bewilderment in its *vikalpa-vṛtti* has been considered in philosophical thinking by the *Yogasūtra* as:

> *śabdajñānānupātī vastuśūnyo vikalpaḥ* । — Sutton 2019: 43

The *Yoga-Bhāṣya* has defined it in this way as:

> *vastuśūnyatve 'pi śabdajñānamāhātmyanibandhano vyavahāro dṛśyate* । — Patañjali 1988: 20-22

This means that the capacity of linguistic information creates mental modifications in the absence of the corresponding reality. The grammatical forms of language frequently deceive us into believing in facts that do not exist in the mind or in that form. Vyāsa uses common phrases like "consciousness is the true nature of the soul", which should be interpreted with caution. As a result, when we argue that consciousness is the soul's true nature, we can compare it to a cow related to *citra*, which would be entirely misconstrued (*yathā caitrasya gauriti*). The cure for this kind of mistake is described as *śabda saṅketa smṛti pariśuddhi*, which means purification of the mind from memory associated with linguistic coincidence, only after which *nirvikalpa jñana* (purely indistinguishable absolute knowledge) arises.

The Problem of Definition

Because the grammatical patterns of language, in which we must articulate our ideas, have reinforced the perception that it is like a chair or bench, absolute consciousness is sometimes confused with restricted and objective consciousness. Since all known objects are presupposed by pure consciousness, it is impossible to define. It must be assigned to a more significant class (a higher genus) and distinguished from other objects of the same class in order to be described. Once it is recognized that the soul is self-manifest and unique, it must also be acknowledged that it cannot be defined. Furthermore, the defining process must culminate in something that cannot be defined; otherwise, the process will never be completed.

As a result, only equivalent statements can be produced in defining a term like consciousness, even if under the guise of a name change, because people ascribe and label it similarly as they see, feel or know it. As Tulsīdās says:

jākī rahī bhāvanā jaisī ।
prabhu mūrata dekhī tina taisī ॥
— *Rāmacaritamānasa*, Bālakāṇḍa

Pure consciousness is indescribably distinct from definable things; hence, it is impossible to define. We do not have to repeat ourselves at this juncture because pure consciousness cannot be defined, as is mentioned several times before. Nevertheless, it is not our prerogative to believe that it is unknown or unknowable because all we can deduce from a thorough examination of the Vedas and Upaniṣads is that there have been seers who have tasted the absolute, which is bliss and ecstasy.[27] Estimating this type of conclusion would be indiscriminate in the same way as counting your friends but forgetting to count yourself in a numbering attempt for the whole is indiscriminate. Therefore, although absolute consciousness cannot be defined, its presence is undeniably understandable.

Because it is not something that can be confined to qualities

---

27 *sato bandhumasati niravindan hṛdi pratīṣyā kavayo manīṣā* ॥
— *ṚV* X.129.4

or limited manifestations, the descriptors *sat-cit-ānanda* do not define it. As discussed earlier, they merely emphasize the positive aspects of the eternal and infinite. Since language can only describe the contrary facts of the empirical world, the ultimate unity of consciousness must be a mystical and incomprehensible universal. Absolute consciousness cannot be deliberately nominated or defined in any other way because there is no contrary truth about it (because it is non-dual), as mentioned in *Chāndogya Upaniṣad* 6.2.1:

> *sadeva somyedamagra āsīdekamevādvitīyaṁ taddhaika āhurasadevedamagra āsīdekamevādvitīyaṁ tasmādasataḥ sajjāyata* ।
> — Radhakrishnan 2019: 447-48

It is illusory to propose that everything that exists is observable only through the senses, like pot and that something which is not visible in this way is like the horns of a rabbit. The supreme consciousness itself, before which all matter is present, cannot be meaningless, although it is true that its definition is not possible like a finite substance or object. Consciousness is *anīdam* and it can only be perceived in the form of *idam*, which is impossible. Thus, it should only be understood in this way. A piece of knowledge can be separated and described as being related to other knowledge, but knowledge's fundamental consciousness, which cannot be tied to anything outside of itself, cannot be impacted in the same manner. Consciousness is unique and eternal in itself; it cannot be recognized since knowing it requires distinguishing it from any other object. Because the infinite cannot be divided, dividing the entire consciousness, which is everlasting, into the forms of the knower, knowledge and the known object is to destroy its infinite form.

The Problem of Pramāṇa

Consciousness is a self-evident, self-existing reality that is complete in its own right. It is a prerequisite for all proofs and disproof debates, and it extends far beyond the realm of logical rebuttal or fortification. It is unlike any other item that the senses may know in this aspect. All other items of knowledge rely on evidence to be established as accurate, but because it is axiomatic, pure consciousness cannot rely on universal rules and techniques of proof. For the infinite, no such logical fortification of epistemology is possible. It does not rely on any *pramāṇa*. They call it *pramāṇa-nirapekṣa*. The self-luminous aspect of the supreme consciousness gives rise to this self-proven nature of consciousness. All deductive methods for proving the presence of pure and absolute consciousness are deceptive because proofs and other means of testifying and the confidence in authenticity itself must be certified by the illuminating self-consciousness. According to Vedic literature, the willing mindset of catching consciousness through rational means is as foolish as a person who requests to touch the shadow of his head with his feet but discovers that the shadow would fall away before his feet reach there.

Consciousness is the foundation of all knowledge, yet it is also a cognizer and any object cannot cognize it. It is the foundation of the cognitive process and anything established as an a priori of cognition. The process of cognizing a *pramāṇa* is built on the foundation of consciousness. It is also established before the process of *pramāṇa* cognition.[28] Nature can only be critiqued in its incidental and relative forms, not in its pure, primary and essential form. According to the Anekāntavāda teachings and the classic story of the elephant and six men, what we know about reality is only a percentage of the whole story. Our knowledge is very restricted, and what we do know is a product of chance, either through critical thinking or meditation. As a result, what we know is very relative because our understanding of something beyond our direct consciousness can never be complete.[29] What is pre-offered by all proofs cannot be proven by the same set of proposed proofs

---

28 *pratijñāhāniravyatirekācchabdebhyaḥ* । — Śaṅkarācārya 2000: 2.3.6

29 Any system is based on some true, yet unproved axioms which serve as the basic assumptions for that system. Consider it as a pre-requisite for the system.

because how can that basis be established and proven by other explanations on which the proof itself is based. This is what was meant by Gödel's incompleteness theorems.

The Problem of Activity

The dualist Sāṁkhyans and the non-dualist Advaitins believe that transcendental consciousness has existed in an eternal and immutable form and is not in motion (*akṛta*). The principles of motion, activity and evolution originate from *pradhāna* in Sāṁkhya-Yoga philosophy and, *puruṣa*, since it is pure and detached, is eternally constant and sustains its identity with the self. The *ātman*, according to Advaita Vedānta, is entire and absolute, and cannot alter, evolve, increase or diminish. It is neither ascending nor descending (Radhakrishnan 2019: 280). Śaṅkara rejects any form of doing or principle of activity in terms of the *ātman* since the activity is non-eternal and *dhruva* by nature. Because everywhere there is activity, there is a mutation of form. Therefore, the *ātman* can never be the residential seat of action (activity). The principle of change is activity (Gautama 1939: 42). Desire stimulates all functionality and activity, which presupposes egoism (a sense of self).

To the extent that he perceives the changing world, the eternal seer (*draṣṭā*) cannot be a part of it. According to Sāṁkhya philosophy, the cosmos is divided into two parts: *akṛta* (*puruṣa)* and the evolutionary *prakṛti*. The supreme consciousness should act as a non-successive witness or seer of the mind's alterations. If the seeing soul is transformed, no knowledge of the mind's altering modifications can ever be gained. The ultimate consciousness is unchanging and eternally continuous because it exists beyond the temporal divides of past, present and future. The eternal consciousness is *acala* and *akṣara* in and of itself. When pure consciousness is referred to as the agent of anything or the doer, it is solely in a metaphorical sense. The supreme consciousness is not a knower and it is only referred to as such in epistemological discussions. Because the action of knowledge is entrenched in the process of knowledge, which is susceptible to change and transformations, similarly, he is not a doer and is unaffected by sadness or gladness, and it is only socio-ethically that he is viewed as such. In this way, the entire quality of change is related to consciousness, but not in its true form; instead, it is only tied to this element in the context of restricting adjuncts.

Furthermore, the concept of limitation is intertwined with the concepts of utility and activity. There can be no agency without being limited by the soul, the body and other instruments. Because phenomena like cognition of activity and change reveal that consciousness is levels above action and there can be no action in transcendental consciousness. In transcendental consciousness, there is no movement or activity. As a result of its association with active titles, the action appears to be linked to inert transcendental consciousness (*upādhi*). Change and action cannot be the final concepts since even an activity need someone to understand it and present it to unchanging consciousness. When the ultimate consciousness is embellished with action or development, it is only possible due to a misunderstanding of the notions of *vr̥tti* (modification) and *bodha* (cognizance). The *vr̥tti* is the part of the body that changes, evolves and grows. At the same time, the *bodha* remains unaltered and unchanging. The development of the mind is not the development of *cit-śakti* and mental change is not the development of the state of consciousness; it is a change within consciousness. The concept of evolution of consciousness is based on the idea that various stages of an evolving thing should be spaced out throughout different periods.

Conclusion

In this chapter, we have attempted to demonstrate that there is a transcendental part of consciousness associated with it, which also happens to be its most fundamental manifestation and primordial form. Consciousness is one, everlasting, unchanging, undifferentiated universal in its transcendental nature, which is established continuously, much like the base and support of a continually changing stream of external and internal variations. It is a presupposed prologue to all knowledge and experiences multiplicity and unity. Despite permanently residing in the background of empirical consciousness, this transcendental consciousness stays stable and apart from it, *kevala*. It is a substrate that does not get mixed with the base it supports or share any of its characteristics. As a result, it is referred to as "pure" and *kevala*. It is free of the contaminants of empirical consciousness and undisturbed, yet it provides the foundation for an empirical representation of experience. However, because the truth is that which is never interrupted or sublated, this detached consciousness is the only existing consciousness. Empirical consciousness is like the actuality of a dream flower, which exists only as long as the dream does but vanishes once the dream is through. People under the influence of *avidyā* lose sight of the distinction between transcendental consciousness and its practical expression, and mistakenly believe they are the same. However, just as true knowledge (*vidyā*) destroys false knowledge (*avidyā*), transcendental consciousness becomes illuminated as the only truth, and the daily phenomenal consciousness merges like a dream sequence.

2

Understanding through Contemporary Western Thought

In the previous chapter, we laid out a framework for the mind-body problem. Next, we discussed the Indian perspective on the mind-body complex and the pertinent problem of consciousness. With the problem of translations and varied developments in logic, the problem of ontology concerning the present issue grew multifariously. Types of different theories came into existence, a collection of which can be found in the famous paper by David Chalmers, "Consciousness and Its Place in Nature" (2003). The way we are going to proceed in this chapter is by focusing on two stances, viz. dualism and monism. Then we shall be dealing with their types in individual sections. Both these perspectives have developed into various full-fledged lines of thought, but their treatment is based on the stance they posit on three fundamental questions as are laid in Table 2.1.

Substance Dualism

Dualism can be seen as the oldest thought in Western philosophy, right from the time of Plato down through the ages which inherited

Table 2.1: The Mind–Body Problems

The Ontological Question	*The Causal Question*	*The Question of Consciousness*
What are these states?	Does the mind influence the body?	P-consciousness?
Are they entirely distinct?	Does the body influence the mind?	What is the nature of this subjective experience?
Is one a subset of the other?	Or do both influence the other? If so, how?	How is it related to brain and mind?

René Descartes in the modern era of advanced sciences. The common underlying thread joining them is their belief that there is some reality beyond what is perceived, the material and that reality should be something beyond what is perceived, the immaterial. We shall start with a modern thought experiment called the "brain-in-a-vat", whose core idea is similar to the evil demon thought experiment by Descartes wherein he believes that there might be an evil demon causing him to make errors whereby he concludes that "the demon can bring no effect upon me until and unless I think I of me as something", concluding the argument with "I think therefore I am something".

Let us discuss the modern argument and then delve into its historical context. The brain-in-a-vat thought experiment asks us to imagine a situation wherein, by the advance of science, we reach a position where we can have our brain dumped in a vat (water tub) filled with life-sustaining liquid and somehow, by again using some scientific tools, we sustain the neuronal activity so that it simulates a frame of reality. Now in such a sci-fi scenario, we would never be able to distinguish between what is real and what is not. Descartes initiated the same thought in his *Meditations on First Philosophy* (Ariew and Cress 2006: 1-39). He proposed a scenario wherein all the perceptions conceived by him were an illusion created by an evil demon. After much thorough deliberation, Descartes concluded that he might doubt everything, whether his body or his thought, but one thing was sure: his mode of thought, the thinking being, could not be questioned. This prompted him to coin the phrase *cogito ergo sum* (I think, therefore, I am). There is no uncertainty about the thinking substance. Let us return to the brain-in-a-vat thought experiment. It has the same meaning in the sense that one can doubt the perceptions of the world, yet he cannot doubt that he is the one who is doubting. This line of thought is similar to the one in the *Matrix* film series.

Let us now reconsider the brain-in-a-vat experiment differently. Instead of having a life-sustaining liquid, the vat would have been with acid, dissolving the brain. Just imagine if this could happen. Now ask yourself the million-dollar question: Could you survive this incident? If you have accepted that you are something different from the physical body, call it the mind. This leads us to conclude that you are not your physical body; you are something immaterial, i.e. your mind.

Now let us move to a structured formulation of dualism. What is dualism? Dualism is the simple claim that there are two fundamental distinct ontological entities in the realm of reality. After establishing two distinct ontological entities, we conclude that one should be material and the other immaterial. Let us now name them in our context and call the material entity the body and the immaterial entity, the mind. Hence, the ethos of dualism can be summed up in three propositions. One, there are two ontological entities. Two, the body is a material entity. Three, the mind is an immaterial entity. A safe derivation from these propositions is that they must have their existence independent of the other. If *x* and *y* are different, they should also have different properties. Descartes moves one step further and calls the individually existing entities "substances". Note that this term was not new in the history of philosophy; instead, it is used here to signify that a substance (earlier referred to as an entity) is an individual entity capable of existing in its own right "independent" of the nature of other substances. Hence, summing up the whole argument, substance dualism is the stance which states that the material body and the immaterial mind are distinct ontological entities since they are individual and different "substances" capable of existing entirely independently from the other. One could wonder what is new about this position. Since Plato's time, this type of dualism has been familiar; the belief in two different ontological things. It has to do with the second question: how do these things interact with one another?

Here comes the full version of Descartes' account of interactionist substance dualism. The view is that these two ontological substances or entities exist independently of each other and have a "causal" interaction. Do we experience such an interaction in our daily life? Yes, we do. Suppose you had a low day and your mood seems off. One way to elevate your mood can be meditation. You regulate your breathing, and in a scientific account, the increased oxygen level in your blood elevates your mood. The same is the case with alcohol or other psychotropic substances. What happens then? According to an interactionist dualist, the material body seems to be interacting with the immaterial mind. Your act of regulating your breath is a physical process involving the physical body but the effects can be felt in the mind, which is immaterial or non-physical.

Your body may survive even after all the functionings of the mind cease to exist, as in clinical death. Can we imagine this the other way around? Can the mind survive death? These questions have been the loci of discussion in Eastern traditions, especially in Advaita Vedānta, but let us take an empirical standpoint on this. Sure, we can imagine our mind in some other world while dreaming asleep. We can even construe ourselves (our minds) as surviving death in a dream. Of course, our mind does work even when all sense perceptions provided by the physical body cease to exist.

One can do a simple thought experiment and imagine being 1 o'clock at night and feeling tremors. One watches himself in the mirror and finds that his body does not exist. The person then comes out of the house, he opens the door but he still cannot see his hands which opened the door. The person can hear the birds cooing and police sirens wailing; he waves his hands to them but they do not seem to respond as they cannot see the person. The person sits and can feel the ground and thinks:

> ... But all my bodily sensations even seem to be there, exactly where they should have felt to be. But why is the body missing? The body surely seems to have gone, but the immaterial mind has stayed behind. And now in such a state one can safely accrue

> with Descartes. Indeed, my body and my mind are distinct. That's the obvious possible deduction for this elaborate thought experiment. Remember that it all can be imagined and it is not as contradictory as one may think. The rational and logical basis of all thought experiments is not their imaginability but their nature of being free from contradiction. If there is no contradiction in the repertoire then the event is possible, at least in the logical sense. The imagination of an event is just an account of whether an event is describable, there is no guarantee of it being in actuality but the describability of an event in a genuine sense free from contradiction is the true measure of possibility.
>
> — Stuart et al. 2017: 1-21

It is this possibility, the possibility of waking up with a mind tacitly intact but with the body gone, that is the founding pillar of dualism. Hence, using the earlier stated thought experiment, one should derive the possibility that the mind and body are distinct ontological entities that can exist without one another. In our account, it is quite noteworthy that the claim is not that they *do* exist independently; as further elaboration in the next few passages will tell us, they can exist independently. The mere possibility of *can* does in no way imply that they *do* or that the stated existence is simultaneous. The pinnacle of such a line of thought would be that they do exist independently and, at the time of demise, they get dismantled simultaneously. But such a development can happen by two different sets of forces, call one the material force and the other immaterial or non-physical force. All this is to make sense of the idea that something immaterial can exist.

Let us now come back to Descartes' account of the causal interaction between the two entities. In his account, the material and the immaterial exist and they do exert causal influence on each other. What Descartes brought new to this account was the concept that the pineal gland of the brain is the interface of such interaction. Modern science may refute such a claim but then it was because Descartes had his observations, particularly that it was for him the single organ, unlike the two cerebral hemispheres and many organs in the nervous system that came in two. Now that we have a fair account of most claims coined by Descartes, let us do what philosophers do best, find loopholes. Though we shall not be the first ones to do that as they occurred well during his own time precisely in the letters of Elizabeth of Bohemia. Her issue with the Cartesian account pivoted on the causal mechanism ensured by him (Ariew and Cress 2006: vii-xix).

Immaterial mental properties like thinking and reflection are the propriety of the immaterial, which by definition lacks spatial attributes. On the contrary, being located spatially, and having shape and size are the attributes of the material (the physical body). How then can these two distinct entities, the material having a spatial extension and the immaterial lacking it, interact? How does something spatial affect something non-spatial? These questions render Cartesian dualism impossible to hold as a logical option for philosophers. But does the story end here? Maybe not.

There have been some attempts, later to Descartes, which made substance dualism work. One famous resolution came when Hume, a later empiricist philosopher, brought into account the solution for the interaction mechanism; he argued that what we see as causal relations are just subjects of human assumptions which in any case can prove to be fairly wrong and may not always yield certain demonstrative knowledge. Hume was always sceptical of the claim that like produces like and questioned such a stance throughout his life. If the mental were spatial too, then there would have been no issue with accepting that mental and physical have a causal connection. Hume, however, says that there is no rational basis to believe that causation may not be accounted for between dislikes, and hence he finds no rationale behind refuting the causal mechanism of Cartesian dualism.

It was centuries later that an Oxford philosopher E. J. Lowe came up with something that he called non-Cartesian substance dualism.

He states that mental properties are the domain of the "subject of experience", being human persons an example of such a case. The physical body is the bearer of physical properties. Hence the two substances. But contrary, Descartes states that a person can too be the possessor of psychological and physical properties, in the sense that a person cannot be regarded as separable from the body in being capable of disembodied existence since it is in the essence of being humans that we have bodies. This is to say that many mental states could exist in our bodies too. Take, for example, yourself, when you are depressed, the lack of enthusiasm which is a part of the mental state, is also felt by the physical body.

He envisions that the causal chain in this complex system is intertwined, which means that he refutes the causal closure of the physical. Imagine this as a tree that, instead of having branches as ends, has branches intertwined. Causal events do not cause their effects at the ends of the branches; instead, they act upon the whole system, i.e. they activate the whole tree of causation rather than ending at the branches, for there are none. The job here assigned to this tree is to mediate the relationship between mind and action. The point is that mental events communicate not with the ends of the tree but with whole tree by activating the entire tree of causal connection or at least some part of the tree. Hence by filling in the gap caused by the concept of causal closure through looping the whole tree, Lowe dissolves the problem of interaction.

Though there have been various problems in this attempt too as every philosophical stance does. The soundest philosophical theory is the one that has the least ramifications and in some sense this account does the same.

Parallelism

We have seen how bringing in interaction to the account of substance dualism causes many problems, most importantly the question of how; how do the mental and non-mental react?

Fortunately, no problem is unresolvable, especially in philosophy, the fallacies of one account bring in alternative solutions and the one in our case is called parallelism.

Parallelism is another possible iteration of dualism which, like substance dualism, theorizes that there are two distinct entities. However, but contrary to interactionist substance dualism (Cartesian dualism), parallelism does not claim that these two entities interact. This refutation itself solves a major chunk of issues associated with the interactionist stance. As far as the basic premises of dualism are concerned, adherents of parallelism believe that the immaterial mind and the material body both have an independent existence. When asked why they do not interact, the answer they provide is fairly simple: the material and the immaterial cannot interact. This seems especially fair when we consult the arguments by critics of Descartes, particularly Princess Elizabeth and Pierre Gassendi. Though the other premises remain the same in this account too, the only change is in terms of the stance on the causal mechanism.

No matter how big and accomplished a philosophical palace may be, it still has to come down to earth and face the high tides of actuality in the world. Rationalism has to always face the empirical realities of the real world. The picture must be coherent always, or else it loses its meaning. The same is the case with our stance, parallelism. It has to account for the phenomenal appearances of interaction between mental and physical. Despite the picture painted by accounts of parallelism, it seems lop-sided and contradictory to our belief and experience that interaction between physical and mental is not possible for such a development is very common and so ingrained that its familiarity is undeniable.

Though parallelism may refute the claim that the material and immaterial can react and while it may seem fair in all accounts, it still has to explain real-world experiences like why a change in mood is followed after one takes a drink and gets inebriated. Not only does there seem to be a physical or mental effect, but there is also a fair evidence of an interaction vice versa. Take the example of being in depression and anxiety, both cause effects on the physical body. An episode of depression is often followed by a lack of will to work or even to move, and many cope with such mental phases by excessive eating. An episode of anxiety is followed by heavy palpitation and sweating. Even a fit of anger has undeniable physical after-effects, most of them unwanted. Such an interaction is the foundation of all accounts of psychology. One cannot deny the big industry running on such iterations of interaction, especially in the field of psychiatry.

So, back to our question: How does the account of parallelism solve our present dilemma? One may be especially amazed that despite all these examples and accounts of interaction, parallelism is comfortable in its own way and there seems to be no threat to it. Why? The parallelist simply asserts that though there can be no interaction between the mental and the physical, this in no way should mean that there can be no relation between them. Parallelism hence asserts that there is a correlation between the mental and the physical in every instance when we thought that there was an interaction. Alcohol consumption is followed by inebriation; this should not mean that the mental and the physical have interacted. Instead, it should be understood that drinking alcohol is *followed* by inebriation, or in parallelism, is correlated with it. Thinking that the body has somehow filled the mind with alcohol or is activating some kind of neuronal firing in the mind that it has caused physical messages to be sent to the mind is all absurd juggling of possibilities. The picture of interactive neuronal firing in the brain and the mind is pure nonsense in the parallelist account. Why? Since signals are something physical, it is to be accounted for by the laws of physics considering the mind is physical. Believing otherwise that something non-spatial like the mind has contained in itself spatial signals, you are back to ground zero. A.J. Ayer (1951: 73-74) may have very well observed:

> Physiologist's story is complete in itself. The characters that figure in it are nerve cells, electrical impulses, and so forth. It has no place for an entirely different cast, of sensations, thoughts, feelings, and the other personae of the mental play. ... Nor are there such temporal gaps in the procession of nervous impulses as would leave room for mental characters to intervene. In short, the two stories [mental and physical] will not mix. ... Each is an interpretation of certain phenomena and they are connected by the fact that, in certain conditions, when one of them is true, the other is true also.

The refutation of the possibility wherein the material and the immaterial interact does in no way refute the possibility of them being correlated and hence the hypothesis that the events of the material body have some correlation with the events of the immaterial mind. The objection of the parallelist lies in the refutation of the Cartesian idea pertinently; the belief in the imagery wherein neuronal activity slides alongside the mind and somehow there seems to be an interaction between them due to their contiguity (remember the idea of the pineal gland as the interface between physical and mental suggesting proximity). The rationale behind this idea is simple and quite the one we have been discussing all along; there can be no spatial contiguity when there are two contradictory entities.

Historically, parallelism was a counterintuitive approach to Descartes' idea of dualism which had the flavour of interaction sprinkled over it. Mere awareness of the problems that ensued with the Cartesian account was enough to spark resentment against his famed approach. It was the interaction between the material and the immaterial that made dualism an unbearable philosophical opinion and hence the Cartesian approach went downhill, i.e. instead of solving the mind-body problem, it made it more complex. But then parallelism is also a commitment to dualism. So, what is new?

Indeed, the mind and the body cannot interact, due to dualism.

However, one should not forget that they do seem to act in pure synchronicity, in tandem per se. It is only when one desires to have a beverage that one's body reaches out for it to quench that desire. And when one has had enough, the mind calls for no more. The catching observation in this synchronicity is this question, why at this moment, why did my mind ask me to stop at that exact moment? How did the mind ring a bell for me to stop, and why at that moment only? This was the observation that led Descartes to propound interaction, wasn't it?

Well, this is the beauty of philosophy. A single observation can lead to a million interpretations. The parallelist argues that what Descartes deemed as causal interaction was just *synchronization*. One of the most celebrated metaphors given for the word *synchronization* was by the wave of parallelism in France during the post-Cartesian era, in the seventeenth and eighteenth centuries. The image of clocks striking in tandem, every movement in synchronization, was the epitome of the French desire for order, peace and harmony during the period. When one clock would strike noon so would the other. It was signifying the inner unconscious desire for order, the way God would have wanted, the way the French needed it.

Imagine the same scenario but with a twist. What if one clock somehow was delayed, i.e. experienced a time lag? It would then appear that the striking of the first one *caused* the second one, with a delay, to strike the latter. That would be a fallacy of inference, named *post hoc ergo propter hoc* (after this, therefore because of this). It was this observation that struck Gottfried Wilhelm Leibniz, the famous philosopher, mathematician and, more importantly the celebrated parallelist, while he was sitting beside his ill teacher Huygens (a pupil of Descartes and inventor of the pendulum). It was there that he saw the pendulum of two separate clocks, which were mounted in a single encasing, move in synchronization. This observation moved Leibniz, so much that he applied this synchronization to his philosophy, particularly to the mind-body problem. He postulated that the mind and the body act as if synchronized and that too in a way to give the feeling that one affects the other, but this is an illusion. For synchronization, when taken in a literal sense, would mean that there is causation, which he very adamantly denied.

In his philosophy of monads, he had earlier posited that substance in itself formed a kind of unified system wherein there can be no addition or subtraction. In this respect, it was more like an indivisible atom. He called such an individual unit a windowless being. For him, the physical and mental pendulums were in synchronization, not by the law of interaction but by the will of God. Synchronization is brought about by the will of God and is initiated the moment a substance comes to be. This synchronization is very well ingrained in the complete individual concept of the substance itself, wherein all the probable possibilities that the substance will encounter in the life it is about to see are already present. Every detail is fine-tuned in its minuscule detail very well before any substance comes to be, so much so that the being is just playing out of those details. Leibniz called this the *pre-established harmony* and gave the example of a clock working in tune with another clock, not by the virtue of the clock itself but by the virtue of the maker who ingrained this fine-tuned setting in them (clocks) right before they were what they are now (from machine to clock). This account does seem to have implications for the freedom of will but that is a topic for another debate, not to mention that Leibniz too took into account this problem and gave what he thought of as a probable solution to the problem.

The important takeaway from such observations and accounts is that the universe is somehow fine-tuned and so well arranged that what we observe as interaction is just an account of the pre-established harmony, that synchronization that God had ingrained in each being well before it came to be. This tuning is not just limited to our mind-body conundrum but the whole universe so much so that the universe by the will of God will ultimately evolve into the best version of itself.

Parallelism strikes a brilliant chord with the occasionalists in believing that the interactions of the body and the mind are events when God acts to bring the so-called tandem, synchronicity. Occasionalists use the clock thought to show their desired philosophical point. Their belief in God was so adamant that they propounded a philosophy that needed a god to intervene every time an action or interaction was carried out. This view sustained and garnered so wide patronage is a testimony to the need for faith and where it can lead. This claim calls for an unflagging and very overworked God, something religious monopolies at the time condemned wholeheartedly. Both, the for and against accounts of parallelism have their pros and cons, but then this was parallelism, a very well-welcomed thought in the philosophy of mind.

Property Dualism

Previously we discussed the stance that substance dualism exists due to two different substances and also talked about the problems that accepting such a stance brings about. For those perplexed and puzzled by the stance of substance dualism, there is another version of dualism that we are here to discuss and it is not a dualism of distinct ontological substances, but of the properties, they inhere, hence the name property dualism. The focus here will be on properties rather than things or substances. Therefore we have to imagine that perhaps there is just one substance but it has fairly distinct properties, two in particular: the physical properties and mental properties.

The basic proposition that we have to start from is that there is just one kind of substance. This position can have two variants. The first variant, the physicalist version asks us to imagine that this one kind of substance is physical. In the description, even the mind is physical (that is one way to say it) or, the mental phenomena are dependent on the physical, in the sense that the mind is the corresponding part of the brain allowing for causal interaction.

Take the example of a painting, such as *The Starry Night* by

Vincent van Gogh, an oeuvre d'art. The painting is a masterpiece, a great work of art; derivative of the painter's dreams, his magnificent perception of an ordinary everyday scene, vivid colours striking happiness and cheer, and that something which immediately strikes the heart. All these are something that is there in the painting in the sense that these aesthetic properties would not exist if the painting was absent. Nonetheless, they are mental (aesthetic) properties not physical in a sense. Maybe if one were to strike a hole through each of the stars in the painting, then it would certainly lose its appeal and much of the aesthetical properties mentioned. What one must keep in mind is that the higher-order properties, i.e. the magnificence and vibrancy, are in no way something that can just be attributed to the colours or canvas used, but one fair conclusion would be that they (aestheticproperties) are dependent on them.

This image experiment is just to show how mental properties such as perception or thoughts or ideas are grounded in the physical sense that they can be derived from them. The physical aspect we are concerned about here is the brain. But this in no sense implies that these mental properties are reducible to physical properties in the sense that just the whole bokeh of imagination that the painting has brought about cannot be reduced just to colour in itself. There is a possibility that damage to a particular part of the brain could change after our perception of various mental properties, but this in no case should be an excuse to derive the conclusion that mental properties such as the perception of magnificence or feeling of peace could be reduced to strictly physical terms.

This stance solves a major problem that was earlier brought about by substance dualism, the "pairing problem", i.e. if there were a realm of mind, affecting the physical, then why does it specifically affect my body only, and not others? More specifically, why does my mind affect my body rather than someone else's? rather (Robb and Heil 2021). For the property dualist, the mind and the body are not distinct for there happens to be just one substance and the mind too is a physical substance. Remember that, initially, we said that there are just properties. Hence, there arises no problem for like can interact with like and thus the issue is resolved.

Let us now look towards the second variant of the property: dualist stance. In this stance too, the first position does not change that there is just one kind of substance and that it has both mental and physical properties. What changes here is the claim that mental properties are something above and beyond physical properties. One way to make sense of this claim is to think that mental properties have real causal powers that are in no way dependent on the physical in the sense that their independent causal powers can produce an effect in the physical world. Take, for example, the desire to have a cup of tea; this desire in itself has the causal power to bring about motion in your body so that you go to the kitchen and plan as well as implement how to make a cup of tea. This case is to be understood in contrast to the physicalist variant wherein it was the physical event that led to an effect on the mental domain, i.e. some neuronal firing making us go to the kitchen. Another way to understand this is to think in the sense that mental properties have the power to bring an impact in a way unaccounted by the physical realm, i.e. independent of the physical realm. This implies in the real world that one may have the same brain state but a different mental state that may indeed differ, that is to say, that one might experience pain while others may experience pleasure.

Despite such a fruitful account, property dualism does have its repercussions. Though in earlier accounts mental properties like aesthetic ones do not pose any effect in the physical world in the sense that they even lack the causal power to initiate any effect. But in the real world, will or intention is what initiates physical actions; in this sense, the mental is not ephemeral. This is something that no property dualist has been able to account for.

Epiphenomenalism

The advent of the nineteenth century saw a resurgence of interest in dualism albeit with more sophistication and vigour.

Epiphenomenalism as a variety of dualism arose in the wake of advancing physical sciences and emerged as a distinct object of study rather than belief. The word itself is very much a derivative of two words "epi" and "phenomenon". "Epi", the Greek prefix, means "upon the occasion of", while "phenomenon" means a situation or an event that is observed to exist or happen (Westphal 2016: 44-45). For epiphenomenalists, all mental phenomena and even the mind are epiphenomena in this context. In the epiphenomenalist's terminology, the basal phenomena are the ones of the physical world while the mental ontology, i.e. the phenomenon of the mind, is what comes in addition to the basal physical phenomenon. However physical phenomena cause mental events, but the reverse is not true. Downward causation is not possible in the epiphenomenalist account.

Take an example of shadow play. The master artist can fashion out any object he wills just by the clever movement of his hands, say a dog. The shadow dog is purely dependent on the movement of the shadow of the master's hand and that too is the extent to which he can change the dog to an eagle. But in no way can the shadow dog bite him off, i.e. the shadow can cast no effect on the hand for the projected image of the dog is just a shadow.

This thought is an enough testimony to the epiphenomenalist case in the sense that no epiphenomenalist would dare to argue that mental phenomena could somehow affect the physical one. To understand the thought process behind such an assumption, it would be sufficient to consider the age at which the thought came to be. It was the age of phrenology and advancing physical sciences (Wikipedia 2022c). People believed that physical knowledge about objects and events could solve all their problems. This age also saw the case study of Phineas Gage (Wikipedia 2022b). Understanding such a background would surely help in finding out how this view of epiphenomenalism ultimately evolved. Epiphenomenalism is in deeper instincts a physicalist's notion who cannot see their way around the actual being of mental events but are somehow lured into the relief that physical sciences like behavioural psychology and neuropsychiatry have brought about. For them, mental ontology is something real but to see how it comes about is the challenge. Hence, with such profound bias brought about by the comfort of physical sciences, they fail to comprehend the power (causal power) of the mental on the physical and like always, what one does not understand, he fears or at worst, neglects it.

Thomas Henry Huxley, a nineteenth-century English anthropologist and biologist, claimed that consciousness was a "collateral product" derived from the "bodily mechanisms" (Westphal 2016: 47). He was one of the first epiphenomenalists who staunchly believed that consciousness (a mental phenomenon) holds no causal potency when it comes to affecting the physical realm; for this, he cited the example of a locomotive hooter, which though accompanies the working of the locomotive, in the sense of being a part of the train, but casts no effect on the locomotive engine (Huxley 1874). But as with all analogies in nature, this analogy too breaks. A crafty mind can surely imagine the old days when locomotive hooters on their application were used to slow down the train by releasing pressure produced by the steam engine. There is also a way to rig a normal engine to do such a job. This is just to make a point that the whistle (a metaphor for the mental) can have a particular effect on the locomotive (a metaphor for the physical). And as can be assumed, the nature of the physical world facilitates this, so much so that there is nothing in the physical world to break such a causal loop.

Hence in Huxley's account, the realm of the immaterial consisting of entities like consciousness, mind, and soul is ruled out of the causal chain of events derived from the immaterial. For questions like why the realm of the immaterial is causally inert or why it is not possible for immaterial mental phenomena to cast an effect on the physical, Huxley has no answer. Epiphenomenalism, in the end, should be viewed as a variety of dualism that allows for unidirectional interaction, i.e. only the physical can cause the mental events, not the other way round. This view seems to reduce much of the mind-body problem by saying that the mind does not act on the body, but then again, the question arises how does the body act on the mind if one is material and the other immaterial?

Emergentism

Emergentism another account of dualism that can be attributed initially to John Stuart Mill. He articulates the concept in his 1843 book *A System of Logic* as a concept that could explain the phenomena occurring in the scientific world wherein there were abundant examples of properties arising from what he calls lower-level phenomena in such a way that they could not be reduced to the lower-level phenomenon. Strictly speaking, the emergent outcome (of properties) is something over and above the basal phenomenon (Mill 2002).

Emergentism also postulates a similar relationship between the mind and the body as epiphenomenalism, as it views the physical as the basal substrate while the mind and the mental are additional by-products at the phenomenal level. What is important to notice here are the differences these two thoughts account for. For epiphenomenalism, the mental and the physical were somehow causally related but this link fades to a great extent when it comes to emergentism. A detailed discussion of the "how" in this perspective will be attempted here but clearer answers will emerge in the next chapter when we discuss physicalism. However, a brief explanation will be provided in the next few paragraphs.

One peculiar mystery at the very roots of the contemporary mind-body problem is the question of why there is pain associated with the brain regions activated and simulated by *A*δ (to be read as *A* Delta) and *C* fibres. (One should know that Aδ fibres are associated with intense pain while the *C* fibres are with burning-pain sensation.) For the emergentist, which also includes people from the physiological background, particularly those who study the brain like neuro physicians, the question is very poignant in the sense that they too have no definite answer as to why the pain emerges from these regions only, not some other. This is such a daunting question that even neuro evolutionists cannot pinpoint an exact finger why, how and where down the evolutionary scale did it come to be that pain came to be associated with *C* fibres. What is to be kept in mind here is that the emergence of pain is not talked about here in the same sense we see 1,000 g turn to emerge as 1 kg albeit it goes on to state that pain caused by *C* fibre excitation develops a phenomenal quality which cannot be explained by the basal phenomenon, i.e. the *C* fibre excitation. Neuroscientists try to seek the answer as to why or how the simulation of these only causes the sensation of pain. Well, as always, philosophy does seem to provide some answers and, in this case, the answer comes from the concept of emergence, in the sense that the pain is an emergent property derived from the simulation of these fibres.

Adherents of emergence theory accept that the mind is physical in the sense that it is the biological structures of the brain, such as cells and tissues, that drive the ultimate emergent phenomenon we perceive as the mind and mental states. To make the concept more complex, emergentists also believes that the mind is non-physical (immaterial) in the sense that no physical description can fully account for the mind as an emergent property of the physical. Mental states like pain are truly novel properties of the physical substrate called the brain, but how they come about is the question; the mechanism here is the daunting question. However, by definition and architecture of emergence, the mind is non-physical since it emerges from the brain (the physical substrate). The right question to ask would be if they (mental properties) are non-physical, then how do they emerge and how are they related to the physical domain, and most importantly why?

Coming to the problems associated with the emergentist account, they are the same as with all accounts of dualism. If the mind, as emergentists say, is truly a novel and an unalloyed phenomenal property of the physical substrate in the sense that the butterfly emerges from the chrysalis, then just on the account of being something "over and above" matter, it should not be able to affect matter (the body in this case). Why? Again, the emergent mental properties talked about in our case are non-spatial and, now when matter, as a basal phenomenon, has evolved into something immaterial (mind), why will it then come back to interact with matter, and the bitter question is how. The exact issue how the emergence falls back in the line of evolution to what it was. No case in the real hierarchical world of evolution follows suit of such a kind. Even the emergence of the mind from the spatial matter, particularly the brain makes it spatial (something within the confines of space can only produce that which is in space). And if the emergentist differs from the account and says that there is a *dependence* of the novel property (non-physical matter) on the physical (lower substrate) in such a way that it is cross-engagement, then how are we to differentiate it from the basal phenomenon and how is it (emergent property) any different from them (basal phenomenon).

To conclude, we must ask the question: how does it happen that the mind has emerged and attained a higher-level property, contrary to what the basal level of matter exhibits, it seems to interact with the matter, which is very different in properties (i.e. physical) and existence? This is a question that emergentists fail to answer. If the mind has emerged as something immaterial and still interacts with the basal physical level, we need to understand how such an interaction takes place. Hence, we are back to the basic mind-body problem, once again. The next formulation in the discussion may help to address some of the persistent problems that have followed us. This concept too will talk of properties in a sort of binary sense wherein a property can be both, a basal property and also an emergent one; in the sense of being something "over and above" the basal level, i.e. in addition to the basal property (as discussed above). This concept (which is to be discussed) has been used by many emergentists to throw out the fly in the ointment. How? Well, let us see.

Supervenience

Coming one step further from emergentism, one finds the next stop in the discussion of the concept of supervenience, which takes the prior understanding of emergentism and moulds a new proposition by adding the baggage of a truly novel concept in philosophy, supervenience, and finally says that mind is emergent as well as "supervenes" on the physical substrate, i.e. body.

In a philosophical sense, a property, say *X*, is supposed to be supervenient on a property *Y*, if and only if a change is duly needed in property *Y*, for there to be a change in property *X*. That is to say, there can be no change in *X* without a change in property *Y* (Wikipedia 2022). How do we explain this in the real world? Imagine property *A* as a set of the aesthetic properties of the sculpture and property *P* as a set of the physical properties of the sculpture. Let us suppose that proposition *A* supervenes on property *P*. What we mean by this proposition is that, if we were to first bring a change in set *A*, then we need to make changes to set *P*, in other words, to alter the aesthetic property, or to bring change to the aesthetic properties we need to first bring a change in the physical properties. Without any change in the physical properties, there can be no change in the aesthetic properties. In the emergentist sense, the physical is the basal level of properties. However, quite distinctly from emergentism, the higher-level properties are governed by the lower-level properties in the sense that they supervene on them. If the aesthetic properties are to be modified, the physical properties at the basal level have to be modified first. Hence, in our context, we can safely conclude that properties *A* are causally related to the basal properties *P*. Therefore, in addition to the emerging concept of properties coming from the basal level, the problem of the relation between the two is quite solved, to an extent at least. The emergentist hence believes in the proposition that the body is material. The advance that it makes on emergentism is that supervenience refutes the assumption that the material body and the immaterial mind somehow interact, instead, it claims that the mental somehow supervenes the physical. Mental events or qualia supervene the brain.

Lastly, what are the problems of belief in supervenience? Well, it is the same issue of the causal closure of the physical, something which has daunted us right from the beginning itself. As all analogies break down somewhere, this does too. Imagine in a distant time, much enough to perceive a difference in aesthetic properties, then there must be a difference in the physical realm too. Another way to realize the crux of the issue is to imagine this in the phenomenon of pain. If there lies the mental event of pain five minutes from now, then there must be a difference entailed in the brain too within the given time frame. We can surely imagine there to be causation running from the immaterial (mental) to the material (physical body) even with supervenience in the mind, as shown above. But the emergentist, even so, magnificently accoutred with supervenience, cannot fare any well in explaining this; how does the mind affect the body? No account, no matter, how elaborate, can seem to diffuse this problem. What is the reason behind this? Maybe all these accounts (ones entailed by property dualism), only seem to delve into the domain of dualism, but somehow are a physicalist account that can make sense only in the language and domain of physicalism. The main problem as the reader might have understood by now is the problem of mental causation, more precisely the causal closure of the physical.

The main issue with the varieties of property dualism, particularly emergentism and supervenience, is that, on the one hand, they claim the immaterial to be an emergent phenomenon dependent on the material, while on the other hand, it cannot exert any causal potency on the fundamental substratum from on which it emerges, on which it supervenes. Perhaps this is the problem that cannot be diffused by the extent of dualism, which then brings us to the accounts of physicalist forces, to be discussed in the section on physicalism. But before that, let us take a detour into physics.

Laws of Conservation and Dualism

Till now, we have discussed the problems associated with dualism, mainly those caused by the problem of interaction. All the various accounts and variants presented above are attempts to seek a definite answer to this problem. There is one additional issue posted against the dilemma of interaction, which comes from the domain of physics. The law of conservation of energy and mass is fundamental and is one of the most well-established principles of physics. The law states that in a "closed" or "isolated" system, considered over a gradual peroid of time, the net total of both mass and energy remains constant (Feynman 1970). More specifically, the closed system neither has an increasing gain nor a depreciating loss, either of energy or mass. One may think of particles without mass like photons or gluons but what is to be kept here in mind is that one cannot deny that even such particles are possessed of energy mainly since energy is a function of frequency (Lycan 1996).

Imagine the human body as an isolated and closed physical system in the sense that it contains both physical mass and energy, and remains isolated from energy beyond the limits of the system itself. This basic concept is what we deem as the "causal closure concept" as mentioned and discussed in detail above. To introduce any alteration in the system, either the energy adhering to the system has to be used, or, it has to be brought in from outside the system. When one considers the realm of the immaterial mind, there arises the problem of dysfunction. If the energy inherent in the system is used, then the realm of the immaterial mind can have no effect on the system since it is beyond the system and due to the system being closed, there can be no effect on the system. If we work the other ways round and introduce energy from outside, then it has two implications: first, this implies that the system is not closed; second, if it is closed, then the conservation laws are denied, i.e. the level of energy must fluctuate.

If the mind is to cast the effect on the physical body, then the energy to be introduced must be physical since the system is a physical system (body). But since by the premises of dualism, the mind is immaterial, i.e. non-physical, thereby the energy imparted by it too would be non-physical and it is, for this reason, beyond the domain of physical and any energy expended by it too would be beyond physical. The problem is the same as already discussed and it is the non-linearity and non-spatiality of the forces governing the domain of the non-physical mind. The non-linearity is on account of the difference in defining characteristics of the physical and the non-physical. Mass and energy are supposed to be the characteristic domain of the physical while the lack thereof seems to define the domain of non-physical, hence making it impossible for the two to interact. The domain of the physical does not seem to comprehend the non-physical forces and energy, while the realm of a non-physical mind will not accept and accommodate the physical forces and energy associated. Why? The causal closure of the physical principle does not allow for it.

Granting any account of dualism (without this critique) will imply that there is an interaction between the mental and the physical and by the laws of physics that would imply the interaction of energy as well and that in turn implies that there will be at the least a fluctuation in energy. If considering the causal closure, we think of the physical as impacting the mental, then there would be a constant appearance and vanquishing of physical energy in the brain since it is somehow the seat of the mind. The problem, as would have been clear by now, is that the realm of physical cannot extend its reach to something which it is not, i.e. non-physical, but by accounts of dualism, it has to somehow interact with it (non-physical). The same applies vice versa, i.e. the realm of non-physical (mental) cannot reach out to the physical, but by the principles of dualism, it has to. The inability of the non-physical to impinge on the physical and vice versa is a testimony to the conservation laws out of which blooms the idea of "causal closure", just as an implication. What causal closure means is just that within an isolated, closed and more importantly, uni-porous system (allowing to be affected by only one kind) only that kind of energy can impinge, of which it is composed, i.e. physical energy can affect only the physical system and non-physical energy or mental energy can affect only the non-physical system. There can be no barter of energy from a closed system in such a way that it affects the net total of its contents of either mass or energy.

There is a way out of this. If the mind and body are considered as one closed physical system, that is, the mind is too deemed as a physical entity in the ambit of the physical body, then the issue is resolved and the conservation laws are then restored to balance since this denies the proposition of dualism that the mind and body are distinct. But what is unacceptable to the domain of physics is that physical systems are causally closed. Hence, in all physicalist accounts, the distinction between the physical and mental is denied by taking even the mental into the physical ambit. Hence, affirming the interaction of these two is quite literally followed. To conclude, the failure of dualism hence can be summed up as the failure of positing a "feasible" account of interaction. And it is, for this reason, that various forms of physicalism have seen a surge, particularly in the last century. So, the next section is a step in this direction itself, which will try to follow up on the physicalist line of thought.

Physicalism and Its Variants

The issues, particularly the difficulties that involve the stance of dualism, must be very clear to the reader by now, given the account stated in the above section. For this reason (the problems associated with dualism), one might be inclined to consider the advances in physics that are presented to us. Sciences, especially physics, and their ability to explain the physical world have provided us with unified principles that account for the explanation of various mechanisms in the physical world. This has given a ray of hope at least to "people of science" that it may solve the mind-body problem too, at least someday, if not today. The main reason for such belief in physics and its principle, I think, lies in the fact that apart from giving considerable explanations, it has made life free of hassles that lie in front of a being if he starts to ponder beyond the physical. Our leap in material advances has challenged our belief in the immateriality that lies beyond so much so that an inquiry of what lies beyond belies our instinct which now is very well entrenched and affirmed in material advances. It, perhaps at least for once, may serve us to leave aside the spiritual and go for what may fairly seem straightforward, which it is not, as our discussion down the line will reveal. So, let us dive in.

Physicalism is the view that all that exist are particles and fields of forces and all manifestations of various phenomena are explicable in strictly physical terms. The mind too, in this line of dialogue, is something physical or at least can be explained completely in physical terms. Physicalism, particularly in the last century, has started by explaining the mind in terms of physical attribution and, today, with significant advances in quantum and cognitive science, especially with functional imaging tools, its zenith seems to be a sort of explanation wherein the mind is considered as an ontological substrate in the domain of particles and physical forces, so much so that not only they govern them but a fair picture too can be framed strictly in physicalist terms or, at least, this is the hope.

To start with, physicalism refutes the proposition that the mind is a non-physical entity. This claim subsumes it in the realm of the physical, implying that all that exists, is physical. Subsuming the mind into the physical realm solves the biggest issue we faced with dualism: the problem of interaction. The mind is physical and physical entities can easily interact with each other, the problem of interaction thus resolving. Dualism was asserted to be false because the physical and non-physical could not interact. This, however, is no issue for physicalism since no non-physical entities exist. All sounds good, does not it? But the question that now stands is how and particularly in what ways the mind acts as a physical thing. This is the question that has given us all the accounts of physicalism that we know of and it is all a manifestation of the possibilities as well as an account of how those possibilities of physicalism have evolved fuelled by the sole purpose of explaining how can the mind be a physical substance?

Behaviourism

Behaviour as an object of study has been a psychological domain at least in the sense that it was from psychology that behaviourism made its jump into the mind-body problem in philosophy. Psychology is based on the foundation of a quest, seeking to find answers about what the mind does, at least in the modern sense. An inquisitive observation by psychology was that human minds behave (Graham 2019), at least, in the sense that the behaviour was the verifiable element of the human mind. This angle of treating behaviour as a verifiable was introduced by the logical positivists (Smith 1986). Considerable ideas that are the foundation of the study of behaviour can even be attributed well before the logical positivists, particularly to the British empiricists Locke and Hume. This may lead to the question as to whose domain studying behaviour actually is and who brought it to the scientific domain before. As for the first question, it belongs to both since the latter had evolved from the former. And since philosophy is the mother of all sciences, one can deduce the answer to the second question as well. Though this is not an account of the antiquity of ideas, considerable efforts have been surely made to give a frame of thought and the reader will surely find it down the line.

Behaviourism is a perspective and its basic premise is that the realm of the mind is behavioural. What we understand as the mind is just behaviour. The mind as we see and perceive is just an extension of the physical body and like all parts of the human body, the mind too behaves. To make considerable progress in understanding the mind, it should be viewed from the purview of behaviour it manifests, says the behaviourist. In affirming this view, some hardcore adherents of behaviourism shift to intransigents' claim that the mind does not exist, what does exist is the observable behaviour, so much so that mind and mental events are denied to have an existence over and above behaviour.

For behaviourists, there is no mind or if there is one, it does not matter. What matters to them is just behaviour. This proposition is tantalizingly simple. What then remains is just observable behaviour, so much so that all the dimensions of the mind are boycotted to fetch an explainable substrate that reduces the hefty Herculean task of mental activity and leaves it all to some curious examination of the physical. At least this is how it evolved and attained fruition. All the questions of ontology are shattered in one go to pave the way for an epistemological substrate of the mind, all fuelled by the desire to reduce the mind into something simple, observable and verifiable. Though this angle is neither very well-favoured by the philosophers nor by the scientists, one should have seen the tall bolstered patronage it had seen especially in the heydays of early behaviourists like Ivan Pavlov, John B. Watson and B.F. Skinner (Graham 2019).

There are two facets to the debilitated state of behaviourism as perceived in erudite circles. First, we are so familiar with our mental constructs, events, feelings and thoughts that we feel them so deeply and intimately that reducing them to just behaviour seems a kind of an odd job. The other facet is the one with which we have become quite acquainted during our discussion of dualism, that being the obviosity of the first-person experience of interaction between the mental and the physical, more particularly the body and the mind.

Now behaviourism also has many varieties. Although the basic idea of examining the mind from the perspective of behaviour remains the same, what changes among in these variants is the framework of the thought and the treatment of the idea itself. The next variation of behaviourism tends to be more methodological and scientific in the sense that instead of considering that the mind is just behaviour, the shift has been to the thought that, maybe, we cannot know about the ontological status of the mind, hence, there should be a shift in studying the mind from the first-order domain of study to the second-order domain of study. This view, known as methodological behaviourism, affirms that despite delving deep into the metaphysical considerations of the mind and the ontological considerations of mental events, the paradigm shift should be towards studying behaviour. Why? Well because of the then accepted fact that the mind, the mental events particularly qualia, cannot form a domain that could be directly studied. The distinction between material and spiritual lived on very well then. The belief was that the spirit and its manifestations could not be directly observed and, hence, could not be directly studied. What then was observable, in the sense of academic and more particularly scientific scrutiny, was the behaviour. The mind and the mental events at this time (post-imaging technique period) were inferred based on their material manifestation and that was the behaviour. The creative aspect of these entities was inferentially studied, based on the behaviour it manifested. Therefore, the paradigm shift to this kind of behaviourism is prominently called methodological behaviourism.

The shift was more scientific in the sense that it provided some material for the sciences to play with and explore. By this time, the West had become desperate in their quest for spirituality and the quest was somehow diverted. They still tried to understand the mind in the sense that the pursuit was the same but the path had changed. This surely downgraded the original struggle and hence cannot be deemed as the wisest line of thought since most, or even to say the biggest quests of modern science, are now about things and entities that are not directly observable. Be it black holes, distant galaxies, stars, nebula or stuff like that. An everyday phenomenon like electricity too can constitute an example of things not directly perceived. Even the presence of gravity is such a phenomenon. But we do have laws and principles in physics to study such phenomena. One can understand electricity both by seeing lightning and understanding James Clerk Maxwell's equations. The presence of gravity can be understood both by seeing an apple as well as by Newtonian laws. All these entities are inferentially studied in the sense that they cannot be directly observed. Therefore, the shift from studying the mind as the primary focus to studying behaviour was, I think, due to the sheer desperation of the West in not comprehending the spiritual in the sense of their incapability to drag down the spiritual to a material scale.

There is another perspective to understand the "why" of this sudden shift towards behaviourism. We can comprehend the atmosphere and the times of the early twentieth century, which were clearly defined by a shift towards the material, due to a reasonable degree of failure in being able to drag down the spiritual into strictly material language. Dualism at this time (early twentieth century) was heavily dominated by religious ideas (not to be confused with spiritual ideas) and reminiscence of the ideas that marked the Renaissance had become synonymous with a scientific temperament. The atmosphere was to break free from such religiosity and bring scientific scrutiny to ideas associated with religion. In light of such temperament and with the growth of psychology (an attempt to study the soul materially), perhaps behaviour was the first site of scientific material investigation in the sense that it provided something material for the physical sciences to play with, something that newly-evolved sciences like psychology could play with. It should be remembered that the spiritual world in this period had seen a sort of uncongeniality due to a long history of exploitation and the unyielding nature of religion inflicted upon the masses. Hence, the shift was to studying that which was direct to the observational faculties. All this was not a new endeavour but the culmination of despondency religiosity had instilled in people. This is not to insinuate that the original subject matter did not exist, just that it was not observable, at least with the material spectacles.

This view is all the more reasonable since it reflects discouragement but not despondency in the quest for the spiritual. The shift was scientific in the sense of finding something material about this all-spiritual line of dialogue and hence the search led them to something available for material scrutiny. It was something directly perceived and something which could be sufficiently morphed to satisfy the inner instinct which had grown wary of preaching by religions. This was the time when the utility of an object was justified by the ends it could serve to meet, thence the form of behaviourism.

Following this line of thought, there is a variety of behaviourism that considers the study of the mind as an effort in vain. Fuelled primarily by vexation that was brought about by trying to reduce the mind to purely material terms or an equation the approach to studying it shifted. As stated earlier, behaviour was seen as a physical manifestation of the mind or at least this was what the physicalists could get hold of in the sense of bringing the mind to physical scrutiny.

This angst manifested into an approach that dispassionately considered the mind as something futile, uninteresting and hence inconsequential. But then something had to take its place since the will to study the mental never dies and that will then take up the study of behaviour, morphing its angst it said, "Well mind is not interesting to me, the behaviour is what excites me more". I think that is a great way to a rebuttal of the cumulative angst of centuries in failing to understand the mind in physical terms.

This line of thought in its most aggravated form suggests that the study of the mind should be completely disregarded to the extent that the basic consideration of understanding the ontological nature of the mind is dissolved. The quest should be completely halted, leading to a state where the truth or falsity of the premise that the mind is non-physical is beyond scrutiny. This, I think, is the Western prospect of academic peace.

There is a form of behaviourism called analytical or philosophical behaviourism which was culminated past this attitude of bringing everything down to material terms and was much favoured by some of the most brilliant philosophers of the age like Gilbert Ryle. It too starts from the same considerations as the ones by earlier forms of behaviourism in the sense that in their endeavour to understand the mind, rather than starting to study the mind from a metaphysical view the perspective, is to study the mind by what it does. And what is it that the mind does? Mind behaves. What this view articulates next is that every proposition about the mind should be seen as a proposition about its behaviour. What this line of thought tries to explicate about the mind, while looking at it from the perspective of behaviour, in a deeper sense implies that all propositions about the mind should be translated in such a way that they manifest as propositions about behaviour. In this sense, they are propositions about the mind in a way that they tell us what the mind is about, in terms of its dispositions.

Imagine a person saying, "I am tired". What does this proposition imply? This proposition is more than just being an account of the inner qualitative feeling of lowness brought about by hard work. For the behaviourist of this line, it is a proposition about the propensity and proclivity of the person to halt, take a break, maybe lie down for some time, take rest and gather energy. These proclivities tell us something about the behaviour that behaviour which the mind has projected on account of its inner qualitative state, that which the mind is feeling so much so that it has become a mode of its being, hence is the projection. It is this projection of the mind as behaviour, which is directly observable and perceptible in terms of scientific scrutiny. It gives something material to both the people trying to observe the mind as well as to those who are trying to understand the mind on a material scientific scale. This brings the mind under the domain of science in the sense of giving the behaviourist something physical to play with.

To understand this viewpoint better, let us take a look at an excerpt from Gilbert Ryle's magnum opus, *The Concept of Mind* (2002: 14):

> When we describe people as exercising qualities of mind, we are not referring to occult episodes of which their overt acts and utterances are effects; we are referring to those overt acts and utterances themselves.

One may think that these passages and a few others like this in the book are a clear demarcation that Ryle was a behaviourist. But an in-depth reading of his works and his standpoints clear out this incertitude. Though he might be attributed as an analytic philosopher (Tanney 2021), what is the actual takeaway from his ideas on the topic is that when he talks about the mind, he does not intend to talk about it in a sense of mystery, as something that the human realm cannot comprehend. He tries to deny the realm of the mind as being something belonging to the realm of the occult. This was a great leap in the way we understand the mind in the sense that it was philosophers like him who challenged the mystery that had been built around the concept of mind and it was in such small efforts that there culminated the whole idea of physicalism, that men thought that mind too can be explained in physical terms. Ryle in no way, while writing the above paragraph, wants to refute the existence of episodes of mind, what he tries though is to diffuse this occult mysticism that had surrounded the mind and hence get its study (of mind) rid of such mystical elements that had been infused into it owing to the temptations of earlier philosophers.

What Ryle is trying to point out is something we have already discussed above and, that is, that when we speak of a person as being tired or being angry, what we are trying to imply is his disposition of either trying to halt or take a break (when tired) or inflict damage (when angry). This is in no way (at least in Ryle's thought) a portrayal of the inner emotion or feelings or even an account of first-person private experience (what we now call qualia). What Ryle is trying here is to remove the mysterious subjective element of the mind that is the cause of all the fuss that is involved in the debate about the mind and replace it with something that can be subject to objective scrutiny, something that can be validated on the third-person scale. This is in no way an attempt to deny the qualitative subjective first-person experience since it is felt a way too intimate to deny. The whole effort is actually about having something that can be subject to third-person scrutiny, a process Daniel Dennett (1991) (doctoral student of Ryle) terms heterophenomenology.

One should ask at this point if there is something wrong with the stance that the mind is just behaviour, in the sense that all the multiple facets and manifestations of the mind are reducible to some physical behaviour that is observable and hence subject to scientific scrutiny. Is there something left out of this account? I think there is, and that is the spiritual dimension of the mind. The inner first-person subjective and qualitative experience is what is left out. Leaving this out should have been fairly easy if we had not felt this inner world of subjective experiences so deeply and intimately; my point is that we simply cannot leave out this qualitative account. It is this problem of the existence of the inner life of all emotions, thoughts and feelings that needs solution. Behaviourism does address the issue (the mind-body problem), at least to some extent, by denying the existence of the mind or one can say by subsuming the mind in the ambit of the physical. This solution as should be remembered is more fulfilling to the temperament of logic in the sense that though it does solve the logical problem of causation and duality, and so on, what it fails in doing is giving a reasonable answer to the problem of qualia. Behaviourism conceives of a case where there can be "behaviour" of being tired and an absence of the inner feeling of tiredness. Many forward stances of behaviourism believe that the behaviour can be reproduced without the inner first-person phenomenal experiences of it, that which we call qualia. We can imagine even a machine replicating behaviour as well as humans do, say respond in some way when seeing red, in the sense of manifesting a behaviour but what it leaves out of the account is qualia. The behaviour may be replicated but the same cannot be said about qualia. This is what is known as the problem of absent qualia (Tye 2006).

Even philosophers like Ludwig Wittgenstein have tried to address the problem of other minds which is in some sense key to behaviourism. For behaviourists to make an impact in the real world we need to have a standardized behaviour shared by a large group of people. However, it should be thoroughly remembered that his (Wittgenstein's) arguments, especially regarding ordinary language, are a demarcation of his search for a language that could standardize the manifestation of human mental events whose external observation we perceive as behaviour. This should be clear from his famous "beetle in the box" argument published in *Philosophical Investigations* (1953):

> Suppose everyone had a box with something in it: we call it a "beetle". No one can look into anyone else's box, and everyone says he knows what a beetle is only by looking at his beetle. Here it would be quite possible for everyone to have something different in his box. One might even imagine such a thing constantly changing.
>
> But suppose the word "beetle" had a use in these people's language? If so, it would not be used as the name of a thing. The thing in the box has no place in the language-game at all; not even as something: for the box might even be empty. No one can "divide through" by the thing in the box; it cancels out, whatever it is. That is to say: if we construe the grammar of the expression of sensation on the model of "object and designation" the object drops out of consideration as irrelevant.

This thought experiment forms the core of Wittgenstein's private language argument. The box in the passage is a metaphor for the body and the beetle represent inner sensations. What Wittgenstein is trying to imply is something that has been present in Eastern traditions for a long time. The crux of the argument is that there can be no language in which we could report our inner sensations in exact measure with all the details and vibrancy. It is so because when we try to report something, the primary factor we take into account is to make sense to the person in front of us, and hence we have to use his vocabulary. Here is where everything goes wrong. In an attempt to correlate vocabulary, we forget that each word means different to different persons because their feelings are different, and their intensity and vibrancy share different tones and colours. Language is an attempt to convey inner sensations, but over time, language has to get normalized for all persons to make sense of. We assume that in a common language, similar words spoken by different persons should imply similar meanings even in terms of inner sensations since the language is the same. Now that is something impossible and too much to ask. Just because we share a public language does not mean that we share a public inner sensation too. This is the reason many times we feel at the loss of words and this can happen even with the masters of a language. This led Wittgenstein to conclude that there can be no private language and, in this attempt, to deny private language what becomes derivative is a standpoint where behaviour becomes the New Testament of inner sensations. Somehow, we have come to respond in a certain way to a variety of feelings we comprehend.

Though while writing this, Wittgenstein was in no sense thinking of implying behaviourism but since what he implied was that there can be no private language, it became a precursor to behaviourism as it tried to find a common denominator (behaviour) that could bring the immaterial mind and its manifestations (qualia) into the ambit of the physical domain. Although Wittgenstein later clarified the sense and context of this thought experiment which was aimed at the disambiguation of meanings in philosophical language, primarily motivated by the search for a universal language, in whose ambit philosophical problems could have a clearer reflection.

Behaviourism does seem to provide a valid solution to the mind-body problem by bringing the so-called non-physical mind in the ambit of the physical by explicitly denying the non-physical. After knowing the context in which behaviourism culminated and having an idea of what it tries to propound, one should try to seek the plausibility of this view. An inquisition down the line should answer, "Not exactly". Why? The first reason for this can be cited as the problem of absent qualia, one that is discussed before. The other reason is a sort of derivative, or say an extension of the same (the problem of absent qualia) presented through the *inverted spectrum experiment* which shall be discussed in detail when we deal with anti-physicalist arguments. Since the same experiment is used to bring out the frailties of other physicalist conceptions, mentioning it now will just result in redundancy. At this point, I think, it would suffice to know just the crux of the idea, i.e. it is possible to have different mental events but similar behaviour. Experiencing a mental event is not just a matter of producing the right behaviour. Behaviour, as one might conclude by now, is just what society teaches one as a response to events. And as far as the search for the right behaviour is concerned, it is only a parameter set by society in a quest to bring order which is in no way a reflection of what happens internally at the level of mental events that one feels. This is the reason why a behavioural disorder has a variety of manifestations at the level of feelings in an individual. One can teach behaviour but one for sure cannot teach mental events. This is to imply the basic objection against behaviourism that the domain of mental events does not supervene behaviour.

Expanding on behavioural disorders, we may find many intriguing insights from psychiatry and psychology. It was an evident truth from these fields that it was the brain where mental processes get realized, thus validating mental processes in a way by finally addressing their locus. Now, that we came up with this, the probability of having different mental events (even when stimuli remained the same) similar to behaviour was realized. Considerable evidence came after analysing the victim of the two world wars, which showed that it was the brain state (and its corresponding mental event) that made people behave the way they do. Mental hence again gained prominence in the sense that mental events gained hierarchy over physical explanations. Phineas Gage's case study was piling up (Wikipedia 2022b). It was when there came firm accounts of causal explanations of behaviour or abnormal behaviour (which concerns the above fields), to say the least, that behaviourism began losing its impulse. At least as a philosophical movement, since today all psychiatry verily treats is, is abnormal behaviour whose parameters are determined by society.

This had colossal reverberations, especially when one considers the line of thought that if we say a mental event is just the disposition of behaving in a particular manner (which is the basic premise of behaviourism) and now after validating mental states we derive behaviour from mental events in the sense of explaining behaviour via mental events, then that would mean, the behaviour is an explanation of the disposition to behave (in "that" particular manner). This would simply be a tautology. In our quest, it would be great if such trivialities are avoided. Explaining the physical body via mental events will simply drag us further back.

THE IDENTITY THEORY

The current theory here in examination has been called by various names (type physicalism, central-state materialism and psycho-neural reductionism) apart from the identity theory. This theory should be considered as an advancement from the behaviourist standpoint in the sense that after we had sufficient evidence piling up to showcase the fact that the mind was something of an inner property arising out of brain processes. As insinuated earlier, the mind found a home inside (as its locus is the brain) and the search for explanations of the mind too turned inward. Hence, this theory can be seen as a quantum leap, in the sense that it gave a new direction to the search for explanations of the mind. Now instead of searching for explanations based on alien factors of alienated spiritualism, the whole expedition turned inward. This theory is hence a landmark in this sense.

The world wars had ended and as discussed in the above section, we had pieces of evidence coming from across the world pointing to the fact that the mind, as conceived until then, had some correspondence with the brain. Following this account, it was in the 1950s that things began to change dramatically. One of the pioneers of this change was Ullin Thomas Place. His 1956 paper "Is Consciousness a Brain Process?" changed the view most people had about the mind-body problem. This and many more such attempts by both philosophers and scientists began to change the hitherto view. Somehow a consensus arrived, that the behaviour of people, what they do, how they respond to stimuli (which is what drives behaviour), and the related internalized experiences, all have their locus of explanation in the brain. This was a huge advancement for the time. It is this advancement that we are dealing with here now, "the mind–brain identity theory" or "the identity theory" in short. As the name itself suggests, the identity theory is the claim that what we deem as the mind and what we know as the brain (along with pertinent parts of the central nervous system) share a relation of identity, i.e. they refer to the same. For them, the mind is the brain and what is deemed to be a mental state is, in fact, a state of the brain.

As one might have guessed by now, this account of physicalism also solves the mind-body problem with a single stroke. How? Well, here too we have subsumed the mind within the grasp of the physical by outright denial of the mind as being non-physical. And this does solve all the issues which were brought about by the belief in the premise that the mind is non-physical. Every mental state (ordained by certain mental events) corresponds to some physiological state (ordained by that physiological state) within the central nervous system (CNS). Hence, the identity theory derives the name "central–state materialism" since the mind is here considered to be the brain itself. If we imagine a circle showing the manifestation of the mind and its realization, then it is the brain and corresponding part of the CNS that will be at the immediate level of such a realization. On the outer periphery, this similar realization of the state of the mind will be manifested as behaviour that was once thought to be determined by the peripheral nervous system (PNS). Hence, behaviourist materialism is addressed by some people as "peripheral–state materialism". This might sound confusing. The key to understanding this is that the realization and manifestation of the CNS correspond directly to sensations (the inner account of feeling) while on the other hand, the manifestation and realization of the PNS correspond to external behaviour. One reason for this could be that the PNS links the CNS with organs, skin and other parts like limbs, which determine how the person reacts, ultimately culminating his/her behaviour.

The theory even now (almost sixty years after being conceived) seems to be very appealing to the inner wit. One can only imagine its charm in the heydays of emerging neuroscientific studies, let alone the emergence of imaging techniques and electrophysiology. Equipped with case studies of brain damage, laboratory lesion experiments and the effect on behaviour surely did simplify (or rather oversimplify) things for us. And with imaging techniques, the theory certainly picked up a notch. Each manifestation of the mind gained a place in the brain (in the sense of being lit up in image scans). Things were supposedly getting easy for the scientists, but they certainly got much easier for the philosophers working on the philosophy of mind. Such a line of thought gained full maturity in Nobel laureate Francis Crick's (1995) work, *An Astonishing Hypothesis*. The astonishing hypothesis is that all of a person's mental life is just a manifestation of brain activities (including nervous cells, glial cells, ionic interaction between membranes, etc.). This led to his further search for neural correlates of consciousness. Now that the mind is just the brain and all of mental life is just "brain life" (the activity of the brain), the problem is fairly solved. How? Well, since the mind is just the brain and the brain being a physical entity solves it all. Does it not? Now that we have just physical entities in the whole scenario (the mind being the physical brain) the problem of interaction hence stands resolved too. Is it as impeccable as it sounds? Let us weigh the solution.

The first and foremost objection is fairly counter-intuitive. How and when did the so seemingly physical brain (composed of physical attributes) turns mental in a single stroke. If the physical could just interact with the physical (without causing fair philosophical problems), then how did we arrive at attributes contrary to the physical. How did this physical set of entities and activities produce something so non-physical as the mind?

Another difficulty that is more philosophical in nature arrives when the central–state materialist tries to identify the states of the brain with certain states of mind. An example of this is the famous argument associated with the theory that the "sensation of pain is identical to stimulation of *C*-fibres". This is an example of an a posteriori identity statement in contrast to an a priori identity statement like "water is H_2O". This means that it is not sufficient just to know the meanings of the relevant words to figure out the truth of identity in the sentence. By definition, statements such as on these talk about a posteriori identity that needs scientific scrutiny. And as for scientific scrutiny, it has long been known that pain cannot be simply just *C*-fibre stimulation since there has been some significant evidence for the involvement of *A* δ-fibre too. As far as scientific shreds of evidence are concerned, both these fibres are not parts of the CNS (Puccetti 1977). These facts, by default, are then empirical refutations of the basic tenets of central–state materialism.

Hence, given the above arguments, most central–state materialists try not to claim that the "mind" means "brain" since the "mind" does not mean "brain". Had it been so, it would have been an a priori identity statement, whose truth could be known just by knowing the meanings of the relevant words. This claim of central–state materialism is subject to a posteriori identity whose truth is a matter of scientific scrutiny. Francis Crick was among the first central–state materialists to endorse this line of thought in the scientific domain too. The famous example that Crick used to give was that though gene transpired out to be deoxyribonucleic acid (DNA), this could be known only after rigorous scientific scrutiny and not by simply knowing the meanings of the words, "DNA" and "gene".

There seems to be another problem coming from the domain of logic. This is the problem of identity, which in our case is a necessary phenomenon. Imagine $x = y$. By the laws of logic, x is essentially identical to itself, i.e. x. Now after considering that x is essentially identical to x, try swapping the second x with y. This should not be daunting since at the beginning itself we supposed that $x = y$. By the laws of logic, the conclusion now follows is that x is essentially identical to y. Now let us get back to the claims of central–state materialism. As earlier stated, if the central–state materialist claims that the mind and brain are not essentially identical a priori, the claim must be false in itself, as shown by the above line of logic (Kripke 1980). Let us take this thought a bit further. If $x = y$, that by the laws of the commutative property is suggestive of the fact that $y = x$. Let us apply this observation in our context. If the mind is the brain, then by the laws of the commutative property, the brain is the mind. So far so good. But upon further analysis, the assertion that the brain is beneath all the mind is very much suggestive of the stance of idealism (all that is, is the mind), contrary to the belief in the discussion of central–state materialism.

Another objection regarding the a posteriori nature of mind-body identity statements was given by Max Black. By nature, the two-component expressions in an a posteriori statement must refer to (or be associated with) essentially distinct properties of the denotation. This nature of an a posteriori identity statement is an indicator of property dualism, which is contradictory to any form of physicalism, let alone identity theory. Consider the famous statement of the identity theorists that "pain is the firing of the *C*-fibres in the brain". There seems to be no issue arising for the identity theorists since they have been fairly using it for long enough. But then let us have a closer look. Distinct properties are being referred to here. As for the firing of the *C*-fibres, the relevant property being referred to is neuronal and electrochemical property, which is subject to scientific scrutiny in the sense of it being a purely physical activity. Pain, on the other hand, is a referent of the inner qualitative feeling of painfulness, the qualia of being in the state of pain. And this is a non-physical, albeit, mental property. Hence, the supposed physicalist (identity theory) statement turns out to be a statement enforcing the idea of property dualism in actuality. What is the identity theorist (aka central–state materialist) to do?

One probable solution comes around by taking into consideration a difference that has been there in philosophy for a long, particularly metaphysics and the philosophy of art. There is a difference between "type identity" and "token identity". Consider the famous poetry (*qawwālī*) *chāpa tilaka saba chīnī* by Amir Khusro in Rāga Bhairavī. It has been there for centuries, sung by many Sufi singers (*qawwāls*) and professionals as well, that includes its famous recording debut in Bollywood in 1978 sung by Lata Mangeshkar and its popularized, heart-touching version recorded by Nusrat Fateh Ali Khan in 1993 at a London private concert. Now one may ask how many Khusro's *qawwālī chāpa tilaka saba chīnī* are there? An answer could be, hundreds. Or maybe there is only one *chāpa tilaka saba chīnī qawwālī*. Then, there arise some serious questions, like how did it come about in all sorts of places (from temples to huge auditoriums) during different periods (since the fourteenth century) by different singers and in such a lot of renditions? Well, philosophers do seem to have a clue, an answer and the one forwarded by them goes like this. There is just one *qawwālī* type albeit many *qawwālī* "tokens or occurrences". This can be understood very much in the same way that there is just one *Bhagavadgītā* but it has albeit many copies. The copy of the *Bhagavadgītā,* both is and is not, the *Bhagavadgītā,* in the sense that it is a token of it (*Gītā*), but not the original type.

Such a distinction comes with its difficulties, but to one's amazement, it has been fairly used to discern between these two variations of the identity theory, viz. "type identity" and "token identity", sometimes also known as "type physicalism" and "token physicalism" respectively. There exists a "type" (say a mental state) of "pain", but there is an independent and individual "pain" that happens to be a "token of the type, pain". In one such variation (albeit a stronger one) it is the type or attribute (property) "mental event/state" that happens to be identical to the type or attribute (property) "brain event/state". While a less plausible but more sweeping version says that it is just a specific instance of a "mental event/state" that happens to be identical to a specific "brain event/state".

It might come to be that two distinct entities feel the same pain (pain in a similar part of the body) but they might differ at the level of brain states. But one thing is for sure: they are in virtue of some brain state. Now it is highly unlikely that all physical and mental systems work similarly considering the huge variations in the realization of such (mental and physical) systems, i.e. different entities' systems (brain) are different. Now it is highly likely to identify "a" pain with "a" brain state/event. Following this line of thought, it becomes all the more plausible as a consequence (of this line of thought) that two entities may share the same mental state but differ in their physical state. Now there is a hypothesis that daunts us and it is that these entities must be in some physical state with which the mental state of pain share identity. Thence arise the questions: how these tokens of pain are tokens of the same type pain? How come all these happen to be tokens (instances) of pain? This is what is known as "the problem of multiple realizability" first formulated in Hilary Putnam's "The Nature of Mental States".

Hence, following this line of thought and many related examples, it was fairly concluded that not only did an extension of such a logical framework of thoughts and argument, put forward in opposition to central-state materialism, work for type identities but also for token identities and that too fairly well. Although a lot of fair arguments against central-state materialism were postulated in the 1960s, it was only in the 1970s that the whole charm and aura surrounding it began to fade away. But was it just a failing of the theory on empirical grounds and the victory of a long tradition of logical validation or was there more to it? Well, as it comes out, it was the triumph of time above all as it had brought forth a more intricate and heftier view that took on the purview of earlier central-state materialism. All thanks to the might of time and the scientific advancement that came with it, particularly the arrival of computational machines in the daily domain. Next came the era of "functionalism".

FUNCTIONALISM

This was the era of computing machines. Machines were on the rise in the sense that they seemingly had the potential to make human lives better, more efficient and easier. At the beginning of the last century, this was due to rapid advances in sciences like biology, physics and engineering. Now it was the age of computers. Though it was not all a fresh start or an abrupt advancement, it had its beginnings fairly earlier, particularly during the world wars. The idea of computation was already conceived, most famously in the works and thoughts of Alan Turing and his code-breaking machine (used for breaking Nazi encrypted codes). Let us now try to have a look at how such ideas of computing and works (computing machines) began to influence the realm of philosophy.

It all began in the late 1960s, starting with a pioneering paper by Hilary Putnam titled "Psychological Predicates" (1967) which was later compiled under the name *The Nature of Mental States.* This can be said to be the first paper (or amongst the first) on the philosophical concept of functionalism. In the paper, he first takes the statement of identity theorists that pain is a brain state (firing of the *C*-fibres) and diffuses it. The first objection is that if the mind and brain are the same entities, then a brain event like pain should be realized and associated in the same spatiotemporal area, say the leg (if there is pain in the leg). Second, a particular brain state can at best be said to be correlated with a particular mental state, but not equivalent to it. Since considering them equivalent leads us to a situation of dilemma wherein we can have no way in principle for the preference of one above the other.

He then goes on to argue that the mind and its states (mental states) are not simply brain states, as in the case of the common belief that pain is a brain state (*C*-fibre stimulation) but, rather, a different kind of state altogether. He compares them (brain states) to be the states of a probabilistic automaton or more refinedly the states of a Turing machine. The Turing machine as originally conceived by Alan Turing (1950) was an automatic machine that allows for computation in a deterministic style with a given set of instructions and a machine table defining how the internal states of a machine interact with one another, and also governing how it responds to inputs again based on the set of given instructions. While a probabilistic automaton is similar to a Turing machine, its transition between distinct states in response to an input is determined in an unpredictable (highly probabilistic) fashion. The essential take away from these two systems (machines) is that their states are functional ones. Their job is to function (according to a set of instructions) or compute, for lack of a better word. Their response to input stimuli is characterized by their functional behaviour governed by a certain set of principles. The next take away is that these states talked above, functional or computational states are not physical states, not even when considered to be the states of the machine itself.

This thought was a big revolution for both the sciences and philosophy. Machines were now truly on the rise. For the first time, we had in principle and practice a machine (a physical entity, a computer) that exhibited non-physical states in the sense that these states were not made of matter. We have had machines before say a watch, it could be in different states (corresponding to different time indications) but those states were ultimately made of matter. A state of being at 9 o'clock was ultimately gears and arrows on a dial with markings on them. But this was a revolution. At least in the sense that now a particular physical state (the state of its components) could exhibit hundreds of other states that in no way could be said to have underpinnings in the physical substrate. We finally had non-physical arriving from the physical in such a way that the non-physical was not reducible to the physical. Since there can be no single particular physical state to which a particular functional state could be reduced. This hence solves the issue of multiple realizability too. How? Well now, we can have two or more Turing machines exhibiting the same physical state but they can be on their way with distinct computations, solving different problems. This is certainly an advantage over the traditional type-identity physicalism since now a particular state could be realized in the sense that now even a single physical state could have multiple renderings of internal (functional) states. There could now be several distinct computational or functional states even at the same moment when they happen to be in an identical physical state. Hence, the take away in our perspective is that mental states as we understand are just states of computations taking place and, hence, they cannot be supposed to be the physical states of the entity exhibiting these states.

The power of explanation that functionalism deploys is due to the computational distinction between computer software and hardware. The most interesting development brought about by functionalism is the paradigm shift in the view that mental states are not something to be compared to or thought to be reducible to the physical (hardware). Minds are active and working functional software. The rigidity of the mind in terms of physical hardware has been eliminated. With the advent of computers, one had to very rarely think of the physical or chemical structure of the computer. What excites us now is the software, the programs. The set of rules governs how things are done. What excites us now is not the hardware (since there is a fair similarity between them) but the software. It is this which governs how things are done, and how the tasks presented before the physical are executed. What matters to us is the explanation at the level of software, which is seeing how the tasks are done, irrespective of the physical substrate which happens to be doing them. The fact that a certain task is being done is just a measure of the program that is being followed. Hence, the relationship between the mind and body is redefined here as the relation of functions to what exhibits that function.

Let us imagine a simple computational problem, say the multiplication of 2 into 3. This one problem, a rather simple one, will turn out to be executed in different ways in different machines (say laptops), based on the computer program they are running on. A computer running on a Java program will do this very computation in a different way than say a computer running on a Python program. One can also consider two entirely different computational machines say an optical computer vs an electronic computer. They work in different ways. While the optical computer works by sending and pushing photons around the logical gates that form the central processing unit (CPU), electronic computers do the same but they use electrons instead of photons. These two computing systems cannot be deemed to be the same as they do not exhibit similar physical states due to the obvious difference between an electron and a photon. But what about the results, the output? That remains the same (6), till the problem, the input that goes in is the same. Distinct machines may exhibit similar functions, even with different architectures that go into the execution of the problem. And what is more astounding is the possibility of the fact that two machines running on different programs may happen to be just in the same physical state at a given point in time.

There was a fair level of anticipation in both the scientific and philosophical communities that with the advent of modern machines, especially computers, there would be a strong inclination towards materialism, particularly reductive materialism. There was fear and anxiety that a kind of vulgar materialism would hijack the whole scenario. The view that we are ultimately some kinds of machine, the belief that everything about us can be reduced to the component-building blocks of chemistry and physics was supposed to take over the domain of philosophy. But thankfully this was not the case. More advertently, the scenario was more or less in reverse. It is specifically due to the employed concepts of machine hardware and machine software that help us consider computing machines in a sense of abstraction, distinct and regardless of the physical state in which they happen to be. This is what helps us to differentiate between purely functional computational states (the non-physical Turing machine states) and the physical ones.

Combined with the rise of superior computing machines (equipped with better transistors) and newly-emerging cognitive sciences, functionalism became the preferred go-to choice for interdisciplinary academics trying to study consciousness, particularly from the angle of the mind-body problem. Behaviourism had seen its peril and identity theory particularly central–state materialism was also on the way downhill. With such a wide variety of applicability and a better ability to account for the behaviour of both machines and humans as well as their interface in Artificial Intelligence, functionalism had the upper hand, leaving lasting impressions.

Let us now deal with some questions that concern the mind-body problem. In what ways does the functionalist approach solve the issue at hand? What are its implications for us as readers of philosophy? Well, as for the first question, the stance of functionalism goes on to deny the mind and its states as being physical. This happens so, but not in the traditional physicalist sense by subsuming the mind in the ambit of physical, but rather by likening the mind to computer software, a program per se. The traditional Cartesian approach of considering the mind a mere object, a thing, is here profusely discarded. Just as the software cannot be considered a thing or an object, the same way mind too (for the functionalist) cannot be categorized as such. What is indispensably consequential about the computer program is not its physicality (since there is none) but the way it gets things done, the way it solves a problem, and the functionality it (the program) exhibits. Similarly, what is pertinent about the mind and mental state is not the corresponding brain state but the functionality they exhibit. The inherent quiddity to bring about a change, the functional whatness, is hence the crux of mind in the functionalist elucidation.

In later years, Putnam began to disregard his view of functionalism which he had formulated years earlier and of which he was once the most vigorous voice. One of his most famous arguments was put forward in his 1988 book *Representation and Reality* which became more vocal by the early 1990s. This argument stems from what is now understood as the problem of holism. Any description of the non-physical, in a sense that is purely computational or functional, can be successfully applied to any set of physical entities that happen to be able to realize that non-physical state. This seems to be fairly peculiar, especially coming from Putnam himself, since in his early years he used to claim that the functionalist account of physical systems (at the hardware level) along with encompassing mental systems (at the software level) does have a distinctive description at the level of computational functionality. It is this certitude that led him to arrive at the truth that computational descriptions are not physical descriptions. With this idea, Putnam would have surely come to the conclusion (which seems fair) that the mind-body problem stands solved since the mind and its states, as one might have guessed, are non-physical in nature.

An extension of this holism argument can be conceived as follows. Until now functional states were typified by the role they played in the postulation of a psychological thesis. These psychological theses are an assimilation of a vast array of mental states motivated by beliefs, wishes and similar idiosyncrasies developed and exhibited individually or collectively. If the state of pain is defined just as an amalgamation of these beliefs and wishes, then in the case of entities that do not share similar internal states, as characterized by the role of those beliefs and wishes, they cannot realize the same *type* of "pain" as exhibited by human individuals. The same applies vice versa; if the *type* "pain" is not realized (say due to incapability to feel pain), then there can be no sharing of those beliefs and wishes. Also, on account of such distinctive diversities sharing a similar mental state between individuals is highly implausible. Two persons sharing a similar kind of pain (say a snake bite) may react in highly different ways. But in the account of functionalism, since the outputs are related to a wide array of internalized mental states, there is a very low probability of sharing something in common at the level of these internalized mental states. This seems fairly counter-intuitive since they happen to share the same pain, regardless of the reaction they offer towards the pain.

This account surely has its implications when we attribute the problem of qualia to functionalism: the characterization of mental states based solely on causal and functional roles seems to disregard the experiential element of these states. The "what it is to be like" experience of any internal state: this leaving out the phenomenal attributes of experiences is leaving out of that which is human since it is the kind of first-person experience that governs our ontological categorization, not the epistemological functionality of experience which is subject to third-person scrutiny.

An extension of this problem of qualia comes from the idea of inverted spectrum qualia to be discussed later. But for now, the crux can be understood as follows. It is fairly easy to think of two different machines sharing the same functional state based on similar input stimuli but exhibiting inverted spectra. Though the computation, the inner functionality and the relative output (say behaviour) remain the same since the input is perceived to be the same, there is for sure a difference in the qualitative account. Hence, this qualitative experientiality cannot and should not be equated with the functional states. It is fairly plausible that a machine (Turing machine) may compute, without knowing what it is computing, say colour green. It computes, taking in the inputs, looking at the rule book manual (the program) as to how to do the computing and, finally, gives an output with not having even the faintest idea of what it is computing. This is the crux of another famous thought experiment by John Searle (1980), "The Chinese Room Experiment". The argument remains the same, that is even if a computer is fairly well-versed in performing a task that seems to be an exhibition of intelligence, this in itself is not enough to arrive at the claim that the machine is intelligent or that it has the kind of qualia as is felt in humans.

In spite of its shortcomings, functionalism still seems to be the go-to theory when it comes to the mind-body problem. It combines the ideals of both behaviourism and the identity theory and happens to leave out the undesired part. This allows for the multiple realizability of mental states while leaving sufficient scope for scientific scrutiny of such states. Functionalism demystifies the "subjective" element of mental experiences by deeming them as simple functional events playing a role in a larger cognitive system.

ANOMALOUS MONISM

Functionalism was a revolution in the way we perceived the issues revolving around the mind-body problem. It could be said to be a healthy combination of behaviourism and identity theory, taking the best of both worlds and marking great strides towards a more realistic and feasible approach to the issue at hand. It was around this functionalist epoch that was the advent of a new theory proposed by Donald Davidson. He, at the time, was working in solitude to come up with a new approach, a new line of thought aimed at an inquisitive inquiry of the association of the mind (the mental realm) with the physical realm, the body.

It was in 1970 that Davidson came up with his paper titled, "Mental Events", which came to be the foundational basis of his stance, later contrived as anomalous monism. He posits in the paper that there are irreducible mental descriptions of events in the world, in the sense that they make use of a mentalistic vocabulary. These descriptions of the world in such mentalistic terms cannot be transcribed into a physicalist vocabulary, one that concerns physical states and events. It is in this sense that the description is deemed to be "irreducibly" mental. Hence, it comes to be that he endorses in "essence" the position that the mind is not physical while the body is.

Davidson starts to build his theory of anomalous monism from three individually conceivable propositions, which, when seen in tandem, offer a contradictory view. First, he posits that there exist causal relations, at the least, connecting some (if not all) mental and physical events, thereby affirming that mental events do have a causal potency. This is to say that mental events partake in causal relations and, sometimes, into ones that we are here considerate about, the ones that cause physical events, as in the case of actions guided by intention. It is in light of such (mental) events and states that we ascribe the rationale behind physical actions.

Following this, he goes on to assert the idea of "nomic

subsumption". The idea is that two events share a causal relation and must have some deterministic laws behind them as the governing principles. Causal relations are rooted in laws that govern them, so much so that if there is an event say *A* that is the cause of another event say *B*, then there will be a law that describes the happening of event *B* by the happening of event *A*. For example, the shattering of glass by a cricket ball. These events can be related by a law that states that when an object with such and such mass combined with such and such velocity, strikes an object (our window in this case), it will cause it to shatter. Hence Davidson comes to the conclusion that causal relations have generalizations based on laws governing them. He then refutes the possibility of causation in singularity, i.e. causal relations will follow causal laws just at a singular instance not in another. He already mentioned generalizations based on law, which is to say that every instance of event *B* followed by event *A* will share causality based on laws, exhibited in the earlier instance. Every time the same ball strikes a similar window, possessing similar velocity, etc. the glass is bound to shatter.

These propositions are easy to comprehend until there comes the problem of the anomaly, our third proposition, particularly called the principle of mental anomalism. This principle fairly remarks that deterministic laws are the domain of physics. It is only in the description of physical events that compelling deterministic laws seem to be at work. But when it comes to generalizations of mental events based on strict deterministic laws, there are none. There can be no generalization of descriptions in terminologies other than physical. This is to say that mental events cannot be predicated on generalized laws as is done in the case of physical events. No laws and deterministic rules govern the domain of mental events so much so that they can be used to predict the occurrence of such events based on causality. This implication of mental anomalism leads Davidson to conclude that there can be no deterministic laws that can be used fairly well to describe relations between mental and physical events. There is no law, no deterministic set of principles that demands my neuronal activity to work a particular way when I go to see my friends or my parents. No set of physical laws seems to govern my neuronal firing, i.e. to fire in this way or that way when I make my visit. It is hence called the anomaly of the mental, the deviations from the set pattern of physical explanations by physical laws.

This view (anomaly of the mental) can certainly be challenged by citing some "laws" from the realm of psychophysics as strict deterministic principles governing the realm of mental states and events. The Weber–Fechner's law and the Hick–Hyman's law are some of the examples aimed at proposing deterministic laws in psychophysics. The Weber–Fechner's law governs the perception of weight. It states that when it comes to human perception of weight there lies a relation (logarithmic) between the strength of the stimulus weight and the strength of the response towards the stimulus. The relation seems to be directly proportional in the sense that to see an increment in the response, there has to be a corresponding increment in the stimulus. While Hick–Hyman's law states that the stipulated reaction time towards a given stimulus increases proportionately with the bulk of information that needs to be processed. This is to say that an increment in the number of options (stimulus) will thereby logarithmically increase the time needed to come up with a decision. There are counter views to such laws as well. These laws are not as strict as they seem or as they should be. The Weber–Fechner's law, for example, applies only somewhat fair when it comes to human perception in the sense that it works well and sounds only for certain scales of perception, like higher pitches when it comes to auditory impulses.

Following such examples, one might conclude that there might not be any strict deterministic laws governing the events of the psychophysical realm. But a closer look at the laws of physics will lead us to follow this conclusion for the same as well, i.e. no strict deterministic laws exist in the realm of physics too. Take the

Newtonian laws of gravitation for example. They assume these laws to be taking place or rather acting when there is a vacuum. But a vacuum in the strict sense never exists. With quantum physics coming into the scenario, we even have an uncertainty principle, one that says that we cannot account for the exact momentum and position of a particle simultaneously. Similarly, light exists both as a wave and a particle, which is a clear defiance of the laws of physics whereby an object can exist only in one form at a given instant in time. All this is not to degrade the sanctity of physical laws, but to point out the aberrations in physical laws as well. Said all this, one can concede that the laws of the physical world (that of physics and chemistry) are more constant and sterner than the psychophysical laws.

Coming back to Davidson's original quest, his primal interest was rooted in understanding quintessential mentalistic laws and how they are applicable in understanding human conduct, particularly the rationale and conscious coherence of an unexpurgated human behaviour. The types of questions that concerned him were like my decision to visit my parents back home, although not in perception, just the thought of it, and the rationale behind it. But later he relinquishes his quest and concedes that there can be a set laws governing the intent and the rationale of such events or such a described event. The rationale of human conduct aimed towards an end is described by the intention concerned, but the point is that it is too insurmountable a task to codify that rationale in such a way that it can be accounted for by the laws of science. To make the case more despondent is the fact that all of our mental constructs are tethered with rationality. Our mental constructs of reason, belief, thought, desires, etc. all find their roots in rationality (our sense of being rationale) which seems impossible to tame, in a way, in such a frame that they happen to be governed by scientific laws.

As has already been said, Davidson believes in the causal relationship between the mental and the physical, while exerting confidence in the general belief that causal relations follow unbending deterministic laws, but he also does simultaneously cite that there are no such deterministic laws that can act as a bridge, as a strict material law like affirmation which works, always, in such a way that they can connect the mental and the physical. It is now that we have stated our propositions of causation and that it (causation) follows deterministic laws, and summed up that there can be no strict laws when concerning the mental terminology, we find ourselves stuck in an inconsistent trilogy of propositions. One that goes on like this:

- Physical and mental events share a causal relation, that of interaction.
- Causal relations are governed by consistent deterministic laws.
- No strict laws govern how the physical and the mental will interact causally.

Hence, in Davidsonian conception, we have struck a conflict, a contradiction in the stances. What has happened? How did this problem come to be? Well, one way to put this in perspective is to think of Davidson's original propensity and that was that the physical and the non-physical do not interact. If they would have done so, there should have been laws instantiating such an interaction. For this reason there are none, he concludes, that they (the physical and the non-physical) do not interact.

What he notes next is something very common and at the same time peculiar to such a line of thought. Peculiar because if one had followed the earlier line of thought (that no strict causal laws exist for the mental and the physical) one would have left the stance altogether, that the mind does have causal potency. The fact that he did not and the fact that he moved on following this line of thought led him to concede that while the physical body and the non-physical mind do interact, such an interaction does not follow the contemporary vocabulary of the physical world. Such descriptions (of interaction) happen not in the terminology of the physical, but then neither do they happen in the terminology of the mental. What he is trying to say is that such interactions (between the physical body and the non-physical mind) are to be described in terminology that is both non-mental and non-physical. What are we left with then? Anomalous mental elucidations with no systemic scientific narrative. This, I think, had something to do with his academic training, early in English and comparative literature, and later his doctorate in Classical Greek philosophy which made him more responsive to the abundance and variety of the language concerning the mind.

Are there examples of descriptions that happen to be anomalous but do not fall under the domain of mental events? A careful examination may lead us to things, other than mental events that share an anomalous description. Take for example the predicate "lavish". People share an interest in things that seem to be lavish without even sharing the faintest idea if such things share something in common, in such a way that they could be linked to the world of physical entities so much so that one could instantiate and correlate them with strict deterministic laws. One's attempt to find a law of lavishness is bound to fall into peril. No stern deterministic laws of lavishness exist. "Lavish" is fairly hazy, idiosyncratic and a highly relative (in terms of usage) predicate. It mirrors our daily attitude, behaviour and exercise but in such an uncanny way that not even in the realm of economics can the word (lavish) attract strict governing laws and regulations. So, it is with all our mental vocabulary. They are so ingrained in our behaviour as a means to behavioural explanation, as a reflection of our so-called sagaciousness, but can nevertheless fit into the physically lawful framework.

There happens to be another line of argument that Davidson follows: one of token identity. What he argues is the token identity of the mental (events) with the physical (events). The vital element in such a line of dialogue is the interpretation of our first proposition, one that mentions the causal potency of mental events — the idea that not only do such (mental) events enter into causal relations, they do so even with physical events. Davidson comes to concede that tokens of mental events share identity with tokens of physical events. The key here lies in subsuming tokens of physical events under strictly deterministic laws. Now coming back to our first proposition, i.e. mental events have causal potency to share causal relations, we add the striking Davidsonian dictum — they (mental events) do so under a physicalist vocabulary, under a terminology that takes into account physical description rather than mentalistic ones.

As it happens to be, mental events are not the domain of strict, deterministic laws, but since they share causal interaction with events of the physical world, there must be physical laws that cover them up (Davidson 1970). Now that physical laws cover such events, they must be tokens of physical events. But there may arise one question, why token identity and not type identity? To answer this, one should note that though anomalous monism talks of identity, it is an identity of tokens, one that relates a particular instance of mental with a particular instance of the physical, rather than of types, i.e. a linkage between general (universal) kinds of mental event and general kinds of physical events. Furthermore, this identity (of tokens) does not subscribe to reductive bridge laws, the laws that connect predicates vary across an array of scientific domains via a relation of identity. To exemplify this, try to understand an instantiation of the same. Suppose I have a pain in my head, it would resemble a corresponding instance (particular) of a state, i.e. physically inherent in me. Now suppose you have a headache or pain felt by you as a mental event that would correspond to some pain physically inherent in you. Now, look conjoined at these two types of pain. There is no reason to believe that we share the same physical state. As already stated, those corresponding physical states are inherent to oneself. This demarcating line was something we drew even before placing our whole argument. The realization of the same pain differs at the physical level in each of us. There even lies the possibility of change in such realization over time. What is even more interesting is the plausibility of the fact that even a single person with two instances of pain may share different physical states in the two given instances. What Davidson tries to argue by placing forward such instantiations is that there cannot be an identity between types of mental events and types of physical events. Why? In his version of physicalism, mental concepts cannot be reduced to physical concepts, which is highly suggestive of a kind of non-reductive physicalism or non-reductive materialism.

It is hence that the aforementioned mental events cannot be a physical event, at the level of description as such, at the level of concepts, i.e. at the level of types. Take the case of a physical event *P* being caused by some mental event *M*. In a typical Davidsonian account, these events will be instantiations of some deterministic causal laws, in some particular description or the other. Now that we have become accustomed to the principle of anomalism of the mental, it is only fairly easy to understand that such a law will not take into account the mental description of *M* but a physical description, one that uses physicalist terminology, hence deeming *M* to be a physical event. It is only after we keep in mind such differentiations that we can refuse the idea of type-identity shared between mental events and physical events. It is in light of this idea that we should acknowledge the subsumption of mental events under physical ones since it is the one that provides us with the true Davidsonian essence.

To sum up his overall argument in light of the mind-body problem, it would help to categorize his argumentation in the following propositional structure:

1. There lies a non-physical mind.
2. There lies a physical body.

3. They (the mind and the body) interact.
4. The realm of the physical and that of the non-physical cannot interact.

Proposition 4 would seem contrary to the above three propositions, but when seen in alignment with our thoughts a little further above, it would sound fairly logical since the affirmation of our fourth proposition would require the existence of strict and deterministic psychophysical causal laws. Hence, it is in tandem with our earlier set of observations, particularly one that we took note of while discussing the idea of nomological subsumption.

The catch here however lies in the interpretation of our proposition 1, i.e. the ambiguity of the assumption of the meaning ascribed to it. What Davidson is trying to imply here is that under a distinctly human lexicon, the descriptions of events deemed to be mental are by nature non-physical. The sense implied by the claim of non-physicality is one of non-usage of a vocabulary inherent to physics. The mentalist vocabulary is devoid of terminology and symbolism ascribed to the domain of physics. What it rather constitutes is a terminology inherent to the psychological domain. It is hence that the description is said to be mental. A strikingly peculiar addition to this Davidsonian claim is that such events can, in one sense, be deemed as physical, while also sharing a non-physical terminology. "That cellphone is too lavish an investment — let us not buy it for now", one says. A cellphone is a physical object. There is no question about it, but the description hence chosen (lavish) is a non-physical one that is a member of a non-physical lexicon. The mind is hence non-physical not in the sense that it is not a physical object, but in the sense that mental descriptions are formulated in non-physical terminology.

There have been various criticisms levelled against the physicalist version but one that strikes the most poignant chord is epiphenomenalism, particularly the claim that such a version of monism (anomalous monism) entails epiphenomenalism. The defeat in such acceptance comes from mental events — for such an acceptance would mean that they lack causal potency. One way of deriving such a claim is by asserting two claims, one that says events share causal potency only under a physicalist terminology, while the other states that only the physical properties of such events have causal potency; this, in turn, implies that its other properties, which are non-physical, are causally impotent, i.e. epiphenomenal. Also, when we consider the principle of mental anomalism, it comes to be implied that the only descriptions that are possible in terms of their strict and deterministic causal explanations come from the domain of physics.

There have been some promising counters to this line of criticism too. The first one, majorly capitalized by Davidson, is the refutation of properties per se. For him, only events share causal potency. Entities called by the name property are causally inert, in the virtue of not being able to cause anything. Hence, they should be deemed as neither causally appropriate nor vice versa. He is fairly sceptical about such a line of thought which considers that events have causal potency relying on the virtues of instantiation of some property or the other. What Davidson is talking about is the causal efficacy of mental tokens in virtue of their identity with physical tokens, which are subsumed under physical laws. The Davidsonian dictum is that causation is an account to be held event *relata* (Davidson 1993). For him to debate on properties is actually to debate on predicates. It is hence a conception of predicates that Davidson endorses rather than one of the properties. This should be understood as central to his ontology, in light of which his whole framework of causation and non-reductive physicalism is to be seen.

Apart from this technical objection attributed mainly to epiphenomenalism, one should also remember the difficulties of identities, whether of types or of tokens (as in our case). One should also take cognizance of functionalism and its account of the heterogeneous nature of multiple realizability for which Davidson has provided no answer. Additionally there is overcarching the criticism for all variants of materialism, i.e. the problem of qualia.

In our case of explaining anomalous monism, qualia seem to be an issue when we report a subjective qualitative experience in a vocabulary that is inherently human, like alluding to colourfulness or loudness, we have no intention of just framing a new vocabulary for purposes of fun. It (this vocabulary) has a functionalist regard, i.e. apart from expressing the physicalist phenomena of electromagnetic radiation or high pitch and decible, it has the function of expressing our shared experience of events to help in a shared way we approach and deal with the world. This new vocabulary not only helps us to talk about the phenomena of electromagnetic radiation or high pitch and decible for that matter but describe our experience of the phenomena, particularly how it feels to be affected casually by such phenomena, in such a way to produce behaviour. Both colours and sounds have non-physical properties. Colours have the property of brightness while sounds have the property of loudness. Neither brightness nor loudness is a physical construct. But luminance and pitch are. They are physical concepts defining physical constructs like radiation emission or the rate of vibrations. When we describe white as a brilliant colour or 120 Hz as too irritatingly loud, we are expressing an intangible meaning, one that in (mentalistic) principle can be ordained, understood and felt by observation, not by measurement. These (brightness and loudness) are not concepts of physics, but fall under the domain of psychology. And as far as human history goes, these concepts were felt first (mentally) before there came law-like generalizations to govern such experiences.

For all its shortcomings and logical soundness in terms of highly academic deductions from the three principles, one needs to view the larger questions like how in actuality (rather than principality) we acquire knowledge about the world. Are mental predicates anomalous? One may be frightened if one doubts the probability of shifting laws, which is highly plausible in an evolving world like ours. Imagine the shifting of justifications we derive from such laws. Issues like causal closure of the physical are especially daunting to a position like anomalous monism. However, despite all such questions and pertinent issues, anomalous monism is a perfect exploit of logic and its possibilities in the capacity of solving an issue like the mind-body problem are based solely on assumptions and deductions derived from the science of logic.

ELIMINATIVE MATERIALISM

Anomalous monism was a completely new approach to an issue as bewildering as the mind-body problem. With all its logical epiphanies, it was, I think, a zenith of logical reasoning. Along with its highly structured argumentation and logical justification, it was a milestone in terms of how far such a line of thought could bring us. Even then, with all such efforts, one may get the feeling (about anomalous monism) that it has somehow left the mental realm behind. But maybe that is what it is with physicalists, they tend to leave the mind behind, not that it is unnecessary, but that the challenges it bestows on any theory of mind are overwhelmingly great. The uncertainty of the mind in terms of its multifarious components is bound to leave any physicalist amazed. Or maybe our science is too young at this stage to comprehend the mind in all its multitudes. Did Davidson think that the mind deserved to be left out? I would say no. A review of the postulation of anomalous monism would surely leave us with a negation in response to the question. It would be better and would make more sense for physicalist aficionados to completely deny the mental realm, as many of them have done. Even with such a denial of the mental, as an independent realm in itself, almost all share a common denominator when it comes to talking of terminologies that are inherently mentalistic in nature. The problem arises when such mentalistic terminology, comprising vibrant mental descriptions as explanations of such concepts, is attempted to be swept under the guise of an opportune linguistic flavour, as a way of expression.

This seems to be the case with the theory hereafter in examination under this section called "eliminative materialism", also dictated as "eliminativism", is a clear insinuation in this regard for it believes in the notion that such a mentalist vocabulary cannot be anchored alongside the physicalist elements supplied to us by the physical world. For people who hold this doctrine, the essence of that (vocabulary) which is truly mental is bound not to fit in the explanations of the physical world, be it the way it appeals to sciences or the way it applies to humans.

Eliminativism, as a form of physicalism, is quick in denial of the proposition that states the existence of things which are inherently mental, more typically a wide array of phenomena that are by description mental. For the thinkers of this thought, concepts and terminologies, deemed to be mental, are irreducible in terms of a scientific one, one that employs physiology at its core. They, like Putnam, found it absurd to scratch around for mental connotations in the realm of everyday psychology of propositional attitudes. Since all propositional attitudes had plain opinions, faith and wishes, none of which had its ground in empirical science, particularly the science of the brain. Hence, the conclusion that they arrived at states that once we have a fair neuroscientific picture, one that fills in all the loopholes of our understanding, one that paints a fair picture of mental events in the colour of the brain and its neural mechanisms, both the need and the room for terminology that contains and describes mental concepts will dissolve. When we reach such an epoch, we shall find the existence of the mental realm and its manifestations to be truly falsified.

Eliminativists found in such concepts a mournful reminiscence of the past. Statements describing these concepts are old fossils, relics of futile sciences (like primitive psychology and psychophysics) that are now surpassed by new methods in brain sciences. They are no more useful to us than the concepts of angels and demons. Just because they were once a common belief is no reason to cling to them. They are simply outdated views regarding the nature of humans, having no seed in them which could promise us fecundity in dialogue. With sciences progressing and beliefs evolving, we have overcome the concepts of angels and demons proving that they are no more than superstition and all they are just a matter of sharing a propositional attitude. There are no discovered physical states (employing empiricism) that correspond to concepts like angels and demons in a way that they can be said to be related. The take away from this point is the crux of the eliminativists' philosophy. There is a plausibility that this take away may sound a bit of a long stretch, but that is what eliminativists go for.

The eliminativists argue that there are no states (physical or otherwise) that one can come across and find concurrent to belief in the concept of belief itself. The problem for eliminativists is belief itself. It is the act of believing that seems to be the root of all dilemmas. It is the belief in psychological concepts, ones that we use in our ordinary life, that is the intricate fallacy here. It is the act of belief in something (as in concepts), i.e. belief in some belief itself, which gives us concepts like hope, dread, wishes and, maybe, a wide variety of such credence, all derivative of the same fallacy, i.e. belief. Belief is a muddled concept for eliminativists. Its philosophical fallacy lies in its incoherence. If a particular belief does not correspond to an empirical fact, then it has an extreme plausibility of being fallacious. If one deduces something, albeit anything, based on that belief, then there are for sure exponential probabilities of it too being fallacious, ad infinitum. Hence all such derived concepts like hope (which are talked about above) have no empirical basis, and no roots in science, and hence they fail to provide explanations that are at par with the ones provided by sciences. It is their fallacious and parochial inherence that makes them so too. Thus, they serve no true purpose, argue the eliminativist.

It is not oblivion though, they affirm. There is a silver lining and it stems from the emerging sun of rising sciences. The answers for such regard, say the eliminativists, will rise from emerging sciences like cognitive science, neuroscience and other similar allied brain sciences. Hence, the attempt should be to partake in exchanges, from the ones offered by psychology and philosophy to the ones offered by such sciences. Answers from such evolving and promising sciences will eliminate the ones that have hitherto been offered by naive psychology and such pseudo-sciences. Just as it happens in sciences, in their progression, they subsume and eliminate older theories with new ones by proposing better and newer models (to be read as theories) having higher correspondence to real-life facts. Dalton's atomic model was replaced by Thompson's followed by Rutherford and a number of others. What led to such a cataclysmic change was the rise of empirical pieces of evidence thought to be correspondences of real-life states and events. Such will be the case even for mind-body issues, say the eliminativists.

Contrary to the line of dialogue followed by Davidson, leading eliminativists like Stephen Stich and the Churchland couple (Paul Churchland and Patricia Churchland) argue that statements involving everyday psychological semantics such as those referring to hopes, dread and wishes are a theory of some sort, albeit a fallacious one, a pseudo-theory based, not on logic, but unestablished beliefs. It is this theory, these groups of extinguished mental constructs form what eliminativists call "folk psychology".

> The common-sense conception of psychological phenomena constitutes a radically false theory, a theory so fundamentally defective that both the principles and the ontology of that theory will eventually be displaced, rather than smoothly reduced, by a completed neuroscience. — Churchland 1981: 75

It is the kind of psychology based not on empiricism and experimentation, but on non-scientific tendencies to explain the behaviour, based mainly on the tool of prediction. It is more implicit and normative than erudite and scientific. Similar examples can be found in all walks of knowledge and even sciences like physics and chemistry. Concepts like phlogiston, elixirs and elan vital are all renderings of such pseudo-bygone narratives of sciences. With better theories coming up, which are better abled at explaining and predicting phenomena, the posits of the older ones get eliminated. The eliminativists hope for a similar miracle in the domain of philosophy of mind with pioneering work done by newly evolving brain sciences like neuro and cognitive sciences (Stich 1983).

As far as folk psychology is concerned, Paul Churchland is quick to note down the antiquity of the idea, which dates back to the Grecian golden age of philosophy, particularly that of Sophocles. What is frustrating for him is its inability to explain the realm of the mind even then and even now.

> The folk psychology of the Greeks is essentially the folk psychology we use today, and we are negligibly better at explaining human behaviour in its terms than was Sophocles. This is a very long period of stagnation and infertility for any theory to display, especially when faced with such an enormous backlog of anomalies and mysteries in its explanatory domain.
> — Churchland 1981: 85

Befuddled by the explanatory failures of folk psychology on a preposterous scale, in the same article he goes on to state:

> Folk psychology suffers explanatory failures on an epic scale, that it has been stagnant for at least twenty-five centuries, and that its categories appear (so far) to be incommensurable with or orthogonal to the categories of the background physical science whose long-term claim to explain human behaviour seems undeniable. — Ibid.: 79

Now there may arise one question. What does the wider philosophical community have to say about this eliminativism? Well, a significant number of the philosophical community disagrees with the claims put forward by the eliminativists. The philosophical community has particular allusions against folk psychology. There is a wider disregard for calling out the existence of folk psychology in the affirmative. Most philosophers (particularly those contemporary to the Churchland couple) disagree with the concept of something as folk psychology, moreover, the claim of it being a "theory" that goes around making mind-reading predictions is predominantly disregarded. This stance otherwise refuted is what is known as "theory theory". The basic essence is that folk psychology is a theory that employs theoretical reasoning regarding the behaviour commonly attributed to humans as is represented in the reasoning brain. It is reasoning as to how the reasoning goes (in the subject's brain). Empathy or an attempt towards it is the highest epoch such a line of reasoning can lead us to.

Well, then, what do philosophers agree on? It is a hard line to pick out in systems as chaotic as the philosophical world. But the common consensus on folk psychology is that it "as a theory" employs everyday mental concepts in our daily life having its underpinnings in habitual traits of humans. The concepts vary in different realms of human engagement but, for me, the underlying common denominator is that they talk about cumulative human engagement, i.e. they do not view humans and their activities (however simple or complex they may be) in complete isolation. Whether it is the concepts of the social world like family, class, culture, friendship or of political ones such as state and nation or those we employ in art aesthetics like surrealism and expressionism, none of them are viewed in isolation, instead, they are rather referenced to a large set of individual components. The line of reasoning goes from deduction to induction, i.e. from general principles evolved as a cumulative fruition of common human living to the individualization of such principles on particulars like a set of people (whose vastness can vary) to persons in particular.

There is nothing radically pungent in either such concepts or the propositions employing them. It is by believing in such a language, in such a social grammar that we can condense our thoughts and share them with the assumption that their semantics do not go awry (Carruthers 1996). It is this shared language of highly universalized concepts that enables us to communicate, which helps us share common values, and feel the goodness of universalized ideals. It is these shared concepts that make us the kind of highly collaborative humans that we are today. Thinking of any human feats of achievement without it would be baseless. Imagining a world without such concepts as the eliminativists would want us to imagine, i.e. by first abandoning such concepts and then replacing them with state-of-the-art scientific ones, that more erudite and precisely scientific ones will only lead to a communication gap. Abstract concepts make up most of human thought and language. The pain of heartbreak is not some *C*-fibre excitation or a feeling of an immense void in being cannot be understood by neurological concepts and, hence, should not be seen in such a framework. This kind of reverse engineering of concepts will be an attempt in demolishing all that we know as humans. Engaging in such a barter will be efforts wasted for nothing. It will offer not a human albeit a machine.

Arguments against stagnation put forward by Paul Churchland are not as sound as they should be. Many sciences have a history of stagnation that predates at least the one we are concerned with, i.e. folk psychology. Arithmetic can serve as one such example. In its elementary form, it has remained fairly constant. The basic operators like multiplication, summation, division and subtraction are all stagnant. Does this make arithmetic any less potent in its explanatory powers? No. This fundamental feature of stagnation as a universal phenomenon grants them the power they seem to assume. The whole attempt of mathematics has been to come up with such beautiful "stagnants" both in theory and equations. It is this ontology of mathematics that gives physics the power for such universalization. Mathematics is the language of nature and it is stagnant not because we have discovered it as such, but it is the reality of nature as such (at least on that level of explanation). Even though much of classical physics has been stagnant since Einstein, more than a century has passed thereafter. Have the theory, explanations and equations forwarded by Einstein been rendered useless? No. On the contrary, it is their stability (to be read as stagnation) that has rendered them pragmatics of such wide-scale utility. If such is the ontology of the physical world and the epistemology of physics, and if (as supposed by the eliminativists) the mental realm too, to be understood in such terms (of the likewise sciences), then why should we demand psychology to be of a fleeting nature. The tools we use to understand the brain, at least at the neurological level, are given to us by physics (brain scans like PET and fMRI). Why then should we expect the answers derived from it to be not stagnant, one should ask. If one looks at answers from physical sciences, it would look more like an appropriation towards stagnation. Hence, one should ask straightforwardly: why are the rules biased against psychology? Why is it that stagnation at the psychological level of explanation should reduce its credibility? Why should there not be placid laws concerning ordinary everyday life too?

To these questions, Paul Churchland falters, but not for long, before coming up with his claims. He points out the inadequacies of folk psychology in explaining mental states and events like illness (mental), creativity, sleep patterns, dreams, intelligence, will, visual perception and cognition. To such shortcomings in explanations, Paul says that there is nothing in folk psychology that can be said to have enlightened on such issues. "Negligent light", he says, is shed upon such problems by folk psychology (Churchland 1981: 87).

Is the bar too high? Indeed. How? Well, in many ways. For example, science has yet not definitively answered, why we sleep, why we dream, or more complex questions like how we perceive the world, or what in them causes the illusions? Add into them the conscious subjective element and ask oneself as to why such events are accompanied by conscious experience, one that cannot be subject to third-person ontology, now one is completely bereft of answers. It is this that Chalmers refers to as the hard problems of consciousness (Chalmers 1995). Are there no answers then? Well, there are many, most of them, however, form points of view by looking at events. The more definitive answers seem to have arrived from interdisciplinary studies. One point of view regarding such (interdisciplinary) studies is that what are they if not looking back at glorious years of philosophy when the view seemed to work in unison, when the interdisciplinary components were weaved into one whole comprising the study of linguistics, psychology, logic (which is a precursor to mathematics which again is a precursor to computing sciences) or even physics for that matter. Another point which is the most important is that nothing about humans is stagnant, neither is folk psychology. It is after 200 or 300 years of studies and deliberations that we have now psychology as a fair science. What about the story before this period? Was it stagnant more than it is now (considering the last great pieces of rationale-based ideas came from Sigmund Freud and Carl Jung)? The answers that are new in some senses are coming up from cognitive psychology, again epistemology at work. Even concepts like unconscious that have popped up in psychology were either present in some form in folk psychology or have been subsumed in folk psychology and hence are part of current folk psychology. Discrediting folk psychology would be in some sense discrediting philosophy calling it stagnant and deeming it something that is not yielding any results now. If it seems so now, it is since the human mind has too many categorizations now, not that it is ill to do so, since it has yielded us very good results considering the medical sciences as an example. What these sciences lack is a unified view, which philosophy wholeheartedly offers.

Even mental illnesses of high seriousness like dementia and common ones like depression have been thought to be treatable using music (Hegde 2017). These are signs of progress in folk psychology that remain relevant to this day, millennia after Asclepius, Hippocrates and even Aristotle (Kleisiaris 2014). The current understanding of consciousness in the seminal works by stalwarts and pioneers like Francis Crick points to this fact. Music is considered a harmony of the frequency of sound waves and initial research by Crick showed that consciousness could be just the same, brain waves working at a particular frequency (it is discussed in a later chapter). What is it if not a case of both progress and stagnation? What then matters is not new information but new perspectives to look at the same thing. It is this which gives meaning. It is this that philosophy has contemplated for ages. It is this virtue that should be sought after.

All mental illnesses are concepts of folk psychology as put in eliminativists' perspective. Hence, the existence of mental illnesses too should be fundamentally false. Is it so? Let us leave that as an open question, as philosophers do, since it requires imagination, again a derivative of folk psychology. I hope such insinuations work for now. Then, what is it that is going wrong? Since no effort to understand nature is a waste, they are all noble. At least in philosophy, they are to be appreciated. If not here, then where? The answer to this lies in the progress European philosophy has made through material advances. Even their education was rooted in technological advancement (consider the invention of the printing machine). It was in succession there came a time when science came to be understood as the hallmark of advancement, the highest feats of the human intelligentsia were thought to be the ones that offered tranquillity to the body, not the stirring of the soul. Yes, sciences did great in bringing that tranquillity, but what is a human without the stirring of curiosity. The conviction that followed such advances in sciences was that only sciences have all the answers, only they could succeed at explaining the mystery of nature, forgetting even the clues that came in between. Consider Einstein's work which was based on thought experiments, a remarkable feat of human intelligence. It is when the attempt should be to weave rationale and empirical pieces of evidence that Churchland lets go of faith. For what Churchland argues should have been just a premise, not the conclusion. A synthesis should have been considered. That would be the true revolution if there is a possibility of any.

Churchland should think that if stagnancy is the hallmark of failure, then the whole of arithmetic and mathematics that follows is a failure. It too has not changed for more than two millennia. Considering the timescale and stagnancy, the universe too has not changed much in many respects, the fine structure remains as constant as it was billions of years ago, albeit it has led to the kind of life we see today. For then, the whole of mathematics would have failed in its incapacity to explain if odd perfect numbers exist or if there are infinite perfect numbers. Even the bigger mathematical conundrums which remain unsolved like Goldbach's conjecture would be an insinuation of the same. Should we then formally declare mathematics to be stagnant too, for it has far too many stagnant problems?

Taking clues from Churchland would tell us for sure how a solution to the mind-body problem is approached in such formalization. Negate the proposition that the mind is something non-physical, not because it is physical but since neuroscience has not found evidence of it. The mind is a concept derivative of folk psychology and folk psychology being false should prove the mind to be the same. Let neurosciences do its job, until then it does not and should not exist, as only sciences can be the hallmarks of authentic judgements.

We stand again at crossroads with the same kind of solutions. Ignore the mind or subsume it under a physical entity or physical relationship. The problem stands solved. The solutions such kinds of physicalism offer, when looked at with clear glasses, are as unadaptable and intractable as the problem itself. The solutions and successes within such a framework seem to lie in how obscure they are to comprehend and how they tempt us to fail in understanding of our phenomenal consciousness, our qualia. Reflection loses in such formulations, that too to formulations themselves.

Anti-Materialism

In the last section (Qualia and Reductionism: A Dilemma) of his 2006 published work *Philosophy of Mind*, Ivy League's Brown University college professor Jaegwon Kim claims that the foremost "limits of physicalism" lie in the concept of qualia, particularly its unexplained presence in humans as a first-person ontological feature (Kim 2011: 236). Physicalism can have all its fame until it the issue of qualia steps in. Physicalism can answer all major pertinent issues into the philosophy of mind (including the mind-body problem), but not qualia. The mere existence of it, more than just a concept, as an attribute of being, is a real threat to any variety of physicalism whatsoever. Challenges remain the same, the what, why and how, i.e. what are qualia (in scientific terminology), why do they exist, and how do they exist? This formidable trilogy of qualia-based questions is what can be called, a face-on challenge to any variant of physicalism. Physicalism, as one might have guessed by now, somehow tries to negate in some way or the other the existence of qualia. This tendency to disregard qualia is something that shows the downside of physicalism, and if it were not for qualia, we would have solved the mind-body problem. The only challenge that stands against physicalism, hard enough to daunt it, is qualia.

Like most concepts in the philosophy of mind such as intention, intuition, emotion and will, qualia too escape a functional definition, one that can be scientifically accountable. Kim in the same chapter goes on to claim that qualia are irreducible, in the terminology of the physical categories, particularly brain sciences use (Kim 2011: 237). What is it then that makes such an attempt at reducing a disaster? The answer I think lies in something that makes it such a problem, the first-person ontology. It is on account of first-person ontology that we have not yet been able to define it, at least scientifically. It is particularly poignant in the sense that even after being so ingrained in our daily experiences, it has escaped a functionally scientific definition.

Despite keeping qualia and the challenges it poses in mind, Kim chooses to call himself a naturalist (one who believes that there is nothing more to the biological, spiritual and social realms than the arrangement of their physicalist components as such). But how does Kim accommodate qualia in such a naturalistic physicalism line of thought? The answer I think lies in his another work, *Physicalism, or Something Near Enough.* He goes on to quote here:

> The position is, as we might say, a slightly defective physicalism — physicalism manqué but not by much. I believe that this is as much physicalism as we can have and that there is no credible alternative to physicalism as a general world view. Physicalism is not the whole truth, but it is the truth near enough, and near enough should be good enough. — 2008: 176

There is a clear insinuation here, that physicalism cannot provide an exact account of the actual world, as it has to accommodate qualia. Something so close and personal cannot be negated at first sight. While physicalism does a good job of explaining many mental events, philosophy always seeks improvement. The tragedy of philosophy, therefore, is that one cannot have two contradictions and expect people to believe that it is sound enough to quench the philosophical thirst. Qualia and physicalism simply cannot stand on one side of the argument.

Till now we have seen various arguments trying to posit how the world we view around us is strictly physical. A larger part of the task for their propogators is to refute the realm of the mental and retain what is left, which they call the physical. Hence that which is left forms the world, i.e. physical matter. But here, sees Kim, in this seemingly perfect view, that there lies something that stands as an opponent, a complete contrast of this physical element, something non-physical, something that cannot be in any way reduced to anything physical, be it at the level of an entity or property. And this something is so personal, so intimately felt that it cannot be discarded, at least not at the level of experience. For its commonality, the magnitude of variety and its infinite occurrence, it becomes impossible to negate it as such. The first-person qualitative experiences of seeing the colour red, listening to Sufi music, smelling a rose, tasting a freshly baked cake and all other objects of experiences brought on so forth by an array of other sensory modalities, be it experienced or unexperienced (if such a kind exists) like the ones felt by wasps when they perceive the light of ultraviolet frequency and wavelength or when they perceive polarized light, are all clear indications towards the same. That which is felt only on a mental plane and can be graphed only on a mental chart, this subjective, first-person intimacy of feeling, the feeling of feeling itself is what is commonly referred to as qualia.

The question one should ask next is, is it all? Is it the list that includes all the possible elements of qualia? Is it all-exhaustive? Well, there can be no list of "qualia elements" that can be all exhaustive, but one critical element that figures in them all is rather a question in itself. The question of "what is it like?". It is one question that accompanies all sensory and non-sensory perceptions alike. This is what has been called in the Indian tradition as the *sākṣī* (witness), the witness of all experiences. This witnessing consciousness tells us what it is like to witness the redness of red roses or witness the green-ness of turquoise, by way of illuminating the experience. All the colours, sound notes and all that lies in between them, all the shades of multifarious feelings and their relevant degrees, intensities, their peaks and middle valleys; their exhibition, of possibilities differing in each being is also qualia, albeit the one with which we are more intimately inclined. The intensities of happiness, the lowness of depression, the nefariousness of confusion, the elations of anger and delight, and even inclusions of their mixtures, so on and so forth felt as intrinsic, the ontic subjectivity of all that is understood to be human, the qualitative, subjective and first-order "what it is to be like" content of experiences both inner and outer is qualia as well. One can even go on to say that these ("what it is to be like?") qualia are more intimate, common and more un-understood in scientific vocabulary. This I think is the paradox of qualia, for this being felt so close and upfront personal by each being and that too for more than millennia has escaped definition. Hence, we have a line of thought which includes the stuff of thought itself, standing as both a counter thought and counter example to our experience itself, i.e. physicalism. One might, after considering this, ask oneself, how "near enough" are we and to what. And as for truth, it waits to be discovered.

To understand the problem, the cul-de-sac dilemma, into which all our knowledge goes and yields nothing but more questions, one needs to keep in mind the definite truths handed down to us by physicalism and the infinite possibilities of all kinds of qualia that can exist, colourful and vibrant in their making, be it a product of sound, taste, touch, sight or by the self itself, all together. It is then we face life, our problem, and by logic, a true contradiction, since in the trueness of one, the other gets falsified. Hence, as philosophy demands, it becomes important, more than ever, to have a vision, not a view. A vision that accommodates both perspectives without maintaining sides with a view, for failing to do so one would fail philosophy and, in its failing, fails life. But what happened here logically? Conjoining a true proposition and a false one, falsehood is what we get, by the rules of logic. How close is this falsehood, to the truth? How close is this view to a complete vision? Accepting Kim's view would lead us to something of this sort — "If the physicalist view was 'the solitary truth', which it is not, it would be true". This would suffice for persons, people studying philosophy, but how would it be for philosophy as a discipline, one that is a patron of truth and wisdom, with a heart willing to accommodate both true and false propositions. This truth, of philosophy rather than persons, should hence be the nectar one should wish for.

What did we miss then? What is lacking? Maybe a fresh start. One that begins with a vision, accommodating both (as dualism does), that which one perceives to be true and that which feels to be true. We ought to say to ourselves, "We have got a situation". I am what I perceive, but I am also that which I feel. This, which I feel is a class of ontologically irreducible entities in itself, which means that in no way can it be reduced to any class of ontological categories which are physical in nature. They are something contradictory and in such an apprehension we have struck chords with our contradiction. Now, that we have our contradiction, one should ask, how have we reached here and how is it possible. One should ask how can things in the scheme of nature be contradictory. How has it led me to such a state that a contradiction is obvious in conclusion? The most important question that one should ask is: how come things around me, everything that I perceive, suggest physicalism but here in me, there lies something pointing otherwise? How is it that, that which I perceive seems so earthly, material and physical, but on the face of it, that which I feel tells me that the truth is something beyond? How is it that even when I look at my being, I witness a contradiction? It is when one stands amidst such contradiction does one begin to reformulate that which was the actual problem, by comprehending oneself a vision, one that accommodates and weighs both the truths parallelly. It is this kind of vision that philosophy, particularly of the mind, needs and demands.

The problem lies in how we have proceeded with sciences and in our case, specifically, the science of consciousness. Much of the input and work provided and done surrounds vision. And somehow the community has deemed colours and related qualia to be impotent in a causal sense. Even a wide chunk of Kim's work surrounds the application of causal efficiency to various domains of philosophical issues. It is perhaps in this sense of causal inertia that Kim attributes qualia's "nearness" to non-existence. This I think is a complete bias of the West for two reasons. One, it is predisposed towards non-causal entities (due to the laws of conservation) in the sense that since they do not interact causally, they should not and hence do not exist and, second, it is prejudiced to think of mental events as causally impotent, just to account for the causal closure of the physical.

Next, I would like to discuss some famous and well-known arguments cum thought experiments (five in number) in the philosophy of mind, all pointing towards the same direction, the same set of ideologies and tendencies that has been deemed by its contenders as anti-physicalist or anti-materialist. Here, I would not go into the debate of antiquity of ideas, but the formulation in the present context against the current concerns of physicalism. The arguments to be put into consideration will be discussed in the final part of the section. These arguments are in their way evidences for the existence of qualia. As I unfurl these arguments and put them in a perspective, it will be conspicuous how they have been used not only for arguing in favour of the existence of qualia but also for refuting specific variants of physicalism and in some instances the physicalist explanations of qualia as a whole. It is in their plain existence itself that qualia serve as a counter example to the physicalist claim that all that is, is material or physical. These attempts by the physicalists, which tend to subsume the mind in its ambit, become counter-intuitive in the wake of such arguments affirming qualia. Advocates of such stance affirming qualia are often deemed to be mysterious, well in terms of the physicalist purview. A close look however at the arguments will make it more than clear that nothing about them is mysterious, neither their formulation nor the conclusion they build up to. The attempt is to bring qualia down to the physicalists' mind, not as something mysterious, but as something so intimate, that it needs a mention in our daily physicalist scheme of things. The whole journey is to refute anything mysterious, which includes qualia as well. There is no mystery in saying that there are evident truths, logically speaking, that are clear cases against physicalism.

Hence, keeping in mind the overview and the proposed layout for the discussion that lies ahead, let us begin. The former section will deal with the idea that everything is mental. Three variants can be chalked out as the sprouting of this very idea. In place of a better word and unfair generalization, I have deliberately used the term anti-materialist, rather than idealism. As this section proceeds, the differences and the motif of using this terminology will unfurl. The variants (of anti-materialism) to be discussed are solipsism, panpsychism and idealism. The specific differences and the common ground should be clear by the time we are done evaluating these stances. The approach will be to start with concerns of the self in this scheme and framework of things. This approach is the focal point of the view known as solipsism. Next, we shall move on to accommodate the larger universe itself in viewing panpsychism, and lastly join these loose ends by discussing the general view of idealism itself. And as earlier mentioned, the latter section will be about the five arguments built on the foundation laid down by the former section.

Lastly, just in case anyone gets such a feeling, let it be said here and now that there will be no unfair attempt to undermine physicalism or any stance that stands contrary to the one going to be discussed hereafter. The attempt is just to outline the various possibilities of thought conceived in Western ideological dialectics and debates. Any favour, if said and done, seems to be the course, that would be one of highlighting the fallacies and philosophical shortcomings of ideas, discussed contrary. The attempt is just to highlight what is missing, be it in the act of subsumption or philosophical soundness. The trick, I think, in philosophy is to look upon and reflect on the state of affairs in an unbiased way, with a vision rather than a view. It is then the journey of philosophy starts. Hence, without further ado, I would just like to say that the attempt has been true to philosophy rather than to philosophical views. So let us now begin.

SOLIPSISM

Imagine you are in a dream, all alone, without even the bed you are sleeping on, or the walls that enclose your room, or anything that you know for that matter, anything except you. Imagine yourself to be the only thing there is. Precisely one. That is all there is. You. Sounds impossible? Can you imagine it? Do not worry, if you answer negatively. After all, we are humans, grown up with family, reared and nurtured in societies. The whole effort to be in society was for the simple plain reason that one man was not enough. No one could survive all on his own. Aristotle used to say that a person not in need of society would either be a beast or God himself (Aristotle 2017). Even a minimal human existence would need food, water, air, etc. all things that are not you, that have an existence apart from you. Even if you could withdraw your needs from such externalities and just try to think of yourself, you will arrive at your body, each of your body parts seems to have a distinct existence apart from you. "I have a hand", you would say. This means that your hand is something different from you, as a being. The idea is that even in simple plain recognition of your own being many things, that are associated with it to continue that being, also come to be. Hence, thinking of you, yourself as the only one in existence is a highly daunting task.

What if you could somehow think of it? What if you could ponder over and come to the conclusion that you are the only being that exists? Well, if you can do that you are close to the idea that we are about to discuss. Derived from the Greek terminology, comprising of two words, "solus" and "ipse", meaning alone and self respectively. Hence, as one can now easily deduce, solipsism is the basic idea that you are the only being in existence. The hard part of it though is to conceive of your being distinct from your body, independent of it. You, the mind, only exist. Forget the material body with which you have so long identified yourself. It is very obvious to do so otherwise, i.e. conceive of yourself as the body since that is the way you have your first encounter with the world. But, imagine that these are just illusions, starting from your body to the world you apprehend using it. Just imagine them to be ideas in your mind and next imagine them to be false ideas.

The pious idea is that there is the concept of a "you". The mind creating and perceiving all these illusions is the real entity, albeit the only real entity there is. The possibility of its imagination is the contention of it being true. Since if you can imagine it, in that imagination itself you have witnessed its truth. This was the very idea we delved into while discussing the "brain-in-a-vat" thought experiment. There too what existed for sure was you and the rest was all illusion. All that was there was just the brain's working out ideas of the world, even your physical body which you see in the mirror. You can imagine and hence surely get an idea of what this is all about. The leap here is that there is no brain and there is no evil scientist. Even the scientist and the brain are figments of your imagination. The whole world, the family next door, your favourite car, the pizza you eat, the water you swim in, all of it, is just a creation, a creation of your brain. But with the idea of solipsism, the trick is to go a bit further and imagine that there is no brain, no wires, nothing, just you. Now imagine, if you can. It is a world of wonder then.

This view of solipsism may sound odd to some extent. The loneliness of it may sound depressing or even frightening because if the view is true and only you exist, it is truly lonely out there. All the things and people you have accumulated in your life are mere illusions, creations of the mind, having no existence apart from the one they have in your mind. No friends, places, things, etc. are there to linger on. Only you. This, I think should be an instance more of giving than taking. This aloneness is what gives your being authenticity and freedom. Realizing that you are one of your kind, maybe the only one. This fact should be more liberating than daunting, as it has been in Eastern traditions. The idea of solipsism is not a very favoured one in the West and has mostly been used to point out the fallacies of philosophical opinions, so much so that many philosophies have been addressed as failures since "they lead into solipsism". Nevertheless, for many, it has been the starting point of all. Knowing thyself, before knowing the world. Well, this was the starting point for René Descartes.

Now that we are accustomed to the basic idea and have a gist of what it feels like to be the only one, truly one in existence, let us accelerate our considerations and move on the practical part of the idea. Let us head to the foundations of modern Western philosophy and the father of it, Descartes. The foundations, the building blocks of Descartes' philosophy, are solipsistic, or so they seem. The starting point for Descartes is that one's self is the sole thing that can be known for sure, beyond doubt. This view has already been discussed while discussing Cartesian dualism. The whole motif of Descartes' famous dictum *cogito ergo sum* is that the whole world is open to doubt, everything near and dear, all that you love and fear, everything. Everything, but you. Nothing is certain, but you. The only thing you can be sure about, for real, for true, is you.

A point one should remember is that Descartes may implicitly be a solipsist, but explicitly in his overall philosophy, he is not. His later assertion is that we indeed know about various objects in the world. But this assertion about the knowledge and reality of the external world, apart and independent of us, is derivative of his philosophy. Descartes derives this assertion from his belief in God, that a good and benevolent God would not betray him into believing and being stuck with that which is not true, that which is false. The shape of this argument for believing in God is somewhat circular. Since the belief in God is based on reason, it, says Descartes, is God-given and hence trustworthy. If we question God and his reason for creating the whole world, one that is external to us is in question, leaving solipsism as the only viable opinion, the only takeaway from Descartes.

What Descartes comes to conclude is as erudite as his stature in philosophy. Both, the precursors and this ultimate conclusion, are works of complex reasoning and careful thinking. Is there something in philosophy as simple as the premise we are trying to conclude? Something from the classic old-school deductive reasoning. Let us see our premises and then our conclusion in this way and see what it leads to. Certainty is a mark of existence, i.e. certain things, for sure, exist. Let this be our first premise. My mind is the only thing I can be certain about. The second premise is in line. Consider these premises to be true. Now that you have done so, a safe conclusion would be that my mind is the only thing in existence since my mind is the only thing I can be certain about. A fair deduction, I suppose. The second premise can be attributed to Descartes. It is an indication of the limits of knowledge. Maybe, it is otherwise, but then the first premise as a dictum stops that, and in that midst of affirmation and negation, we deductively reach our conclusion: solipsism. Look at the sheer simplicity of it. This is what attracts validity for such a kind of argument. Occam's razor, we call it (Gibbs 1996). Formulated in the sense particularly remembered and used today by William of Occam, it propagates the idea that simplicity is a mark of the trueness of a hypothesis, i.e. the simpler the hypotheses, the more the plausibility of their trueness. How is it a case of Occam's razor? Well, our hypothesis concludes that solipsism is probably the simplest one since it cogitates for the existence of just one entity, our mind, the mind of the person arguing.

Let us take one more look at how our argument for solipsism fits the criteria for Occam's razor. Well, the proposition that the razor argues for is that the simplest hypothesis is sure to be true amongst an array of competing hypotheses. Let us now bring our contentions, that being, the simplicity of solipsism. Solipsism is the simplest a hypothesis can be. It is the simplest one for it argues the existence of just one entity. Hence, now we can safely conclude that our hypothesis, solipsism, is true. It is an elegant line of thought and the safest way to reach our conclusion. The sheer simplicity of solipsism is the elegance of it.

Occam's razor may not convince all philosophers, but for the same reason, its simplicity. One argument against it is that simplicity can be a measure of probability, not a guarantee. Another question that can be raised for this line of dialogue is pertinent to our second claim that solipsism is the simplest hypothesis. Is it? Nihilism then accounts for no elements to prove, the hypothesis that there is nothing in the world or that nothing exists. But is it simpler? It too has accounted for one entity at the least, non-existence, nothingness. Well, that is a long debate and I think that it should be left to the reader's judgement. But one thing is sure: this (nihilism) stands as contention for Occam's razor, something that needs rethinking.

The victory for solipsism lies in the fact that this argument still lies as a strong contender, an opinion worth consideration, even though the only assertion needed to prove it (solipsism) wrong is the existence of a second thing. One more mind, just one thing beyond my mind, material or anti-material. This should raise more questions and it has the kinds of which lead to a distinct branch of philosophy, i.e. epistemology. The question is whether the world we perceive with our mind gives knowledge of the internal world or the one beyond it, an external one. Philosophy is a bunch of questions weaved intricately with one another but for now, it would help if we stick with the ones provided by the philosophy of mind.

Another famous argument that opposes the view that just a single mind is derived from observations of our world, particularly the regularities of experience in such a world. These regularities are recurring patterns in nature like the day after night and vice versa or things falling down no matter how high you throw them. What is the best that can go into such an explanation? The realist answer is that there must be something out of our experience which has to account for it. Since explaining experiences on account of experiences makes the argument circular. It is in searching for things, forces and events away from our experience that a world beyond us is conceived and known. If everything in the world were a story weaved after our own will and reason, then its correspondent events would be the same, mirrored after our own will. This does not seem to be the case. If it were all in our mind, then we sure would have had the ability to conjure the events we experience in our way, one that brings us only pleasure. But things turn out different, sometimes completely contrary to our will. If it were all in our mind, we would have had better control of it, since it is not, there must be at least one entity beyond our control. Therefore, by acknowledging the existence of at least one entity not working according to our will, we have demonstrated the existence of at least one thing beyond our will.

One might assume, and that too fairly very well, that these aberrations in experiences prove the existence of things beyond our mind and its construction. But there is a glitch in the argument that these arguments do not tell whether such a conceiving, either of things, world or events, is a physical one or again one that is not so, the non-physical. Are there more minds and just minds, observing and perceiving minds? This is an open question that leaves a big gap, which can be filled with just minds apart from physical substances. In this open imagination lies the victory for the anti-materialist. Since much of the objection towards any anti-materialist stance comes from proponents of physical theorists, it would be worth looking at why they have gained such prominence. One reason is its ability to explain patterns in experiences and observation, and that patterns say that the physicalist is a pattern of a world beyond our mind and can be looped in terms of principles and laws governing them. Nothing more is as astounding to physics as is its predictive capacity; the capacity to predict behaviour, events and even the nature of things based on laws and principles. The best explanation for such an astounding predictive success is that things and features they correspond to it must be true, in the sense that there must be things beyond our comprehending minds. But then again if we look at modern physics and even stalwarts like Albert Einstein, a chunk of their discoveries was a result of careful and comforting mental experiments, again a deliberation of the non-physical. This surely raises the question if their creations have a separate existence and if there is a world beyond the one that the mind creates and reveals to us as such. The greatest challenge to the physical world comes not from the physical world, but from minds themselves. Each person claims to have a separate mind of his/her own. This is the biggest apprehension against solipsism, which is again of the minds, one's beyond mine, an issue to be dealt with next theory, panpsychism.

PANPSYCHISM

Let us break it down to "pan" and "psyche". These Greek words translate into "all" and "mind" respectively. The word psyche has many renderings including soul, spirit, heart, consciousness and even life. But the context here is to be decoded in terms of mind and mind-like attributes, particularly consciousness. So, like solipsism, here too the idea is very simple and more importantly all-inclusive. The idea is that there is a universe that has a mind, a form of consciousness that operates at all levels of existence. From the micro-level to the macro-level, there are conscious phenomenal properties in all of existence. The range of inclusion across entities, events and observations that this theory has brought forth, whether in the Indian non-dual philosophies or through the age of coming philosophies of Chalmers (2003), is a testimony to this idea that idealism is now somehow embedded in the philosophical unconscious, one that cannot be easily suppressed. And with physicalism, quantum mechanics and space exploration, our need to be closer to the stars has somehow exponentially advanced. With advanced physical theories and ideas for unified field theory in place, the distance between us and the stars is getting closer. Artificial Intelligence is a quest for such remarkable feats. A divinity, as big as the stars.

What is most striking about panpsychism is its extension of premises and claim that not only is everything mind or mind-like but it also happens to be a fundamental nature, a characteristic feature of reality as we know itself. The opposing arguments mostly go after this claim to say that reality is not fundamentally mental, it may emerge (again, according to the way the matter is organized, as an emergent property of that physical arrangement itself). The first way to refute its rudimentary, fundamental nature is to say, nothing is mental, no mental elements exist and even if there is some high-level mental feature, it will be understood through physics. If we go back, this was the line of dialogue followed by eliminative materialism. The other way has been earlier talked about. The emergentist way, which is to say that the mind emerges from rudimentary, elemental facets of reality, as in complex systems, like human brains. What is striking is that they see this possibility of reflection of consciousness as realizable in modern-day silicon chips too. In this way, even physicalism cannot refute anti-materialism, Artificial "Intelligence" is the quest they say. Is intelligence more than just connections of functional information networks or is there something more to it, an element of qualitative phenomenal first-person reality? The merging of the seer and the seen? The mysteries are never-ending but sure worth reflecting upon.

There are some major arguments for explaining how mentality can emerge from a supposedly chaotic and complex physical system like our brain. Our brain, individually, looks nothing like a consciousness generator when looked at individually. Electrons, gluons, atoms, bonds, acids, cells, tissue signals, processing. Nothing has that consciousness, or so we know. But working together a chaotic system develops that thing; consciousness steeps in somehow (Pepperell 2018). Panpsychism has given mental life to them all. There is a mental element. This is where we draw the line. We shall focus on these sorts of competent variants, of the ontological arguments. Some hold the contention that there will be an explanatory gap, a permanent one. Panpsychist rejects the probability that consciousness can be an emergent feature. It cannot be there unless and until it was already there, all it just did was phenomenally manifested.

Let us look into three arguments by the panpsychism faith and one vital counter argument from the physicalists, the combination problem. The foremost argument rests on drawing analogies between living and non-living, showing that there lies behaviour even in inanimate objects, one that resembles very much like ours, and that too sufficiently so. The second argument rests on the *ex nihilo nihil fit* principle. The principle here explicates the fact that only like can produce like. There has to be consciousness to manifest itself again, the ultimate absence of it cannot produce it, i.e. it cannot be produced if it had not existed. The final piece in this line of argument for panpsychism will be called on the Darwinian ideas of evolution and natural selection. The idea will be to see if there is a line, in an actual sense, between creatures or entities, one that separates those who are in virtue of consciousness and those that are not. The question is also about if we can truly draw a line or if it is just a futile exercise. For, if there is no line or randomization of choice in drawing lines, then that is not natural. Nature is not random. "God does not play dice", says Einstein.

Argument from Analogy

We have all killed mosquitoes at some point in our lives, not figuratively. We step on ants and insects if they bother us too much. We dance in the rain and we think we are alone, without a partner (a conscious one). Entities lacking a communication medium, beyond our comprehension, are apprehended to be dead by us. But higher animals, ones whose language lies within our comprehension, say a dog, cat, or a human? Even the idea of taking their life out is enough to bring a guilty feeling in us. What is the difference? They are all alive in some way or the other, even the rain (as we shall discuss) or inanimate objects of its like or very much so. As for lower animate entities, they are very well possessed by sensory organs. They look for food, shelter and reproduction all the way avoiding dangers, everything very much like us, the mediums can and do vary though. Panpsychism does not draw a line though, despite varying sizes and language mediums. "For it", all the manifestations of nature, be it animate creatures or inanimate entities like raindrops, share an analogy of behaviour and structure with us humans, much enough to call them in virtue of mind or consciousness. Maybe, they all share enough mental elements that they can be deemed to be capable of human affection and non-violence, just like the Jainas thought (Wikipedia 2020).

Let us have a look at the analogies we are trying to find, the common link between "us and them" that would make them worthy to be thought of as mindful. Let us take three important facets of mentality (though there can be more) and see how there can be a sharing of analogy. First is perception. All animals share the faculty of perception. They are possessed by sensory organs aiding them in doing so. They all sense stimuli and respond to them as modern science says these responses are guided by a sense of self-preservation and replication. This reaction towards stimuli can be sometimes beneficial while at other it may be a cause of decimation, nonetheless, there is perception involved. Another analogy can be drawn in terms of memory. All entities in the universe are possessed by information embedded in them (Seife 2006). Animals too learn in their lifetime and share a capacity to store information. DNA is found in almost all life forms including the lower one, which is too a storehouse of information (Wills 2016). All life forms share an ability to learn from the reaction to stimuli and many of them are prudent enough to store it for future benefits. Last in line is the ability to act, manifested as a sort of decision making. This ability arises for most of them via the ability to learn from the reaction to sense stimuli and stored knowledge, and remembrance of memories.

As discussed earlier, a striking feature of panpsychism is inclusion, encompassing both living and non-living. The earlier analogies say that panpsychism extends beyond the living realm in the sense that what we think of as organisms endowed with consciousness is just a little speck on the consciousness spectrum. There are many spectrums of consciousness-endowed entities in the universe, human lineage is just one among them. The whole living kingdom from unicellular life to plants and animals, all share some form of consciousness. Unicellular organisms like bacteria and viruses have specified and developed mechanisms which they use to make sense of their surroundings. Some even mutate as a response to survival inhibitions. There are shreds of evidence of basal patterns of learning even in unicellular organisms (Zimmer 2013). The movement in life forms is guided by survival inhibitions, one that resembles humans, like for food and better survival chances. Plant movement towards sunlight or in-depth movement of their roots either for water or nutrients, all are analogies of human behaviour. These small examples are pieces of evidence supporting the theory that life forms other than humans, low or high, do share some level of a mental element.

Even the inanimate things are to be included in this realm of the mind for there is sufficient reaction from them too, to be taken as evidence of mentality in them. Metals react to temperature; they change shape and some even colour. Even electrons, when supplied with energy, shift places. Common salt can induce a change in the colour of the flame if it were to be viewed as a behavioural transaction. Steel can retain the shape they are welded into. This is deemed to be an evidence of memory in inanimate objects. The existence of quantum particles in multifarious possibilities and the exhibition of a certain one single collapsed state when observed is a sure case of exercise of free will. The adherents of panpsychism view such nature of the inanimate objects as shreds of evidence of mental exhibition in them, quite analogous to humans.

Ex Nihilo Nihil Fit

From nothing comes nothing. This concept was first formulated by Parmenides and described in physics by Aristotle. The essence of the generalized version of this idea is that "like produces like" or "only like can produce like". If there happens to be something, it has to come from something. It cannot arise from nothingness. Seeds come from fruits, heat from the fire and the offspring from parents. The core idea is that if there is something in existence, it must have come from something, assuming an existence otherwise is absurd, i.e. anything or something arising from nothing is an utterly disastrous proposition.

Let us try to bring things back into our perspective of mind, particularly the idea of an emergent mind. At a rudimentary and fundamental level, the basic elements of the universe, according to the emergentist, are physical, that is to say, they show no sign of being in virtue of any form of mentality. Basic elements of such likes include quarks, electrons, protons and neutrons. None of which are said to be possessed of a mental element, says the emergentist. This extends even to our brains. When looked at individually the synapses, electrical signals, chemicals, brain waves, etc. are all devoid of mind-like manifestation or consciousness. Here lies the catch in emergentists saying and, that is, though they (individual compositions of the brain) lack consciousness in isolation, when put together and arranged in a certain way, consciousness emerges out of them. When looked at closely, this will look like a case of something coming from nothing, unlike giving rise to like, physicality giving rise to mentality. Your consciousness has somehow emerged from individual elements none of which had consciousness in them individually.

None of the above talked about individual particles have consciousness as their nature. Let us take a dive into imagination and imagine what if we took all of them in a basket scrambled, would consciousness arise there and then? This is the question we have been asking with machine learning and Artificial Intelligence, and the answer till now has been negative. This is very much indicative of the basic tenet of emergentist philosophy, something from nothing. If emergentism is true, we should have had our mind from that which is not in virtue of the mind, or non-mind, in place of a better word. If we follow the emergentist example and embrace the idea of something from nothing, we are committing a logical fallacy, big enough to reset our steps back to panpsychism.

Argument from Evolution

A basic tenet of the Darwinian idea of evolution is that through the process of natural selection, species of beings show gradual evolutionary and adaptational change over generations. Newer characteristics are nothing but evolutionary modifications of earlier generations' characteristics. Fossils and dug-up remains show their evolutionary characteristic changes. If this slow but constant aspect of evolutionary modification is considered a universal case of characteristic evolution of organisms, then humans should be no different and hence should follow suit. This is to say that the mental characteristic attributes of humans too must have been a subtle result of constant evolutionary adaptation from their past inheritances, acquired from forerunner species, who themselves must have been in virtue of mental manifestations like consciousness, in some form or the other. This is to be supposed as an extension from the earlier argument, that is to say, that since there are just incremental modifications, what was never there could not have been forwarded to newer generations. If mentality had not been there on the face of the earth and in the kind of life it has braced in its bosom, it could not have manifested in the way we see it in modern humans. What evolutionary scientists are now trying to find is a line where they can say mentality has arisen, a line that can demarcate creatures before mentality and hitherto henceforth. The link is to find a predecessor without mentality from which arose an offspring creature having mentality.

This quest can be put in one more way, and that is to say that somewhere in this process of the historical evolution of organisms and species there has to be a point, where we can mark a filtering boundary, one that segregates organisms in virtue of the mind from those that are devoid of it. But as far as science and scientific explanations are concerned, nothing similar, a segregating line, has emerged from such studies (Framework 2018). There has been nothing provided and shown by these studies that can help us point to a conspicuous time and place in the history of evolution when creatures and species first showed mind-like manifestations, particularly consciousness. Panpsychists see an opportunity in this loophole of a story and use this in its favour. Panpsychism argues that since there is no such evident demarcation, it should be understood as evidence of uninterrupted progression of mentality, right from the beginning of the history of evolution itself. It should be taken as a rightful passage of mentality from our single-celled predecessors. Since there is no evident line of segregation, it should be a case of continuity itself. And well, it is, for life began from non-living atoms and molecules like amino acids, and what happened via evolution, through the process of natural selection was just a modification over the past. The consciousness though was always there, streamlined through the whole process itself, the way we see it now. Hence, the quest to draw a line is utter foolishness, says the panpsychist, for there lies none in nature.

Problem of Combination

In philosophy, arguments that favour a theoretical stance the most can well be reshaped in such a way that they become an adversary of the same stance they had begun to prove. One such argument often quoted in favour of panpsychism (against emergentist physicalism) is that physicalist emergentism will never be able to conclusively explain how the individual components of underlying physical substrates of the mind like atoms, synapses, neuronal cells and electrical signals produce consciousness. The main agitation is that since they (underlying physical substrates of the mind) lack mentality, they, no matter how well and proficiently arranged (or combined), cannot give rise to it.

The physicalist response to this problem of emergent mentality of non-mental correspondents has been discussed earlier in the *ex nihilo nihil fit* argument. The panpsychist way out was to include mentality through and through starting from subatomic particles to atoms and human manifestation of consciousness hitherto. What this implied there and then was that all these constituents have their form of consciousness. There may be a distinct manifestation of it, one that is different from us, but at a basal level, they too are conscious. This is where the current problem of combination stems its roots from. Panpsychism too has to answer how does human consciousness, supposedly different from its components' consciousness, arise from them, when human consciousness is nothing but a combination of such individual components and consciousness thereof. If panpsychism says that physicalist emergentism cannot come up with a suitable explanation thereof, then there is no answer conceived, hence, we cannot expect one from panpsychism too regarding constitution of constituent's consciousness combining to phenomenal consciousness.

To put this into a perspective, think of the consciousness of the individual components of human consciousness to be "not-me" consciousness. This is a fair way to do so since the consciousness embedded in them is the consciousness of atoms, neuronal cells, electrical activity, chemicals, etc. These individual consciousnesses are not my consciousness, but they somehow when put together my human consciousness arises. There is no identity between an atom's consciousness and mine. Hence "me" consciousness is different from "not-me" consciousness. Therefore, it is a clear case of "unlike from like" or "something from nothing". This was the case that panpsychism earlier argued against and as a student of philosophy, it should be considered if the argument stands the other way round, since truth, if it exists, should be the truth for all instances covered.

There are certainly conceived ways out. One way out seems to come along by combining solipsism with panpsychism in which the affirmation is that my mind is the only mind and the problematic material constituent components are just ideas in it. This saves the mentality of material constituent components thereby preserving the mentality of "me" consciousness too. This seems a robust idea since the "me" mind is not a composite one, but an individual stand-alone entity in itself. The other way out is the one prescribed by Leibniz wherein multiple minds exist, all of which are simple and non-composite.

IDEALISM

This short section in the description of the anti-materialist view, idealism, is aimed at connecting dots and bringing the whole dialogue to a final loop. We started by coming to terms with the possibility of one mind, a single one pervading the universe. Next, we moved to the possibility of a "all-mind"-like reality, wherein we discussed the arguments for a reality where all that existed, was hypothesized to be the mind. From atoms to humans and galaxies beyond, all existence was in virtue of mind-like manifestation. This part of the anti-materialist discussion will focus on something known as universal idealism, the meeting point of two distant ideas of the same variety. The universality of the idea is in the proposition we are trying to assert and, that is, all that exists is either mind or dependent on it. Hence, this is the confluence of two rivers, solipsism and panpsychism, and where we are now is the meeting point. The negation here is of any reality that is not-mind or not dependent on the mind. The idea has become somewhat retro these days so the inability (if there is any) of conceiving such an idea can surely be granted.

There certainly can be variations of such idealism like limited idealism which narrows down the ambit to some (not all) things being mind or mind-dependent. This idea of idealism has greater implications than one might think and the list is for sure never-ending. One just has to ask oneself and figure out a list of things that derive their existence from the mind. Mental events, states, beliefs, etc. are derivatives of the mind. Constructs like these provide us with fundamental questions about an array of philosophical topics. Take aesthetics into consideration and question the existence of beauty. Does beauty lie beyond the eyes (to be read as the mind) of the beholder? Beauty lies in the eyes of the perceiver we say. Would there be "beauty" if no one was there to appreciate it? Let us consider ethics. Do moral values and concepts of morality have any existence in the world beyond our minds? Certainly, these concepts have no material existence but the question is whether they can be explained materially as social sciences try to explain. Questions like did God have a moral compass in his mind are examples of the flamboyant ramifications of such a theory in place. If such concepts as beauty and morality were out there, then everyone would have perceived them to be the same, such is not the case. There are variations to such ideas across societies, races, civilizations and even persons next door. How could it be? The only explanation is that such concepts are mind-dependent.

Till now, we have become accustomed to the physicalist notions of reality which stated that all that there is, is physical. Now here we stand face to face with idealism telling us that all that is, is mental (mind or mind-like) or spiritual. What is that supposed to mean? This is a question that challenges reality itself and the assertion that follows is that reality, as we know it, is not physical or material. Therefore, idealism is fundamentally different from the view that physicalist adheres to. Idealism is an anti-materialist view, as one might have guessed by now. Let us assume reality to be the only existence. Bodies are just a small component in such a reality. The way idealism differs from physicalism is in asserting the opposite, i.e. bodies too are not material or physical. So, if we follow up on our original mind-body tetrad, what idealism does is the negation of the first premise. The body is not physical, it is non-physical, anti-material. This is coherent with the whole idea idealism stands for and that reality "is not physical". Hence, the dichotomy stands dissolved. Nothing about reality is physical. The reality is spiritual.

George Berkeley has been the most famous philosopher in the West arguing for idealism at an ontological level which is what differentiates him from Immanuel Kant. Berkeley had always been an empiricist and his idealism was an attempt in the direction of his convictions. The empiricist belief was that all knowledge is nothing but a product of our sense perceptions. From this assertion, Berkeley builds up his philosophy, essentially claiming that experience which is the basis of all knowledge is itself rooted in sense perceptions. Thus came his dictum, *esse est percipi* (To be is to be perceived). His convictions were anti-realist, anti-materialist to be precise. In his contention, materialism was the view that stated the existence of a material non-mental entity beyond the attributes of our perception, sense-datum per se, which happens to be the reason behind those attributes, while not being the attribute of perception or even mind for that matter. The materialist view he majorly contended was the one that stated the existence of material entities and material properties beyond our perception. The materialism he was against was something both the dualist and monist physicalists could agree upon. This anti-realism that seems so engrained in his thought was based on some thoughtful convictions shaped in the form of arguments, ones that we shall discuss briefly.

The first argument he gives is one from the sensation of pain. Suppose you cut yourself with something sharp or burn yourself with fire. You must be in grave pain that is for sure, but just tend to yourself and ask where is this pain. Two options should emerge. Either the pain lies in the knife or in the flame or in the perceiver's mind, the one who suffers the pain. What makes more sense, one should ask? The plausible answer, one that makes sense is that pain should be in the mind of the person with the cut. It is highly unfeasible to think that the pain should be in the knife, for then that would mean the knife is in pain. Let us extend this perception a bit more and think of perceptible properties that can induce such pain. Take brightness, for instance. You wake up early in the morning and look at the sun with all its splendour, what a pleasing view it seems. The same sun becomes so blazing by noon that it becomes hurtful to look even with a single eye. If by earlier reasoning hurtfulness exists in the mind and the brightness of the sun is to be equated with hurtfulness, then by the law of identity the bright sun too is just in the mind and if the sun with its blazing brightness is just in the mind, then why not extend it to the cool light of the moon? Why not say that it too exists in the mind? (Berkeley 1948-57).

An extension of this argument comes from a daily experiment involving temperature. Take both your hands and immerse one of them in hot water and the other in cold water respectively. Just long enough that your hands get a feel of the temperature while not affecting them. Now place both hands in lukewarm water. What happens now? The hand earlier in hot water now feels cold while the one out of cold water feels warm. How is the water (lukewarm) exactly? Cold or hot? How can one feel the same water in two different ways? The experiential sense datum is contradictory, hot and cold at the same time. Which hand is offering a better and more accurate measure of temperature? None. The water is neither hot nor cold. It is lukewarm. The take away for the idealist here is that the temperature, at least the felt one, is just an attribute of experiential sense datum, not a property of the external material object, i.e. water.

The next argument that Berkeley gives is of identity. The basic idea behind this stems from what he calls "the likeness principle" (Cummins 2008). The dictum that the likeness principle states is that, "Only an idea resembles an idea". The question he asks is: what lets an idea stand for a material entity?: Resemblance, comes the answer. Ideas represent material entities by resembling them. If the idea you have of a dog is a representation of the dog, then your idea of a dog should resemble the dog itself. But, for Berkeley, only an idea can resemble other ideas for it cannot resemble material entities. Why, one should ask? The answer Berkeley comes up with is that it is only when we compare two things, we come to know if they are like or unlike. What the mind compares is just its ideas for only they can be perceived immediately. Hence, there is no question of likeness between an idea in the mind and a "non-ideal" which would be independent of the mind asserting its materiality. Therefore, it is impossible to form an idea that represents the idea itself, let alone adequately. As a result, if you have an idea that seems to be the representation of a material entity, say a dog, then the dog must be the idea itself (Luce 1968).

Lastly, we have what Berkeley calls the master argument. The reason for attributing it with such a name is the forcefulness with which the argument is put forward, so much so that he is ready to put his whole case at stake. He asks us to imagine a tree or any plain daily object that anyone can identify without any difficulty. Next, he asks us not only to frame these ideas, but also abandon the idea of a perceiver of the former idea, which is the self. This he says is impossible and thus shows that while it is the evidence of the fact that your mind is doing the task of forming ideas, it is not fair to deduct that these objects of thoughts, your ideas, exist independent of the mind. For such an independent existence, he says, one has to conceive the idea without conceiving oneself, which again is highly improbable and repugnant. One cannot shape an idea of an object which is mind-independent; for in doing so, one would have used the mind, proving its existence. The whole gist of the argument is to consider that if realism were true, then mind-independent entities would exist, but again one needs a mind to conceive of the tree, says Berkeley, which disproves the existence of mind-independent things.

Issues against Idealism

Apart from all the questions raised against idealism (the one propounded by Berkeley), two questions stand out in particular. The belief in such a theory seems hypothetically impossible. How can the body be not physical, when pieces of evidence both from daily use of language and experience stand in the way of such a belief? The body we possess is a physical one, a noun. The existence of a separate mind seems questionable, but not the body. This seems an utter contradiction, calling the physicality of humans as non-physical. This ontological issue that arises is one of differentiation, between the act and content of rightful perception.

The problem of ontology gets a linguistic turn when we analyse the second problem associated with it, the problem of phenomenalism, particularly in the works of English empiricists like David Hume and John Locke (including Berkeley as well). Phenomenalism advocates the ideologue that physicality is nothing but a sensory stimulus, a perceptual experience. For Berkeley, there are no things, existing only in themselves, and they have no existence beyond the perceiving mind. The attempt here is to examine assertions about the physical body as assertions about real and probable experiences or "ideas" as Berkeley would like to call them. Having been successful in the attempt would mean realizing the nature of physical bodies while understanding them as assertions about real and probable experiences which for Berkeley is nothing more than perceptual sense datum. To say that there is a slice of bread in front of me is to say that there lies a white square of a certain length and width in my visual perception. To say it will disappear a few moments from now is just a phenomenal elucidation of my body, albeit a part of it, my mouth.

The biggest challenge lies ahead of the subjective idealism of Berkeley is similar to the one discussed in the solipsism section. The objection is stemmed from patterns in ideas and experiences occurring in a fixed order. Not only is it an objection against idealism but phenomenalism too. The problem gets deeper when we look around and find people agreeing with those patterns and orders of experience. Why do multiple people agree on "the idea of white bread"? Why is it that when you close your eyes and look back, the bread is still there? The explanation that the non-idealist tends to choose for such a coherence, spanning various mental states, is of affirming a cause common to those mental states. The reason for bread disappearing is that there exists a mouth (which might have allowed someone to eat it), a physical entity distinct and independent from the mind, entities that are subject to the scrutiny of various sciences.

The last problem that goes way deeper than the phenomenalistic explanation is how the mind and mental contents or mentality interact, given that both are non-physical, for, none of them exists in linear dimensions. This obscurity of causal explanation of interaction is the linchpin deterring the account, away from a full exposition of all the issues involved. In Newtonian philosophy, physical particles interact with their like for they exist in linear dimension and act causally on each other, accountable to the physical forces of sciences. Do ideas work the same way? Are the physical entities some kind of unknown mind particles? Is there mind–mind reciprocity? Is there a mental currency causing interaction and exchange? They (mind and mental content) are devoid of both mass and energy. This is not only challenge for idealism but also for any stance that holds a mentality dichotomous from physicality. The problem and answer for such a clear mechanism have been the centre point of all such debates surrounding the mind. The last thing to state here is that though the interaction of mind and mentality with its like is a daunting issue, it is not the mind-body conundrum. The issue is the mind-body problem, not the mind–mind problem. Keeping these issues in mind I shall lastly attempt to present some famous arguments (five in number) that despite all physicalist challenges stand face to face with any version of materialism that forgoes the mental element.

Anti-Physicalist Thought Experiments

It was in the second half of the last century that theoretical physicalism faced many questions, particularly ones that no account of physicalism could help answer. This period was characterized by a deep inquisition into the know-hows of qualia, something that was a hard-hitting point for all anti-physicalists. By the end of the last century, physicalism had reached a zenith of explanation, in the sense that there was a period when it could not answer some hard-hitting questions raised by anti-physicalists. Although most in modern philosophy of mind chose the physicalist side, some arguments and questions raised are still a testimony to the anti-physicalist presence and the explanatory gap that lies in physicalist explanations. Here, I would like to discuss five arguments touted as staunch opposition to a unanimous physicalist purview of things.

It should be kept in mind that none of these arguments is ultimate. There have been past systemic debates and dialogues into the intricacies and implications of the arguments, which continue to date. The importance of discussion of such anti-physicalist stances is that they highlight the explanatory gap that has eluded physicalism. These arguments should not be understood as the final answer to the problem, but rather as insights pointing out the deficiencies of current approaches.

The core idea and the scenario behind each argument are short. Each thought asks us to imagine a case scenario and asks us to deduce the anti-physicalist theme in there. I shall be discussing both of these. It should be noted that not all arguments were framed in the context we are going to take up now. The derivative idea is a result of long philosophical deliberations ranging over to date. Lastly, I shall delve, in brief, into the implications of these philosophical deliberations, and how they have given us an anti-physicalist approach to the whole debate. This will be the summing up of this discussion on the Western approach, leaving the reader open to ponder over both, the prevailing physicalist views and the deficit in their explanation.

INVERTED SPECTRUM THOUGHT EXPERIMENT

Initially conceived by John Locke (1689/1975) this thought experiment has undergone many iterations. The version here asks us to imagine two persons. For the sake of explanation, we shall name them Mr Normal and Mr Inverted. The distinguishing feature that concerns us now is how these two persons visualize colours. Mr Normal on the one hand has normal colour vision. Mr Inverted, on the other hand, has a condition called an inverted colour syndrome. What this does for Mr Inverted is that it causes him see colours inverted. If we look at the colour wheel in *fig.* 2.1, we can have an idea. What Mr Normal and other "normal people" like us see as green, Mr Inverted sees that as red. What is orange for us (Mr Normal) is blue for Mr Inverted. The colours get inverted

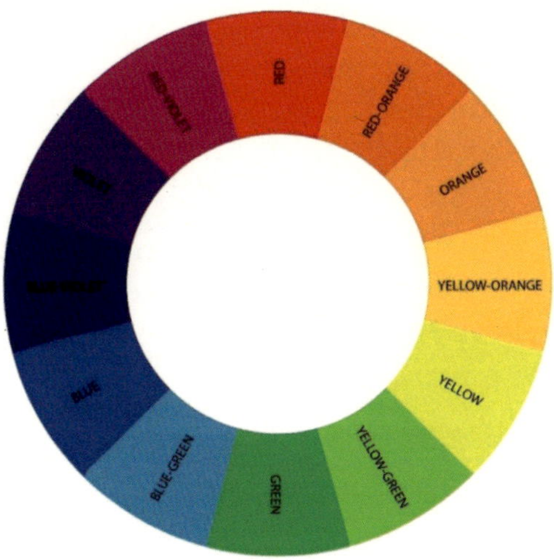

fig. 2.1: Colour wheel/hue circle

180° on the colour wheel for Mr Inverted. This is just to say that they have different subjective experiences of the same colour.

Next, imagine that when you show spinach to them and ask for the colour. Both call it green. You place an apple they call it red. This means that they have the same objective colour behaviour that manifests in their verbal behaviour too. They are functionally alike. How does this happen? How come they have different subjective experiences but alike objective behaviour? The answer lies in the way they were raised. When young, both were shown spinach and told it is green in colour. Red for strawberries and tomatoes. That is how they learned colour. Although Mr Inverted literally has a completely different subjective experience, he learned a common reaction, a common response to colour, one that matched Mr Normal and all normal people like us.

Let us take things further and imagine that both Mr Normal and Mr Inverted share the same anatomy along with the observed behaviour, i.e. to say they have similar biology and brain chemistry. When shown a bundle of spinach, similar part of the brain lights up in an MRI scan. This happens when there is a qualitative and subjective difference in inner experience. But as the science and its tools would say, they are objectively similar. Hence, one can conclude that they are objectively similar in all aspects, yet qualitatively and subjectively different (at least in experiencing colour).

This, if imaginable and conceivable is a testament to possibility and if it is possible, then it means that there can be persons with objective physical similarity, yet differing in the inner qualitative account of the experience. Hence, this "inner qualitative account of the experience", academically called "qualia", is not something physical. Now if there is something apart from "only physical" as the physicalist claims, then physicalism stands negated and falsified. If we come to specific versions of physicalism, then this thought experiment stands against three versions of it, viz. behaviourism, functionalism and identity theory.

Mr Normal and Mr Inverted are behaviourally alike, yet they have a difference in their mental experience. Show them both a bundle of spinach, they behave the same by calling it green, yet have very different perceptions of the same. This shows that there is something more, and perhaps distinctive of the mind than just behaviour. Therefore, there is something more to the non-physical mind than just ordained behaviour. Hence, behaviourism is false.

Functionalism states that the states of the mind are functional states defined by the causal functional role they play with respect to inputs and outputs as in a causal relation. In this case, the input is the picture of spinach and the output is speech "colour green". This demonstrates that the subjects in question are functionally alike. Yet, they have differing inner subjective mental experiences of the same functional states. Hence, the mind cannot be just the functional states and their processing since there is more to it as the thought experiment clearly shows.

Also, the experiment goes against identity physicalism. We have already conceived that the two, Mr Inverted and Mr Normal, have similar brain anatomy, even similar parts of their respective brains light up on similar stimuli. Yet, despite these similarities, they have something very different for something exactly similar. And that is the inner mental experience of similar colour stimuli. Hence this shows that there is something more to the mind than to respective brain states. Mental events are over and above brain events, mentality does not supervene up on physicality. Therefore, identity physicalism is false.

THE ZOMBIE THOUGHT EXPERIMENT

Originally conceived by Chalmers in his 1996 book *The Conscious Mind* the new word for philosophy here is zombies. The zombie Chalmers conceives is not a half-dead, half-living monster, but a being just like ourselves except for the fact that it lacks consciousness. It has no inner subjective feeling or experience when it sees a red rose or smells coffee. To make things simple, we shall choose our old subjects Mr Normal and Mr Inverted for this thought experiment too. So, here is how it goes.

Mr Normal here too has our normal daily qualia. Mr Inverted here, instead of having inverted colour qualia, has no qualia and yet has similar behaviour to Mr Normal and other normal people like us. What does that mean? Mr Inverted, when he smells tea, will say it smells tea, but at the level of inner subjective experience, he has none. It will feel nothing on the inside to smell the tea, no memories, vivid feelings, or experience of being in Darjeeling, that we might associate with drinking tea sometimes. Pure rock, nothing on the inside yet by the looks and behaviour just like Mr Normal, or any of us.

Let us move one level deeper with this and think that the similarity is not just at the behavioural level but also in internal physiology, i.e. they share similar brain anatomy. This means that when we give them tea, similar parts of both Mr Normal and Mr Inverted will light up in MRI brain scans. The same will be for the colour yellow and so forth. So hypothetically speaking, they share similar physical properties and even behaviour, yet there is a difference on account of qualia. While for Mr Normal the colour yellow or tea brings a multifarious inner experience, for Mr Inverted there is no such thing. No qualia or inner subjective feeling, no inner experience will occur. Yet show them yellow and not only will they reply that "it is yellow" but similar physical experiences too will be shared. The difference is qualia and its absence. This may sound like a terrible proposition to accept but if we look at the majority of unconscious processing that goes on; not so much then. Much of our intelligence is unconscious processing, a proposition later at play when we discuss the science of consciousness.[1]

Even after such consideration, the argument is hard to digest that both Mr Normal and Mr Inverted have similar physical

---

1 See the discussion on "Global Workspace Theory of Consciousness" in the next chapter.

structures and manifested behaviour, yet only one of them has qualia. But if you can digest the idea as being a coherent plausibility you may come to understand the deeper gist of it all. The situation, if possible, shows us the fact that qualia are not physical properties since they cannot be reduced to any physical attributes and no matter the physical similarity, both internal structure and behaviour, there can be differences in qualia. This leads us to our main conclusion that qualia are non-physical.

The argument can be spelled out in the modal format. If a philosophical zombie is conceivable, one that shares physicality like normal beings but lacks inner qualitative experience, then it is plausible for such a being to exist. And, finally, if such a philosophical zombie is possible, then that is a testament to the fact that inner qualitative experience is not reducible or dependent on physicality. Therefore, inner qualitative experience (or qualia as we call it) is independent of physicality.

THE COLOUR MARY THOUGHT EXPERIMENT

Originally conceived by Frank Jackson in his 1982 paper "Epiphenomenal Qualia", the argument put forward now has also come to be known as "The Knowledge Argument". The argument asks us to think of a neuroscientist named Mary. She has lived all her life in a locked black and white room and never got out of it. She has gained all her knowledge about colour vision from black and white books and black and white videos all available in the room. Despite it she specializes in the neuroscience of colour vision and knows everything there is to know about colour vision, both the biology and the physics of it as well. She knows about the wavelengths of light including each specific colour in them and how they react with our brain. She knows how light reflects off surfaces and stimulates the inner organs of our eyes like cones in our retina. Being a neuroscientist, she also knows how the electrical signal then travels down to the brain via the optic nerve where again it stimulates patterns of neural activity which finally causes colour perception experience. In summary, Mary knows every detail about the perception of colour vision, encompassing all its objective physical details.

The knowledge argument version of this thought experiment stops us here when Mary is still in the room and requires us to ask some questions. Is the knowledge that Mary has of colour vision in captivity complete? Is there something about colour vision that she does not yet know? Is there something about colours like yellow and red that she does not yet know in her subjective experience of them? Will seeing colour bring her some new knowledge about colour that she does not know?

Let us now imagine that one day she steps out of the room. What happens when she steps out? She experiences a whole new world of colours. The question that now stands in our face is, does she learn something new, particularly new about colour? Though she has already known everything about colour and colour vision, seeing colour for the first time brings her something new at the level of experience. Does she grasp something new about the nature of colour?

Philosophers of the mind often tend to answer in the affirmative. Yes, she has now learned something about the colour yellow or red (or any colour) that was not known to her even with all the knowledge of the neuroscience of colour vision. What is this new knowledge? It is the intrinsic experience of colour, an experience that lies beyond simple physical knowledge of the colour red, the inner subjective account of the colour red, as to what colour red looks like, what it is to see the colour red. This is something that was till now not available to her and suddenly becomes known to her. This is what "qualia" is all about.

To put the argument in perspective, we can move forward like this: If Mary knows every physical fact about colour vision and her knowledge is complete, then there can be nothing new about it that can be known to her. She moves out of the room and sees red and then feels something new both at the level of knowledge and facts.

She has now gained some new knowledge. This means physical knowledge is not complete and there is something to colour, beyond the physical knowledge of colour, the quale of colour.

There is another way to put this argument: Going by a physicalist attitude, all attributes are physical and Mary knows everything physical there is to know about colour vision. Once she steps out, she comes to know something new about colour vision. This means her earlier knowledge was not complete. Then not all attributes are physical. Physicalism is hence false or not the complete account of reality, at the least.

What this means is that if all physical facts about colour vision are known to Mary and yet experiencing colour teaches her something new, then there is more to mental states than just objective physical facts. This implies that there is something non-physical (both at the level of properties and knowledge) that constitutes a conscious experience. Hence, the physicalist proposition that mental states can be completely physically explicated is wrong. Therefore, there are some qualities (at least for colour vision) that transcend physical explanation. The argument extands beyond colour vision to represent the entirety of conscious experiences. We may know objectively everything there is to know about a person's brain and yet not know the intrinsic experience of being the person himself. This is the basic idea behind our next argument. Let us see.

NAGEL'S BAT ARGUMENT

Originally published in 1974 "What Is It Like to Be a Bat?" can be said to represent the first wave of anti-reductionist attitude in modern philosophy of mind. Thomas Nagel, the author of this article, asks us one simple thing, to imagine what is it like to be a bat. "I want to know what it is like for a *bat* to be a bat", he says (Nagel 1974: 439). He says the inner subjective experience of being a bat is an experience that is closed to us, even with our external objective knowledge of it. Objective phenomena are something that can be explained in an objective language that is purely physical, but the subjective conscious experience of the bat is something beyond objective explanation. He further says:

> It will not help to try to imagine that one has webbing on one's arms, which enables one to fly around at dusk and dawn catching insects in one's mouth; that one has very poor vision, and perceives the surrounding world by a system of reflected high-frequency sound signals; and that one spends the day hanging upside down by one's feet in the attic. Insofar as I can imagine this (which is not very far), it tells me what it would be like for me to behave as a bat behaves. But that is not the question. I want to know what it is like for a bat to be a bat. — Nagel 1974: 443

A reduction of the inner mental experience in terms of physical concepts is highly improbable, says Nagel. The inner subjective experience cannot be analysed in terms of functional or intentional states since even automata have them yet they lack consciousness. This does not mean that mental states do not have behavioural and functional characterization but just that such characterizations are incomplete in lacking subjective analysis (of the corresponding mental states). Leaving this crucial element out of the picture makes a reduction more improbable, for, in giving an objective physical explanation of the subjective character, we have to leave out the specific point of view and come to terms with the over-generalization of the phenomenological nature of subjective experience.

Maybe, we can have a psychedelic experience of being a bat or imagine ourselves to be a bat. Would that help us? Nagel says no, because our experience is determined by "our fundamental structure" which is different from that of a bat. Even imagination is not sure to help since it is bound by our experience and our experience by our physiological structure. Nothing in our present constitution of the physical structure is going to help that. We may ascribe types of experiences like hunger, but we cannot know the subjective nature of such experiences for the bat himself. But it would be wrong to negate the subjective experience of a bat just because we cannot know it by the limits of our knowledge. This comes as an implication of the problem of other minds (Avramides 2020).

The problem, says Nagel, is not just an epistemological one, but one that goes way deeper, i.e. the ontological incapability of forming concepts that are ontic a posteriori. Such knowledge is closed to us. There is no way to know it. An objective reduction has to be separate from subjectivity and be more generalized, all-encompassing, one that even a being from another planet can understand. However, in doing so, we are moving further away from human experience or bat experience in our case. We may map the physical functional processes behind a subjective experience, yet cannot know what it is like to be an exhibiting witness of those processes.

This argument too works on the line of others, namely, giving an account of the experience of reality that is not accountable physically, the subjective inner experience. This argument, how it was originally conceived was not an argument for idealism but the inefficaciousness of attempted objective reduction. It was to serve as a critique of the methods of physicalism more than physicalism itself.

THE CHINESE ROOM ARGUMENT

John Searle (1980) came up with this famous argument in the budding age of Artificial Intelligence. That era had seen functionalists like Hilary Putnam, and computing machines becoming more practical and available. It all in some sense started with Alan Turing and his enigma decryption machine. Much of the theoretical base of modern computing machines came from him. This particular argument has been presented in several ways by Searle himself. But if we look back this argument like the last one (Nagel's bat argument) was not directed straight against physicalism but against some other philosophical issue. The issue here was strong Artificial Intelligence, hence for current purposes, we shall be moving in an anti-linear fashion, deriving a conclusion from implication rather than implications from conclusions. The way this argument is being presented here and the implications derived thereof are anti-thesis of functionalism, computational theory of mind and behaviourism.

The thought experiment asks us to imagine a unilingual person. Let us take a native Hindi speaker who knows only Hindi. He sits in a room facing a wall with a hole in it. From the other side of the hole comes a chit of paper with something written on it, presumably in Chinese, a language he does not understand. Our unilingual friend has been provided with a guide manual with instructions in Hindi alongside unfamiliar Chinese symbols and a box of Chinese inscribed paper scripts. He has been told to respond to the incoming Chinese chits with the Chinese scripts he has in the box. The rules as to which chits are to be sent out as a response are given in the guide manual. Imagine there is a person on the other side, a Chinese speaker who is sending in these scripts. Over time, the person sending the incoming scripts will be convinced that the person on the side responding to the Chinese scripts is a native speaker of Chinese too. The reality however is that the Hindi speaker is still a unilinguist and does not know a word of Chinese. He is just following the rules and responding to the incoming queries.

Let us now ask why the Chinese speaker is so convinced that the person on the other side is also a Chinese speaker. Since the person has successfully and sufficiently replicated the functionality and behaviour of a Chinese person interacting. So let us come back to our argument now. Behaviour and functionality cannot be the marks of conscious qualia, which is the inner subjective experience, in this case, the inner subjective experience of understanding Chinese. Why? Because we have shown here that replicating behavioural patterns and functionality do not replicate conscious qualia. The Hindi speaker here has the same behaviour and functionality as the Chinese speaker, but he does not understand a word of Chinese and hence does not know "what it is like" to know Chinese. The speaker has passed the test for understanding Chinese but he does not know a word of it and there is no way one could learn Chinese just by shuffling Chinese symbols, i.e. replicating behaviour and functionality. The bottom line hence is that if the Hindi speaker cannot learn Chinese only by replicating the behaviour and functionality of a Chinese speaker, then neither can any other physical system do so solely on this basis. The behaviour and functionality alone are not sufficient for human cognition which produces the inner qualitative experiences in us.

Naturalism and Its Discontents

Naturalism is the philosophical standpoint that intends to make the claim that all that is nature and, presumably, there are no "supernatural entities" in the scheme of things. As Dubray (1911) puts it:

> Either the limits of nature are also the limits of existing reality, or at least the first cause of its existence is found necessary, has nothing to do with the working of natural agencies. All events, therefore, find their adequate explanation within nature itself. But, as the terms nature and natural are themselves used in more than one sense, the term naturalism is also far from having one fixed meaning.

It was and is a movement that gained its impetus via the rise and fair success of empirical sciences which in other words is called "the scientific turn" in philosophy. The difficulty of this ambitious naturalist project has been to provide a scientific reduction of the evident natural phenomena (Ganeri 2012: 19). But this has not stopped a multidisciplinary approach to the problem of consciousness. For the present context, I shall briefly try to delve into the theoretical account of three living giants with fairly different viewpoints on the same — John Searle, Daniel Dennett and David Chalmers.

THE CHINESE ROOM ARGUMENT

Searle was initially a philosopher of language and is celebrated for his work in semantic philosophy. The times he worked in were overwhelmed by the promises of computer technology and the rising field of Artificial Intelligence. Developing an artificial mind using a computer program seemed to be the next big triumph of technology. The aforementioned Chinese Room Thought Experiment dealt a crucial blow to these hopes after years of efforts by computational functionalists. What is unique about Searle's approach is that he tries to take the best of both dualism and materialism, and preserve it while discarding the rest (Searle 2016). How he does it is the question?

The first crucial point that Searle makes for the dualists is their assertion of the irreducibility of the mental, entirely in a physical vocabulary. The materialist for him is right in contending that the universe is entirely natural consisting of matter particles and fields of forces at the fundamental level, and so on and so forth. Preserving these two statements he takes out the false contentions of both the factions and they are that consciousness is something out of the physical world and irreducibility of consciousness is a delusion. What this means is that he is willing to accept consciousness as a subjective phenomenon evident as a part of nature but what he is not willing to accept is the other-worldliness of this phenomenon. The contention that consciousness exists in a separate realm as a distinct ontological entity does not figure in his scheme of things. Another major advance that we see here is prioritizing the first-person ontology (Searle 1992) that is to say auto-phenomenology as opposed to the third-person ontology or heterophenomenology, as Dennett would like to call it. The point is, how do you create an amalgamation of these two views and here comes the big advancement and that is asking the precise question: "What is the appropriate level to talk about the problem of consciousness?" Herein we come with his theory of "biological naturalism".

The theory postulates that consciousness should be seen as a biological problem. Consciousness is a biological phenomenon arising out of the biological brain processes. The so-called mental states are biological processes, not biological states. To take an example, you go to a movie with your friends and you have a terrible headache. You might have to keep your commitment to your friends whom you are meeting after a long time. All the way the internal subjective experience of even an Oscar movie is going to be not so good or enjoyable because you have a headache. The headache here is presumably generated by lower-level biological processes, generated by the so-called lower systems and perceived by the higher systems of the brain which work in tandem and coalesce together to generate a bad qualitative experience of the movie. To draw an analogy, consciousness is similar to photosynthesis, respiration and metabolism, a biological process. But Searle does not go for naive synthesis. He says that these accounts should not let one conclude that consciousness is nothing but a by-product of brain processes and introduces the distinction between causal and ontological reducibility.

Causal reducibility talks about the dependence of two seemingly distinct sets of phenomena. In our case, he thinks that consciousness as a phenomenon can be accounted for by taking into account the brain processes of electrochemical firing, synaptic connections, etc. This is to say that consciousness is caused by brain processes. Ontological reducibility talks about an identity reduction saying that consciousness is nothing but input–output processing, etc. happening in the brain. This is to say that phenomenal consciousness is not reducible to brain process. So, he believes that though phenomenal consciousness is causally reducible to brain processes, however, it is not ontologically reducible to it. The simple argument that he puts forward to posit the same is that consciousness is auto-phenomenological, whereas behaviour and input–output processes of electrochemical firing are heterophenomenological. But even after saying this, he does not believe consciousness to be other-worldly like a dualist would posit.

The biggest challenge is that holding such distinct reducibility is hard to sustain. What asserting the aforesaid stance means is that though consciousness is not ontologically reducible to brain processes, it can arise out of certain biological brain processes. This implies that we can understand our conscious states through brain processes as well as through our first-person subjective experience. The problem here is an epistemological one. Precisely that one knows oneself through his/her brain processes, but one cannot know his/her brain processes. For that, one needs to have imaging machines. Where does this line of knowing that starts from neuronal processes end up with our phenomenal consciousness. It is perhaps what the higher-level systems decides, demarcating the line before which one cannot assert and after which one can experience (the unconscious) phenomenal experience. The succinct fallacy of the stance is to say that I know sugar is sweet because sugar is a chemical composition of bonds that is interpreted by my brain as a sensation of sweetness and hence this sweetness is nothing but my phenomenal consciousness of sweetness. This is as absurd as the behaviourist saying that what explains my behaviour is my disposition to behave in a certain way. It is so because though one knows one's experience from first-person point of view and knows that it arises out of the brain processes from the third-person point of view, but one cannot know the brain processes from first-person point of view, one cannot know the neurons firing from a first-person point of view. Therefore, causal and ontological reducibility cannot be held distinct and it is for this reason that this theory has been called biological mysticism (Westphal 2016: 137).

Also, one should look into the facts like gut–brain (Carabotti 2015) and keeping the same in mind, one should ask why should just neuronal processing be involved in conscious experience. The evidence suggests neurodegenerative diseases like Alzheimer's are linked to the gut–brain interaction (EMM 2017). What then makes brain the special candidate? To this issue of brain being a special candidate for the seat of the consciousness, the Chinese Room Argument can somewhat be applied. The objection that can be applied is: if human consciousness were just brain processes governed by the electrochemical firing of neurons which at the base level are nothing but atoms arranged in a specific pattern, then what is the problem with replicating it on a silicon chip? To all these questions, Searle probably has no answer and his case lies to rest.

DENNETT AND MULTIPLE DRAFT'S MODEL

Daniel Dennett is one of the biggest minds working on the problem of consciousness. He was a student of Gilbert Ryle whom we discussed earlier. This school of thought is very critical of Cartesian dualism wherein the mind and bodies are considered as separate ontological entities. This is quite understandable for obvious reasons. The idea of Cartesian dualism culminated into serious pseudoscience with ideas like the one of a homunculus inside the mind viewing the movie of your phenomenal experience like a movie (Wikipedia 2022a). Ryle called this a categorical mistake.

Dennett carries the idea forward and denies the existence of the mind as a separate ontological entity in its own right. To put the same in the correct terminology, one can say that he denies the existence of any qualia, a separate subjective conscious qualitative experience in its own right. He takes the four "I"s of qualia, i.e. ineffability, intrinsic, interpersonal nature and immediacy (Dennett 1988), and calls it a vague way of defining an operating definition of qualia by those who believe consciousness to be non-physical. In taking the above "I"s, one rejects the possibility of the problem ever being solved with a whole lot of mysticism involved in it. If an experience is intrinsic, how can it be scientifically studied from a third-person perspective? We at the very outset take the problem to be unsolvable just by having such a definition. Like saying a Cadbury chocolate tastes sweet but may taste sweeter than any chocolate in the world or the worst chocolate in the world to some. And if such were the case, then they would not have been reportable for a verbal report like saying "Chocolate is sweet". Also, even if we grant that such an experience is intrinsic, it surely does not remain the same over time. One may completely ridicule a Cadbury chocolate after eating some other chocolate. This is a fair amount of evidence to suggest that the so-called intrinsicality is vague and relational that changes over time and denies the aforementioned operating definition of subjective experience which is qualia.

He also applies the scientific scrutiny of heterophenomenology which is a way to study the phenomenal subjective experience and other mental phenomena wherein the subject is asked to put his subjective experiences to verbal report which is compared with experimental neuroscientific data and the experimental environment to present a holistic picture of the common denominator that underlies all experiences and also help in gaining a meta approach as to what an ideal theory of human consciousness should be able to explain. These data sets are interpreted based on an intentional stance, which is a methodology to judge the data set based on the intentionality or the belief and desire of the person reporting it. This methodology intends to cover all the conscious phenomena for scientific scrutiny. What he uses this whole set-up for is to claim that the so-called qualia need not have any mystical element in the whole scheme of things. Believing else wise would be similar to putting faith in the idea of homunculi inside the brain.

Continuing his rejection of the Cartesian theatre, Dennett also posits not only there are no homunculi but there are not any clear-cut spatiotemporal divides as to when and where the sensory perceptions turn into conscious experiences after being acted upon. There is no precise voila moment after which unconscious processing turns consciousness. Also, when one goes on to find one will not find a seat of the soul or consciousness. Brain processes are locally-global and globally-local. Meaning that various components of the sensory stimulus are processed by different parts of the brain and are integrated by other parts of the brain, then relayed as a verbal or non-verbal behaviour by a whole different part of the brain and allied mechanisms like speech and gestures. To make things more complex, the brain is a parallel processing machine contrary to the linear one we have in the outside world.

It is here he posits the multiple drafts model which states that there are various representations of the stimulus which can be seen as a stream of content (drafts) running parallelly and quite async. There is no person inside to choose between these inner streams of content all of which supposedly fight for attention. Now the brain is based on its psychological and evolutionary conditioning of survival and reproduction requirements. Now the stream of the content, frame or draft that is chosen stays longer as compared to the other drafts and while others do not become a conscious experience, they are kept in an archival system of sorts for comparing with future drafts, etc. and make better predictions based on the weightage (Bajpai 2018; Dennett 1991). Dennett hence favours the Global Workspace Theory of Consciousness which will be discussed later.

As stated earlier, Dennett refrains from addressing the spatiotemporal question. The spatial question is the locus of consciousness and the temporal question is that when is it in the scheme of all the aforesaid processes does an event become the conscious frame of reality? When and how is that conscious frame of reality actualized? Though he says that one frame of reality is chosen over various others depending on the conditioning brought down by the evolutionary struggle but what is it in the brain that decides which frame of reality is to be chosen over others and why? Because not all of our decisions make sense, but yes, in a particular frame of consciousness, we do believe that that experience in terms of a draft was the right thing to have, and intentionality guided by will towards actions was the best course to take. This again means that while acting we do not have a dichotomy, but yes, the dichotomy is preserved.[2] Though Dennett himself tries to ridicule all such questions considering his disgust against Cartesian theatre, these questions are real philosophical questions that need to be answered and, sadly, the theory is instead of finding answers straightaway neglects them which is against the philosophical spirit.

CHALMERS AND NATURALISTIC DUALISM

David Chalmers can be credited single-handedly with revitalizing the philosophy of mind and the debate surrounding consciousness with his 1996 book *The Conscious Mind*. Being a mathematician and having worked in cognitive sciences, he poignantly points out the deficits which materialist theories suffer from despite their vast power of predictability. It is their reductionist attempt towards which he points his fundamental expostulations and posits them as under:

- The physical explanations do not fully explain the mental states. They do seem to provide insights about them though.
- Consciousness is fundamental.
- The aim of science and philosophy should be to work in tandem towards developing a unified theory of consciousness.

The biggest achievement and the project he set for the academic domain (both philosophical and scientific) is via demarcating a distinction between "the easy problems" and "the hard problems". For him, the easy problem can be worked out in the domain of

---

2 This can be contrasted with the traditional question of *sākṣī* that who is it who has the actual experience and knowledge. In the case of Dennett's theory, it can be understood as such, if an action is taken based on a draft which is chosen based on say evolutionary conditioning, then who chooses the draft and who experiences the draft because the contents of experience cannot choose themselves nor experience themselves.

neuroscience and cognitive sciences, etc. Some of such problems can be elucidated as under:

- How do we make sense of the external stimuli?
- How does the information from the external stimuli, our memories and our sense of "I" coalesce together to give an integrated sense of self?
- How do we record and report our mental states of existence?
- How do we choose to focus on certain things and not others?
- How do we modulate our behaviour?

As we have seen in Dennett's Multiple Drafts model, all the aforesaid questions are answered and they together form what we call an experience or our phenomenal consciousness. For him, our phenomenal consciousness is nothing more than these processes.[3] To this, Chalmers points out the other facet of the issue, "the hard problem". As I understand, the hard problem of consciousness is how materialist answers to the easy problems can coalesce together to give the phenomenal subjective experience of even the simplest of experiences like the taste of chocolate.[4] How does the brain bind the knower, the knowledge and the known into a unified phenomenal subjective experience of tasting the chocolate is the question. This is Chalmers' poignant criticism that despite the vast powers of prediction that the materialist sciences have, which seemingly are fairly quantitative and objective in nature, they do not seem to explain the qualitative experience.

The biggest contribution of Chalmers to the history of consciousness debate in the philosophy of mind is, in my opinion,

---

3 I have briefly summed up the main objections against this position. More issues will be highlighted when we discuss the scientific side of the same later in the book.

4 An understanding of localized brain processes and neuronal systems like the ones governing emotions and attention can provide an understanding of the final experience itself.

this very simple question. The reductionist may solve the easy problem and take it forward as the answer to the hard problem, but the question remains the same and the explanatory gap remains the same. How does all the quantitative data of materialist science converge to give us the "What it is like consciousness".[5] He is very clear about this and says in one of his lectures on YouTube that if you dismiss consciousness as nothing but an evolutionary illusion, then you are ignoring the data, wherein there is nothing that explains the phenomenal subjective experience.

Keeping in mind the above expostulations, he seeks to posit a non-reductive theory of consciousness which again is an advance over the Cartesian dualism since it does not seek to bifurcate mind and matter into two ontological entities, rather, it asks us to take the "phenomenal consciousness" as a new fundamental property of reality. It is fundamental in the sense that it is not physical and cannot be reduced as such. Consciousness for him exists alongside particles, fields of forces and as such cannot be reduced to the latter. The challenge here is different from the materialist challenge that is not one of reducing consciousness to matter but finding how consciousness arises and how it is correlated with the material world. A theory where we can abundantly question and sufficiently answer as to how the brain is correlated with conscious experience and vice versa. What kind of systems can exhibit consciousness and why do they exhibit consciousness and where is that line after which a system can sufficiently "modulate" or "reflect" consciousness? To explain this, he gives us his theory of "Naturalistic Dualism" (Chalmers 2017). Here are the three principles he posits:

- The "Principle of Structural Coherence" state that the structure of consciousness and the structure of awareness are corresponding entities. Awareness and consciousness are two distinct phenomena. Awareness is information available to the cognitive apparatus for utilization in manifesting behaviour and its modulation. It is governed by the same processes

[5] This is what Alok Bajpai (2016) calls as the "translational problem".

that aid in the cognitive organization of experience. Hence, conscious experience or consciousness always corresponds with the direct availability of information available for report, behavioural manifestation and vice versa.

- The "Principle of Organizational Invariance" states that two similar structural systems in terms of their functional execution hierarchy will share the identity of qualitative experience. What matters is not the physicality of such systems albeit the abstract causal hierarchy of functions among the physical parts of the system. Hence, it is the functional organization and its replication thereof that stands as a challenge to artificial general intelligence.
- The "Double Aspect Theory of Information" states that information is dual-faceted and exhibits both physical and phenomenal features. Information can be physically embedded in an abstract space of physical states and could thereby give rise to phenomenal states as discussed in the above principle. Therefore, this information is embedded in both physical and phenomenal states.

Therefore, Chalmers considers a form of Pan-Proto-Psychism (Westphal 2016: 99) wherein all information exhibits phenomenal facets so that every occasion of information processing in a certain hierarchical functional organization accompanies a phenomenal experience. Now, since information processing is a pan-phenomenon, so should be and is consciousness perhaps. This position is similar to what Giuho Tononi and Christof Koch posit in their integrated information theory which will be discussed in the next chapter. One can agree with Chalmers on most points but differ on others. His proposition for a panpsychist position is commendable but how can two opposing qualities share their loci in a single substratum? The points of difference need a better and elaborate clarification, and some background of the prevalent scientific theories. These are discussed at the end of the book.

Summary

We had a look at two kinds of mind-body theories: monism and dualism, and discussed their flaws. Descartes used the explanatory gap argument to position against substance dualism. Descartes viewed that mind, thinking and the self are all the same thing, and it is a non-physical conscious entity. However, it is wrong as there are "parts" of the self that are not conscious; some thinking goes on without the self; the role of "the self" in consciousness is unclear. Minds understand and produce language. How these faculties relate to the physical system is unknown. Explanatory gap arguments beg the question that how minds understand and produce language now; how these faculties relate to the physical system is unknown. Machines cannot produce and comprehend language, and the explanatory gap should mean a "substantial gap". We now know that machines today can produce language. It is comprehension by a machine which is still elusive.

A property dualists believe that mental properties have no causal effect on physical properties, which is absurd because it implies that your desire to drink a glass of water has nothing to do with your action. It faces the problem of philosophical zombies. Nagel contended that the physiological characteristics of a bat differ from its mental properties (qualia). We might know everything there is to know about bats physiologically. However, we shall still have no idea what it is like to be a bat, as the qualia of being bat a alien to us. The laws of conservation state that the net mass or energy in a closed system remains constant over time. The human body is a closed physical system, and because the mind is not within the body, it cannot affect the body. If the energy within the body is not used, either mass and energy are not conserved, or the system is not closed. Even if it were somehow inside the body and non-physical, it would have to use physical energy to change the physical body, also known as the causal closure of the physical. From the time we are conceived in our mothers' womb, there is nothing non-physical. Why should one believe that something non-physical is added among on the way? If so, when?

Physicalist theories deny a non-physical substance and solve the problem of interaction. How is the mind physical? Behaviourism believes that mental states can be known or said in terms of verbal and observable behaviour. Since mental states cannot be observed, they should be inferred from the behaviour. Pavlov, Skinner and Watson developed theories of stimulus-response and in experiments showed that how we behave, think and respond to things can be changed with the proper conditioning. Training one to behave appropriately should be the aim of sciences. However, this provides no insight into the inner world of experience. One does not have to rely on observing one's behaviours to know one's emotions like happiness.

The mind–brain identity theory says that the mental state is the brain state. Issues here are multiple realizability. Different types of physical structures can realize specific types of mental states or processes. The identity that pain is *C*-fibre excitation is contingent, not necessary. It could have been otherwise in some possible world, say *x*-fibre but identities are always necessary. An unmarried man will always be a bachelor. Pain will always be pain. However, will pain always be *C*-fibre excitation? Not necessarily. Therefore, the identity must be false and the mind is not the brain. How do qualia aries from brain states is the hard problem of consciousness. Functionalism says that mental states are computational or functional. Pain is not a brain state, but of a functional state. Such states are not made of matter, but of functionality. One can Concoct 50 using any mathematical operation in an infinite number of ways, i.e. it can be multiply realized. What matters is the software, not the hardware that governs experience. We all have the same hardware, but the information processing manual and software distinguish us. A presentation can be made using a variety of software. The program, not the laptop device, is responsible for how this is accomplished or realized. The Chinese Room Argument demonstrates that the mind is more than merely a syntactic processing of a specific algorithm. They have semantics as well, and syntax alone cannot produce qualia.

Furthermore, the analogy between hardware and software is incorrect. Feedback loops exist. Hardware can modify the software. Exercising, smiling often and eating a healthy diet have all been shown in studies to improve mental health. Yoga and CBT, for example, have been shown to alter mental processes and even brain circuitry significantly. The mind and body interact, and no physicalist theory can account for even the most fundamental of experiences, such as the taste of sugar.

Finally, we briefly discussed a brief accounts of naturalism advanced by philosophers Chalmers, Dennett and Searle. As a deflationist materialist, Dennett explains away mental phenomena and thus contradicts what is ordinarily available to conscious beings such as humans. Material reductionism is thus an ontologically flawed theory because it violates the fundamental concept of the mind's independence by reducing it to the body. Consciousness is fundamentally subjective and first-person, and it must be treated as phenomenal. Because there is no explanation for consciousness, the scientific third-person solution is an easy way out. Something else replaces consciousness. Chalmers believes that consciousness, in its subjective form, cannot be reduced to anything else, raising the issue of qualia. The hard problem of consciousness is complex because we believe that we cannot solve it using scientific methods. How does a personal or phenomenal experience emerge? Even if we can objectively and scientifically explain psychological states, we do not understand how phenomenal experiences arise. The dual-aspect theory of consciousness solves the "hard problem of consciousness" by recognizing two sides of reality: its physical — functional organization and its experiential aspect. This solves the problem on an ontological level because the subjective first-person experience is eliminated. Intentionality is a normative feature of consciousness and the fact that it gives rise to meanings cannot be explained in a pure naturalist framework.

Meanings and intentionality must have a place in the theory of mind and consciousness. To account for intentionality, we must go beyond naturalism in its conventional sense, reductive naturalism. Searle's non-reductive naturalism contradicts the notion of the irreducibility of consciousness, which is ontologically required if we move away from reductionism. If *S* can exist independently and assert autonomy or independence from *B*, it is not reducible to a brain state *B*. How does consciousness gain subjectivity when caused by the brain, a material entity in and of itself? This question remains unanswered in Searle's biological naturalism. There is a logical possibility of a universe with physical reality but no qualitative experience. Such a scenario may give rise to the notion that every piece of materiality is endowed with experientiality so that no part of the universe is devoid of mental stuff.

With this, we can now conclude our discussion on the issue from the perspective of Western philosophy. In the chapter that follows we shall try to have a look at the scientific theories of consciousness and their shortcomings.

3

The Science of Consciousness

For centuries, the question of consciousness has been at the forefront of philosophical discussions. There have been numerous attempts to prove the ontological existence of consciousness. The questions about consciousness in its earlier days were not much guided by materialist perspectives. This is not to say that there were no explanations being sought regarding the question of consciousness from a materialist perspective. The Cārvākas of India and the pre-Socratic philosophers of Greece who tried to explain the external world and the phenomenal world from the perspective of fundamental elements like water, earth and fire stand testimony to this. The point of discussion in this chapter will be the development of consciousness studies that began in the later part of the seventeenth century. It was around this time in Europe that the search for the self or soul revitalized from a materialist perspective with the questioning of traditional orthodoxies and liberalizations in all the fields of study. It involved changes in the study of human body particularly the freedom for body dissection to learn more about how human physiology could influence the body's functions, internal states of mind and ultimately behaviour. The different aspects of human mental expression, including emotions, sense of self, perception, cognition and so on, were investigated and a search for the causes (biological mechanisms) behind them began. It would be prudent to point out that they were not very advanced by then.

Physiologists unsurprisingly found no homunculi in the human body. Nothing palpable within the human body could be identified as the source of this sense of the self. The search for soul was the search for something concrete that could account for all of an individual's psychological and mental mechanisms of experience. Physiologists discovered reference of a pineal gland, which is responsible for many mental activities of the human body in the works of a Greek physician, Galen (*c.*130-*c.*210 CE) (Lokhorst 2021). Many refinements were made over the decades, and many associated organs were discussed, but Descartes, the philosopher-mathematician, presented a comprehensive account of the pineal gland's likely workings and related function in human expression of thought. He discussed how the pineal gland plays a significant role in mental mechanisms. Descartes' account also included the pineal gland, which was involved in sensation, imagination, memory and the causation of bodily movements (ibid.).

The thesis of Descartes drew a plethora of critiques particularly following the publication of his two main books, *The Passions of the Soul* (1649) and *The Treatise on Man* (1810), which explored the relationship between the body and soul through the role of the pineal gland. There was a surge of approval and rejection shortly after these works were exposed in the public domain. Those who agreed with him admired his theory, while others despised him for being so bold. Today, we know that the pineal gland is an endocrine gland that secretes hormones and that it cannot be held responsible for all of the aspects of human expression that Descartes attributed to it. However, the question that might be asked here is whether or not his approach was correct. Was his postulated mechanism relevant, and does it have any practical ramifications for the line of philosophers and associated students of such brain and consciousness science? The answer is unmistakably positive. One can wonder why this is the case.

However, he cannot be held solely responsible for the proposed mechanism's inadequacies. The advanced imaging methods of our time such as computerized axial tomography (CAT) and magnetic resonance imaging (MRI) were not accessible to academia. The technology of the time, i.e. 300 to 400 years ago, was insufficient to fathom the inner workings of such a magnificent masterpiece fully. Moving on to the second point, did his pseudo-science have any practical implications, and if so, what were they? The concept of localization was the most significant achievement. Consciousness and mental expression were thought to be limited to a single part of the body, the brain. This may appear infantile, but it was a great accomplishment. It cleared the way for much of what we now know as the brain and allied neuro-cognitive sciences. In short, it is fair to conclude that Descartes was a forerunner in his own time and we owe him an outstanding debt when it comes to our current knowledge of the dispute. He was the one who gave the study of the brain a scientific bent.

In the words of Alok Bajpai, with physics peeping into biology, giving us imaging tools, and the knowledge of synapses, neurons and various other parts of the brain working as functionaries in human expression, we have come up with various models to understand how this lump of approximately 2-3 kg gives us something entirely different from the material substance, i.e. the brain. We have come up with various models to understand it. After all, the whole issue of consciousness, or the mind-body problem, is now a profoundly philosophical one, i.e. how something material, such as synapses and neurons (of which there are billions), gives rise to something completely different, consciousness[1] (Bajpai 2018). As discussed earlier in the last chapter, Chalmers has touted this as "the hard problem of consciousness".

We still have not worked out the exact process underpinning consciousness. The problem has been in the human discourse for a long time, especially when we consider that we still lack a well established and precise science of consciousness.[2] This is not

1 I do not like to say this but to me this seems like begging the question. Especially since this would mean that we have taken for granted that consciousness somehow emerges from the brain.

2 To be precise, we do not have an equation for consciousness which we can run in a machine and get to see the internal movie of every person, the qualia movie I would like to call it.

to claim that we do not know about the brain or consciousness. We know that brain and conscious processes are related. These processes are controlled by the biological substratum known as the brain or somehow mediated by the brain. In this chapter, we shall discuss problems like: Can consciousness be reduced entirely to neuroscientific terminology? What distinguishes a conscious mental state? Is consciousness merely the result of information processing? Is it paying attention to certain things consciousness? What is the extent to which consciousness pervades reality's very fabric? Moreover, we shall seek to understand the dominant models to understand how phenomenal consciousness comes from the objective brain processes — trying to find solutions or insights to these fundamental concerns (Levine 1983; Tye 1997).

We shall investigate some significant models proposed by various philosopher-neuroscientists and other academics to address the above problems. These models have different names, but they all have one thing in common: they all begin with the supposed objective processes of the brain to explain phenomenal consciousness. Also, we shall try to look at some approaches that try to examine the problem by diving deeper into the quantum dilemma and hinting at the deep-rooted origins of consciousness in an attempt to understand the scientific angle of the problem. Many theories involving the perspective of quantum mechanics on the issue tend to bring quantum mechanics into the problem of consciousness by exploiting the issue that at the quantum level, reality seems to be observer dependent. This for many physicists, specifically Roger Penrose, seems to imply that consciousness is somehow fundamental to reality. His theory is not the first one to claim so, but is the most prominent one in our times. So, the philosophical discourse on transcendental consciousness might not be a jargon even in scientific understanding.

We shall first look at some reductionist models that reduce consciousness to neurobiological processes. This aims to prove that consciousness is nothing more than a series of neuronal activities.

This approach can be called the disembodied mind approach. Second, we shall discuss the embodied mind, a novel scientific approach that aims to provide a more comprehensive view of the challenges and account for the fact that humans, let alone human brains, do not function in isolation. Humans have bodies that are not biologically separate from their brains, and they exist in an environment. Finally, we shall glance at some pretty radical approaches to address the problem of consciousness, not from a neuroscientific perspective, but rather from the fundamental dilemma of modern physics, viz. the quantum problem (collapse of the wave function). We shall then wrap up the chapter by emphasizing the need for a unified theory of consciousness that addresses the neurological component of the problem and tries to go into a comprehensive multidisciplinary approach.

The Neural Correlate of Consciousness Theory

At first glance, the term appears to be self-explanatory, but is this the case? There is always more to it than meeting the eye. After all, the debates and researches surrounding consciousness studies have revolved around this enigmatic yet straightforward approach. One thing is sure: this technique to investigate consciousness, like all sciences, has its roots in the traditional research methodology of reducing a phenomenon to its underlying causes to uncover a chain of correlations. A good example is the link between smoking and cancer. Any physiologist can deduce a correlation by correlating the chemical make-up of tobacco, paper, filter and generated smoke with the biochemistry of the lungs. The benzo compounds, arsenic and other chemicals found in cigarette smoke have been linked to gene mutations, either by direct damage or by adhering to it and delaying damage repair.

So, it is not the act of smoking that kills. It is the chemical interaction of the toxins and body tissues. The point is that if a non-smoker were habitually introduced to these chemicals not by the ways of smoking but elsewise, the damage would be more or less the same. Smoking is correlated with tissue damage but does not have an identity. Similarly, it would be preposterous just because he goes to a railway station that the train arrives. The train arrives because it is scheduled to arrive. The philosophical term for such a fallacy of reasoning is *cum hoc ergo propter hoc*.

Science works on the principle of correlation. We may not know the cause of a particular event but we may have a fair inkling about it. Based on that, we deduce the causes and perform experiments. If the experiments work on the model, we accept the answer that a given event may be the cause of an observed effect. As in the example above, we see smokers getting affected by cancer. However, if one were to be exposed by the same chemicals as in cigarette smoke, elsewise, one would still be affected by cancer. Though cigarette might not be the cause of cancer but we correlate the effect that is cancer with smoking. After repeated sights of smokers getting affected by smoking, we conclude that smoking is the cause of cancer. There are many smokers who do not get cancer and even if it is the smoke which causes cancer. We do not know if it triggered the genes which causes cancer or some other mechanism generated by the interaction of chemicals in the smoke and the bodily tissues which cause cancer in which case that interaction or the triggering of genes will be the cause. Hence, the way science proceeds is by making safe correlations as is the case in the neural correlate theory which we are going to discuss.

A materialist approach to consciousness attempts to reduce consciousness to a sequence of events or causes within itself. This attempt is purely reductionist. This means that the neural correlate of consciousness (NCC) approach hypothesizes that, for one, consciousness has its locus in the brain. Second, specific neuronal processes or brain structures are necessary conditions for consciousness. Lastly, that all conscious experiences on close examination shall share the involvement of either these processes or will share a common activated brain region or regions.

Let us start by attempting to comprehend what the term NCC mean. In a limited sense, it must be the events in our brain following the absence of which a conscious experience cannot arise. They are the bare minimum of neuronal activity and associated brain systems required to generate conscious perception (Chalmers 2000: 17-41). However, as more evidence and studies accumulate, we may reach a point where there is not a single NCC, but rather a plethora of NCC. For example, Metzinger (2000) has compiled several NCCs. One exciting thing that one will note here is that there is no consensus if NCC is an oscillation or feedback loop running via different parts of the brain (thalamo-cortical loop) or is it the connectome (neuronal assembly) or a neuronal process or neurotransmitters. All of these refer to different processes and parts of the brain. Therefore, there is no consensus on what actually constitutes NCC.

We begin to get a clearer idea of how the entire system, which is based on several underlying correlations, operates. Any science, including the science of consciousness, operates similarly. The problem is that we are dealing with the brain, specifically the human brain, which is probably nature's most intriguing creation, resulting from millions of years of evolution, which has layered structures and mechanisms. There are various mechanisms at work here and it is up to science to figure out which processes or mechanisms are linked to which of its counterparts to construct a comprehensive story for ourselves which we perceive as phenomenal consciousness. Following this line of investigation should make comprehending consciousness much easier. The question then becomes, why is not this the case? Without considering the inherent nature of qualia, the solution may be that one focuses solely on the correlations. No one has pinpointed the exact cause of the anomalies in such an explanation. The anomalies that we are talking here are that though there are various processes and neuronal structures which help us understand the nature of consciousness, there is no pinpointed minimal set of neuronal mechanisms or processes which seems to be necessarily responsible for consciousness. If we take out one of these processes, our phenomenal consciousness may not be as it is. One can take the example of aphasias wherein a problem in a part of the brain may cause a deficit like Wernicke's aphasia, a deficit in speech comprehension. Perhaps consciousness, as a non-physical entity, is outside the scope of biological studies. Scientists still believe that within a century or more, refined interpretations will provide us with a better picture.

Francis Crick and Christof Koch (1990) were among the pioneers of this idea discussing it in scientific domains. Their approach to the investigation was strictly materialistic, arguing that consciousness has to be explained at the neuronal level. They assumed that all aspects of consciousness have a minimum set of neuronal mechanisms to which the latter can be reduced (ibid.: 264). Their underlying theory was that consciousness could be reduced and eventually explained by a single entity in the brain — something that distinguished a conscious brain from an unconscious one. They meant that learning more about this would help them grasp conscious and unconscious phenomena. Initially, they discovered that neural activity appeared to be directly linked to working memory's short-term memory and serial attention. They then proceeded to base their research on the aforesaid fundamental assumptions.

Following this line of reasoning, both scientists attempted to construct a theoretical framework based on these assumptions to provide a viable solution for the problem of consciousness. With this in mind, we can consider the following three questions: What type of neural activity is associated with consciousness? Is there a specific group of neurons that has a role in the emergence of consciousness? Finally, what makes these neural connections and the firing between them unique?

They took the first step by locating consciousness in the brain. They then ruled out any brain structures that had no part in the emergence of what we now refer to as phenomenal consciousness.

The theory was that focusing research on them would be pointless because areas like the cerebellum, hindbrain and midbrain lack those unique neurons, and the resulting neural activity which produces consciousness. They then divided the mammalian neocortex and accompanying brain structures into highly plausible places for neuronal activity, including the thalamus, basal ganglia and claustra. They then turned their attention to sensory modalities, particularly vision. The empirical challenge developed at this point: consciousness seemed to be united somehow. But how exactly?

Distinct areas of the brain process different modalities of vision such as depth, colour and shape. V1, V2, V4 and the primary visual cortex deal with colour information. The shape is handled by areas such as the lateral occipital cortex. The middle temporal visual region, called V5, deals with depth and motion. According to common sense, all of this data should be stitched together to create a coherent image. However, where does this happen, and how does it happen that these distinct pieces of data are appropriately overlaid? How do we consider conscious vision to be one despite these different sensory inputs? This is what is known as the binding problem. The next important question was how the brain binds various series of information and sensory input presented by various neural networks that deal individually with distinct components of unified vision that we have of the perceived object (the binding problem). The conclusion was that there was no such binding together of neurons anywhere in the brain. Furthermore, this was only the beginning of a project to which Crick and Koch (1990) would devote their lives.

They proposed early on in their research that some neural activity corresponds with consciousness while others do not, thus distinguishing between neural activity that leads to consciousness and that which does not. In his book, *The Astonishing Hypothesis*, Crick contends that molecular interactions between nerve cells and their related chemicals may explain our behaviour (1995: 3-12, 265-68). Crick and Koch concluded in their 1990 paper "Toward a

Neurobiological Account of Consciousness" that at any one time, a coalition of neuronal activity in many cortical areas meets up to bring forward a global activity, which then translates to visual experience and consciousness. Maintaining this level of global activity requires attention and working memory. Subsequent studies revealed that the neuronal processing in these locations appeared to be in perfect sync at around 40 Hz. They then proposed that by firing at 40 Hz, neural activity binds these diverse components of a coherent visual picture. The distinction between cells that account for consciousness and those that do not, according to them, is the firing of consciousness-composing cells between 35 Hz and 70 Hz; hence the "40 Hz" abbreviation. Consciousness arises when the firing of cells is synchronized or when their membrane voltage changes in synchrony. In the same 1990 publication, they also stated that these synchronized oscillations bring nothing new to the platter of conscious awareness but instead put together previously collected data to produce a coherent whole.

By 2003, both Crick and Koch had come to terms with the possibility that their hypothesis was incorrect. "We no longer consider that synchronized firing, such as the so-called 40 Hz oscillations, is a sufficient condition for the NCC", they wrote in their paper "A Framework for Consciousness" (2003). This acceptance, combined with the facts presented by cognitive science breakthroughs, led them to revise their theory. The idea in their new explanation was that synchrony of neural oscillations could undoubtedly contribute to the establishment of phenomenal consciousness, but only when numerous participating coalitions of neurons put forth the effort to dominate over others. To put it another way, the new idea was to think of cells or the cortical neural networks that run on them as forming temporary functional coalitions. When these coalitions come into being, they create the foundations of consciousness (Westphal 2016: 121). As per this view, synchronicity in these coalitions can only increase their chances in the quest to understand consciousness. This is a development in its regard since synchronicity just on its own can be of no use. This point can be understood by using a simple thought experiment. Imagine a set of orchestral instruments all playing at one time, beat to beat, all synchronized by a conductor. This in no case can help to "integrate" the symphony of music, not even by the slightest measure, if the members were playing their part in the orchestra, say someone playing the cello or someone playing the violin is separated by space, i.e. they are located in different places spatially. There is no binding if the violins are in Australia and the cellos are in India. There is a condition to having a single piece of music playing in a symphony, and that condition is the spatial integration of various pieces of music, in our instance, "information". As a result, synchrony of neural oscillation at 40 Hz, or any frequency, cannot give a satisfactory solution to the "binding problem". However, this begs the question if binding is possible. Yes, if the little cluster of neurons organizes themselves into a specific coalition. Within a coalition, different neurons and their neural activity help each other and stably maintain a form of global processing by inflating the activity of fellow contenders. This finally helps the coalition, which has a more intense and sustained activity, to prevail over others and embody the contents of consciousness (Crick and Koch 1998: 98).

Crick and Koch define the penumbra as another feature of these brain architectures. This property is closely linked to the concepts of snapshots and thresholds. The penumbra refers to neuronal processes such as synaptic effects and neuronal firing patterns that are not directly related to neural correlates of consciousness but are influenced by them. As a result, the penumbra incorporates previous connections and associations of NCC and predicted implications of these neural correlates. They may include movement planning, memories and other activities triggered by NCC.

An instance may be the memory of riding a Royal Enfield, which is stored in a specific NCC and can trigger a memory of the first time one rode a Royal Enfield. The penumbra can ascend to the state of consciousness as this NCC shifts. The network of neurons and the activity of their neurons are essentially dynamic and in flux. As a result, our brain continuously and relentlessly generates snapshots in constant succession rapidly and consistently, providing the perceiver with the illusion of a continuous flow of consciousness. This account suggests an explanation for qualia (Crick and Koch 2003).

Another issue that arises when the 40 Hz concept is abandoned is how these interim coalitions of neurons and their neural activity synchronize themselves and their activity. This was the main point of the study in "What Is the Function of the Claustrum?" (Crick and Koch 2005). This study aimed to look at the claustrum's physiology, architecture and function, a thin neuronal layer that lies under the neocortex. The claustrum's remarkable connectivity lends support to this theory. In the light of such extraordinary physiology, both Crick and Koch advocate for experimentation and research into the role of the claustrum in the generation of consciousness. They quote here in an attempt to make a passing analogy.

> It is like the analogy of a conductor coordinating a group of players in the orchestra, the various cortical regions. The players can still play without the conductor, but they fall increasingly out of synchrony. The result is a cacophony of sounds. — 2005: 1276

The philosophical question here is whether it advances our understanding of consciousness and the mind-body problem; this is the question we must strictly address before proceeding with the claustrum as an NCC. Crick and Koch are now confronted with the same problem that all interactionist dualists have been confronted with all along. When they propose a specific physical structure as the locus of interaction, such as V1 and V2 in the case of conscious visual awareness or the pineal gland in the case of Descartes or the claustrum, in this case, they fail to answer the fundamental question: why only this part, why only the claustrum, why only pineal gland, or why only this particular set of neurons as the site of the interaction above? Investigations in the future will undoubtedly show that the proposal of Crick and Koch is similar to the positions taken by central–state materialists and interaction dualists, albeit with a dash of emergentism thrown in for good measure (Bajpai 2018: 21).

The question they do not address in their initial enthusiasm is how the claustrum or any biological substrate puts forward its activity when it comes to the concept of mind, which is somehow non-physical, or how the physical claustrum activates the non-physical mind, or how the claustrum affects consciousness. If we do not answer these questions, we are back to Descartes, because such expositions are no better than his. Perhaps Descartes' solution is preferable to the ones proposed here. At first glance, the claustrum appears to be a better bet than the pineal gland, but questions remain, such as how these neuronal processes, whether synchronized, at 40 Hz or 180 Hz, produce consciousness. In their excitement over the newly-discovered organ, Crick and Koch, in my opinion, lost sight of the true magnitude of the challenge that lay ahead of them. They neglected to address the logical aspect of the problem, which is more important and should be addressed here before the scientific and physiological aspects. Perhaps they initially assumed that in every event of conscious experience, there are neuronal coalitions and neuronal processes with their firing sequences, as orchestrated by the claustrum. That is how science works, after all. Identifying antecedent causes and connecting them to likely future events. This observation is undeniably correct. However, it does not address the mind-body problem or the associated issue of the generation of subjective consciousness from the objective processes of the brain.

As science and its tools advance, we realize that perhaps Crick and Koch were incorrect in their initial hypothesis that a single set of mechanisms and activity could account for all manifestations of consciousness in isolation. The search should be for NCCs rather than for NCC. According to some neurophenomenologists, the classic Crick and Koch approach is unidirectional. It derives consciousness solely from neurons, neuronal activity, brain processing and embedded architectures, ignoring that consciousness shares social aspects with the environment and the stimuli supplied by it.[3] They believe that neural events and conscious states are bidirectional and have a reciprocal relationship. As a result, this approach oversimplifies a rather complex problem. Any comprehensive account of conscious experience must include such minute but context-forming aspects of consciousness.

Furthermore, any scientific account of the neural correlates of consciousness should be able to explain the qualia problem by bridging the explanatory gap. For example, the rich colours of a magnificent painting depict an array of vast conscious phenomenological dimensions to just the objective dimension of the painting, say colour, shape, strokes and the embedded context of the painting, all of which form subjective dimensions of the wholesome experience of consciousness. Saying that the colour black in the painting is just an objective phenomenon dealt within the brain by neuronal oscillations in the V4 area of the brain does not provide any insight into the raw feelings felt when observing the colour black in its entirety. Perhaps the experience of seeing the colour black is associated with the underlying mechanism, but that does not imply that they are reduced to or identical to the oscillations discussed earlier. Any explanation of subjectivity that reduces it to just brain processes ignores the very thing it was meant to explain: conscious experience. There is a targeted gap between the account proposed, and the phenomenon sought to be explained. Any attempt to identify the NCC that will provide us with a complete account of consciousness is bound to fail because neuronal oscillations are a different phenomenon than a conscious mental event; they may allow for the emergence of a conscious mental state, but they are not the entire story. As a result, we need

---

3 As elaborated to me by Alok Bajpai in our discussion regarding feedback loops. Philosophically speaking, this is the approach followed in the theory of embodied cognition.

to bridge the explanatory gap to provide a complete account of consciousness (Bajpai 2021: 34).

Also, it does not explain the "hard problem of consciousness". Subjective and non-physical aspects of consciousness, according to Chalmers, are beyond the dimensions of physics simply because the domain of physics is the physical world and the subjective experience of consciousness is non-physical. Some supporters of Chalmers' position argue that no account of the neural correlate of consciousness can fully explain the phenomenon of consciousness, that is, even if we find the NCC for some subjective experience, we may never know why a particular subjective experience feels the way it does. We may understand the mechanism underlying colour perception, but we may never understand why a colour feels the way it does to us, and to make matters more complicated, these feelings are private to the individual. Even the most elaborate and refined theories of the NCC can never explain the phenomenological aspect of the experience, which we value above all else. After all, this is what we wanted to account for before we started looking for underlying mechanisms. We wanted to describe the experience rather than the mechanism. Mechanisms are merely a journey that we may be destined to take, but the explanation of the wholesome phenomenological experience was always the goal we sought. There is also a flip side to this; perhaps the NCC is simply the wrong approach that we have taken because if the problem of subjective experience, the raw feelings, is non-physical, then seeking an objective neuronal basis for such subjective phenomena will fail. However, does this mean that the entire exercise we undertook was in vain? No, not at all. We are still piecing together the various mechanisms, architectures, neuronal activities and underlying processes that create a complete picture of phenomenal consciousness, in this case the consciousness of a picture. Perhaps, in the future, when we have better explanations and better accounts of these individual components of the picture, we shall be able to reverse engineer and reconstruct the entire picture. Finding these unique mechanisms has also addressed many issues and challenges in the biological and medical fields, which are entirely different sciences and may have been very much needed before we could solve the mystery of consciousness. However, that is perhaps a topic for another discussion.

The Global Workspace Theory

Before delving into the specifics of Bernard Baars' model, it is best to start with the fundamentals. What exactly is a global workspace? It is a common shared architecture platform, more akin to a "shared blackboard" with many users, used for signal integration and propagation to a large number of loosely coupled agents. In today's parlance, it can be understood as being based on the model of crowd computing (also known as swarm computing), in which people can share, post and even work to alter the limitations of the previous hypotheses posted therein, much like a common chatroom. One example can be Google Workspace wherein coworkers can collaborate on a single project to make amendments therein. A previous model, drawing or written work can be edited by different agents who participate in the project. When a Carnegie–Mellon team was developing a new Hearsay system, tasked with identifying nearly 1,000 spoken words with different variations in the acoustical environment, it showed great promise in the early days of this global workspace architecture particularly in the 1970s. In addition to this constraint, the problem was identifying words whose sounds differed due to different vocal tracts, resulting in a range of acoustical range profiles (Barrs and Alonzi 2018: 122-25). Was this architecture successful under these conditions? Yes, with a 90 per cent efficiency rate. This attempt showed two essential points: the brain is a parallelly distributed architecture with multiple inputs competing to gain prominence. Also, while the brain has vast unconscious processing capacity, it indeed exhibits a limited conscious field.[4]

[4] B.J. Baars (1993: 56) calls it central limited capacity.

The benefit of such a shared common workspace is that new ideas and iterations are constantly shared in real-time and made available to all for further feedback. As a result, the system can adapt, evolve and even change the shared architecture in real-time, giving the workspace more vibrancy and flexibility in terms of usage and future development. A beta version of open-source software can be used as an example of such a workspace (say Android). The software architecture is available to all Android platform users once placed in the public domain (Android play store). The source code is open to suggestions, feedback and even real-time changes from other coders. Furthermore, the changes made and approved therein are edited and adjusted in real-time, reducing the labour involved in the software's further development. Apple's Siri, the voice recognition system developed by Apple that still uses Hearsay's success model, is one success story of this architecture. It employs web-based crowdsourcing to collect words from various languages and create and cater to the user's needs. Interestingly, it still employs the fifty-year-old Hearsay model (based on this global workspace architecture), and guess what, it is one of the best, if not the best, systems in the market dedicated to addressing this issue.

In the 1980s, Baars discovered an empirical resemblance between workspace architecture and conscious processing in the brain, resulting in the "Global Workspace Theory", also known as the "theatre model of consciousness". It should be noted that Baars' account of consciousness is strictly physicalist because the global workspace he envisions is to be conceived of in terms of physical processing occurring at the level of neuronal activity. He sees the global workspace as a vast cellular network within the brain. According to this model, consciousness is like an information doorway to the physical brain because it allows an extensive and widely spread structure of neuronal networks to act upon by integrating, providing access to and coordinating the activity of distinctly highly specialized sites in the brain that would otherwise act as autonomous stand-alone features in the absence of such a mechanism. Baars employs the metaphor of global workspace theatre for this extensive neuronal network architecture, which resembles a cognitive platform with processing occurring at both conscious and unconscious levels.

The above-mentioned blackboard architecture is also present in the brain. Furthermore, in this context, it is a kind of working blackboard where constant inputs are fed, or projected, for lack of a better word. These inputs can take many forms, but the majority of them are images and statements (their form will be discussed below). Many of them fade, but not all of them. Some do survive. Now, distinct cellular networks in various brain parts that deal with various aspects of consciousness, such as visual perceptions, auditory sensations, and even tactile perceptions, feed signals to this global workspace. The signals are then designated, categorized and finally broadcasted by a decentralized network, all in the brain. The final manifestation of the entire process is what we can call information consciousness, which is sent out by these decentralized networks.

The term "theatre" is used frequently by Baars, but it should be noted that this is not the Cartesian theatre (*fig.* 3.1), which Gilbert Ryle first coined in his magnum opus *The Concept of Mind* (2002). This

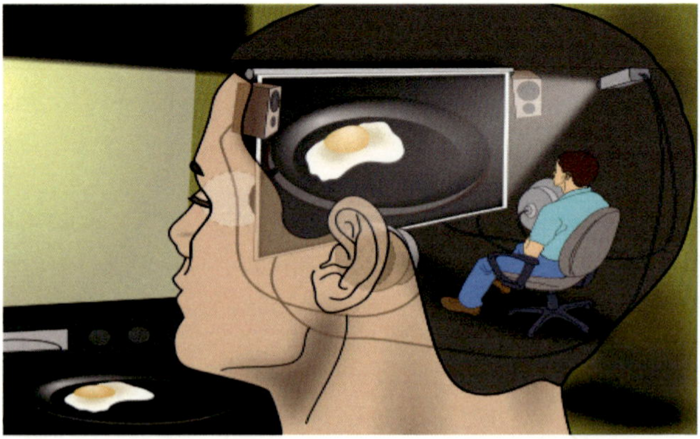

fig. 3.1: The Cartesian theatre (see Wikipedia 2022d)

theatre is also not the same as the one described by Daniel Dennett in his book *Consciousness Explained* (1991). Before proceeding with the discussion, let us clarify what the theatre means in the terminology of these two philosophers and then understand what it does not mean in Baars' theoretical terminology. It implies the following for both Ryle and Dennett

> that there is a specific location in the brain where there is a coherent representation of everything, we are consciously experiencing in a given moment: what we are seeing, hearing, smelling, and indeed, everything of which we are consciously aware. — Talks with Dr. Alok Bajpai (Telephonic Conversation)

In essence, Cartesian materialism asserts that there is a Cartesian theatre somewhere in our brain where a hypothetical observer could "find" the content of conscious experience moment by moment (Dennett 1991).

This imagery, which Dennett used in his magnum opus *Consciousness Explained*, is similar to (though earlier coined) that of Ryle. He coined the term "ghost in the machine" in his book *The Concept of Mind*. This concept also mentioned an "inner observer" watching an "inner theatre". Although the terminology has shifted from "inner theatre" to "Cartesian theatre", both concepts are a critique of the traditional "Cartesian materialism" that served the same purpose. I think it is incumbent up on me to explain the sense in which both these academics use the term theatre. As far as I understand Dennett, the theatre analogy is used in the sense of illusionism.[5]

For him, the brain is playing a trick[6] because it gives one a feeling that there is a consciousness separate from the objects and the allied representative reality that one's brain perceives.

---

5 Bernard Baars' global workspace model incorporates working memory (*fig.* 3.2). For details, see Brooks 2016.

6 Alok Bajpai prefers to use the term story. The brain is creating a story by positing a frame of reality every 500 milliseconds.

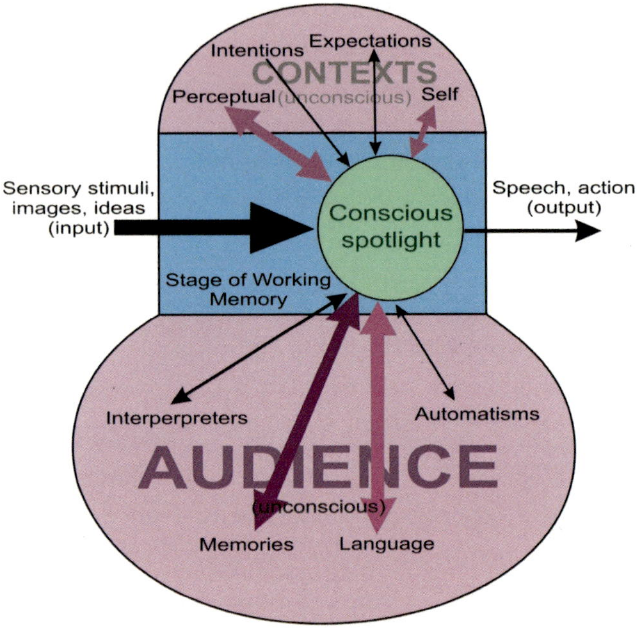

fig. 3.2: Global workspace model, incorporating working memory (*see* fn 5)

Though it gives one the feeling of a person observing the world and one's internal states, the matter of fact, for one, is that there is none. For one, it is just an illusion that the brain is creating to ensure survival within a given frame of external reality. Baars uses theatre terminology to employ a different point. For him, the unconscious mind is like a larger workspace which is the theatre analogy. Access consciousness can be understood as an equivalent of the unconscious mind where much processing is going on that one does not realize and thankfully that never becomes conscious for ordinary humans. What comes to the so-called theatre's spotlight after all the unconscious processing of the access consciousness and being posited as a frame of reality is what consciousness or qualia are. This theory hence is further discussed.[7]

[7] I sincerely thank Alok Bajpai for clarifying the difference in the usages of both the theatres.

Now that we have established what the theatre metaphor is about, let us examine what it aims to explain. It would be helpful, I believe, to inform readers ahead of time that, just as the theatre has many components in place, the theatre metaphor used here has many components that will be addressed individually. Now is the time to let one's imagination run wild and conjure up an image of a theatre just before the action begins. Consider the stage with the audience chatting. A few doors on the side of the stage lead to the play's tiring room for the cast and crew. Assume that the play begins with the lights dimming in the first instance, following the audience's silence. The spotlight now falls on the stage, with the lights dimming throughout the theatre, revealing a single bright spot on-stage for the actors to perform. Is this, however, all? Certainly not. Backstage, many hands are involved who do not appear on stage, but the show would not be possible without them. They include a director and various players such as stagehands, spotlight operators and a supporting technical crew. What is fascinating is the script's plot under strict direction, with everyone working in unison to put on a fantastic show. In spite of their absence on stage, they continue to contribute to the show's success. Now that we are acquainted with the characters involved, imagine the show is going on with the house light dimming and the focal contents of consciousness emerging with the help of nothing but darkness surrounding the central spotlight (Seth 2004).

Let us keep in mind *fig.* 3.3 as we discuss the contents of the figure and our theatre metaphor.

1. The stage of the theatre metaphor corresponds to working memory. The short-term memory component is associated with immediate perceptual and linguistic memory, intimately linked with almost all conscious processing we do (Baars 1997). This minimal cognitive faculty is used to store information temporarily. We rehearse the insignificant details of our lives here and tell ourselves "the story" of our

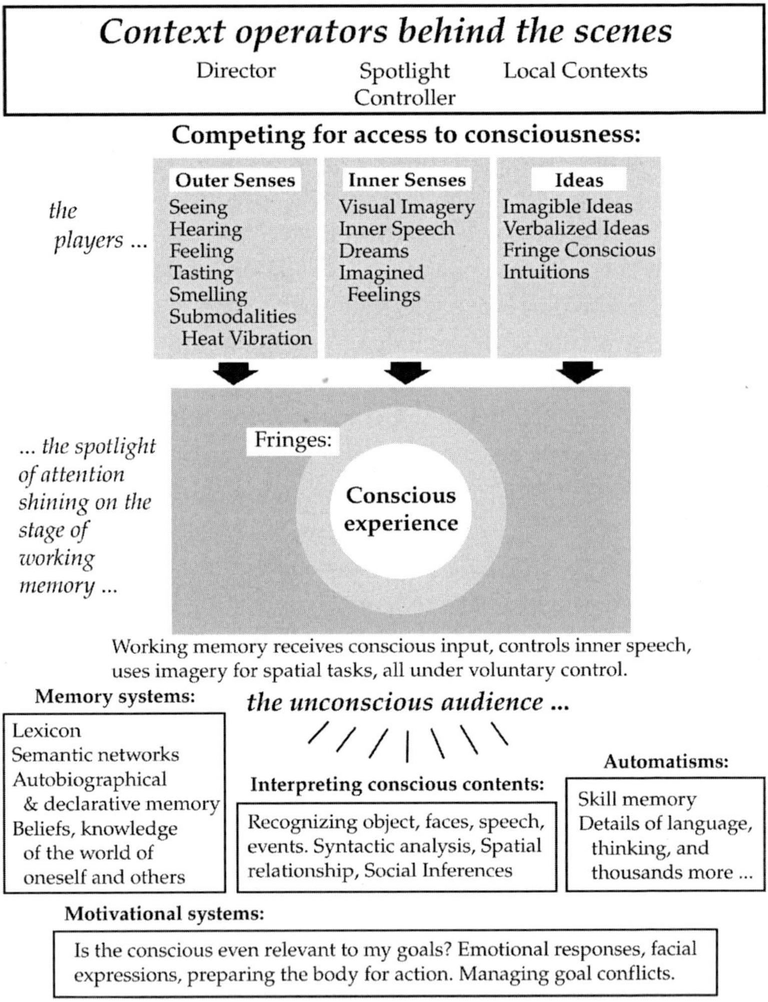

fig. 3.3: Functional representation of the workspace model (see Baars 1997)

daily lives. This "storytelling" takes place on two basic levels: "inner speech" and "visual imagery".

Inner speech is the voice that comes after a heated argument and tells us everything we should have said or not said during the argument. The same dialogue follows one when one reads a book silently, trying to understand an enigmatic passage. It is the same place where we rehearse phone numbers to remember them and store them in our long-term memory. Similar parts of the cortex involved in generating outer speech and listening are required for such verbal working memory, giving it the trifold component of speaking, hearing and inner comprehension. Visual imagery assists us in demonstrating our understanding of spatial problems. Consider a store one passes on one's way home every day. One forgot to buy something from the mall earlier and consider purchasing it from that store. You see what I mean, don't you? This is the mind's eye. Surprisingly, it involves the same parts of the cortex that are required for understanding our surroundings (Morgan et al. 2017).

As previously stated, both of these components of working memory are reasonably limited. According to research, inner speech can only comprehend seven unrelated things, whereas visual imagery can only comprehend four. They operate serially, displaying a series of episodes. This is analogous to a bright spotlight that can only shine on one actor at a time. All of the actors can be in focus simultaneously, but only one at a time.

2. The actors on the stage remain there while performing their roles. In this theatre metaphor, the actors on the stage are the contents that shape our daily conscious experiences. As these vivid sources of conscious experience try to make it to the stage, the phenomenon of consciousness allows for constant competition and collaboration between these players.

   A few examples will help one understand the phenomenon of competition and collaboration. Consider talking to a friend from afar in a crowded place. One's eyes and ears work together to interpret the information being sent by the other side. This is an attempt to make sense of two disparate sources of information. Similarly, watch a movie with a soundtrack that lags behind the action of the actors' lips on screen. The battle between these two information channels begins here. Only one source of information will emerge victoriously. This is the phenomenon of contesting, which teaches us something about the phenomenon of consciousness. It has a minimal capacity. Only one stream of conscious content can be in the spotlight of consciousness at any given time. However, a vast amount of information can be dealt with in that stream, and one can also jump between various streams, such as watching a daily soap and cooking simultaneously. The use of the theatre metaphor here is due to this limitation of consciousness. Because, as the actors on stage, only one actor can be in focus at any given time, and the switch from one actor to another will also accommodate only a limited set of actors.

3. Emphasis on concentration and absorption. Only when there is a spotlight on the actor on stage, do the contents of consciousness emerge. As previously stated, the stage is working memory. This spotlight, like all lights, has a fringe around the penumbra.[8]

   This focus on attention and absorption plays a vital role in the metaphor of theatre that we are using here. What happens if it falls on a specific actor on the stage? It draws the audience's attention to the actors performing their roles. In the metaphor, the same is true. The focus of attention falling on the stage of working memory brings that information from working memory to the conscious mind. Imagine a conversation you had with someone at a given place like a marketplace. Close your eyes and try to remember it. Most probably you will remember the person and the talk you had but you will not forget the place where the talk took place. When you try to remember you will remember the person

[8] This is similar to the elucidation of penumbra that we discussed in Crick's context.

nearby but then the person you were talking to will not be the focus of your consciousness. The people other than you and your friend talking in the marketplace who were not the focus of your consciousness while remembering them forms what you call fringe "consciousness".

Let us now return to our theatre analogy. The actors are in charge of broadcasting information to the audience and they represent unconscious memory resources, daily automatic routines and our knowledge systems. These audience members, too, can form coalitions to disseminate information on the stage. In contrast, actors can only disseminate universal knowledge using the spotlight of attention onstage. The immediate and detailed information would be included in focal consciousness (the centre of the spotlight).

On the other hand, fringe consciousness refers to situations in which we have reliable access to information but lack detailed experience. Such experiences include a sense of knowing, familiarity with concepts and their implementation, or even recognizing that something does not fit in or is not quite right. According to new research, a large portion of our mental lives is spent on the periphery, where we frequently experience a sense of fuzziness or vagueness. More interestingly, the above-mentioned feeling of knowing refers to items in one's working memory that one is unaware of at the time, as in the case of the numbers above (Barrs and Alonzi 2018: 122-30). One is conscious of an individual number only which is in his inner speech. Rest numbers are also on the stage, but only on the fringe (Bhushan 2017).

4. Contexts operate from behind the scenes to mould events on the stage. The context here describes a vast mine of unconsciousness responsible for moulding our daily conscious experiences and beliefs.

Consider you setting out to the sea in a boat. At first, you see the sun moving, but you soon realize that the boat is moving, not the sun. Then you get your sea legs and the world returns to normal. Nevertheless, an hour or two later, you consider returning to land as the sun begins to set. You proceed until you reach the shore and tie your boat to the dock. The setting sun sways once more. Nevertheless, then you calm down and the world returns to normal. What transpired? This is a classic case of context in the terms it is used here. In all the changes we experience, our nervous system makes predictions to compensate for gravity changes and the surrounding visual appearances. The world is deemed stable only when this internal prediction is successful (Baars 1997: 115-29). At an unconscious level, this prediction is aimed at synchronizing reality and expectation. The contextual orientation establishes this sense of an unstable world compared to walking on land. We shape contexts in our conscious experience, which then go to the unconscious, evoking and setting our conscious experience from the background when needed. We employ a variety of such mental contexts without being conscious of them. To sum it up, contexts are those sources of knowledge that shape conscious experiences while remaining hidden from conscious awareness. They include both unconscious expectations and intentions. There are four possible sources for such mental contexts that shape our conscious experience:

- Priming or context-setting effects show how one's conscious experience shapes and alters the mental context for future experiences. For example, the rhythmic structure of a song.
- Fixedness, wherein an unconscious assumption relating to the context stands in the way of solving a problem. For example, grammatical expectations in a sentence.
- Expectations and intentions shape conscious experiences in the case of uncertainty. For example, tip of the tongue sentences. Get. Set ... (Go).
- Violations of expectations cause a frame of unconscious

context to become conscious and reportable. For example, someone "bad" doing good for you.

Hence, these conscious experiences settle down in the unconscious and shape the future response to stimuli. These contexts are the deciding frame of what choices we make and how we perceive an event. Therefore, they are highly needed for us to operate in the world. Imagine how it would be like to learn to balance your bike every time you ride it.

5. The concept of "self" as "the director". The director is also an operator behind the scenes. So, it too should be understood as a context.

   The task this director aims at is performing the executive functions, which include attention (spotlight) control, cognitive inhibition (stimuli filtering), inhibitory control (controlling impulses), working memory (setting the stage) and cognitive flexibility (switching between concepts). These tasks (executive functions) lead to higher functions like reasoning, planning and problem-solving. This "self" maintains long-term stability in our experiences and actions, creating a unifying account of our everyday life. Any fundamental and upheaval change to this frame of self and its associated expectations and intentions are experienced as alien to the self.[9]

   This "self" manifests itself in two ways. In one mode, you are "self as an agent" and in another, you are "self as an observer". The director aims to establish a goal-hierarchy in the "self as an agent" mode, i.e. to organize goals based on various factors such as the urgency or need for the immediate goal. The goal-hierarchy easily distinguishes between long-term goals like survival and short-term goals like finishing this sentence. We judge people and events based on the goals they demonstrate through their actions. For example, one may put his life in danger for his love or children. When called

[9] As in multiple personality disorder.

to the frontlines, a soldier can leave his home even if his wife is about to give birth. Even such essential life objectives are ordered (Baars 1997: 142-56).

The self is deemed "self as an observer" in the other mode. The term "observer" has been used here in a specific sense, referring to an observer of patterns. This means that the self acts as an observer aimed at recognizing patterns. As the sciences now tell us, many of our cognitive systems in the brain "observe" the output generated by another set of brain systems. We try to find patterns everywhere, be it in our visual faculty or auditory faculty or when we try to chalk out some information related to a particular concept or other. For example, we look for patterns in visual images, such as paintings. The need for symmetry is just one of many examples of how the brain searches for patterns, shapes and sizes. There is no need to exemplify our needs. The auditory faculty works in the same way; we try to find acoustic patterns while listening to a song, and it is this pattern recognition that subtly defines our musical taste. As a result, when we say that I am aware of a specific object, event or phenomenon, we mean that I have access to that object, event or phenomenon. This self, engaged in conscious access, is referred to as the self as an observer.

As a result, the self can be viewed as a framework or context that serves as the subtle foundation for our life experiences and situations. As a result, the self is the fundamental intention and expectation shaping our lives. In our theatre metaphor, the director works behind the scenes, pulling strings, controlling the spotlight and shaping actions on the stage using the stage and the actors involved.

6. The audience. What is the point of the theatre, the spotlights, the director and the actors? Its purpose is to entertain the audience. In both practice and theory, the audience is referred to as the *raison d'être* of the entire theatre.

The majority of our daily activities are carried out at the unconscious level. These unconscious functions are so pervasive that they can be thought of as specialized systems in the brain. Our brain is a decentralized network or system, with each component containing specialized capabilities. The question that must be addressed is how to mobilize these specialized unconscious networks to pursue basic human instincts such as reproduction and survival. The answer provided by Baars is the metaphor of theatre, i.e. it is for these pursuits of reproduction and survival that the unconscious networks and functioning of the brain fashion out the various "characters" of the theatre metaphor. In our theatre metaphor, consciousness serves to broadcast small information inputs to a relatively functional society of unconscious audience in the brain.

It is important to remember that all of the composing units of this theatre metaphor are metaphorical and exaggerating the analogy to its limits defeats the entire purpose, as all analogies break somewhere. Routines become automatic for the person experiencing them when daily dealt with. Not only are such automatic routines specialized and autonomous, but studies show that they collaborate with other such faculties to carry out our daily activities. Audience members can have a vast network of nodes connecting them all, allowing them to carry out daily tasks without much assistance from the conscious brain. According to evidence from new sciences, many of these unconscious processes do not require consciousness (Kissin 2011: 175-80).

However, the routine collaboration between separate brain systems may have its origin in unconscious processing, implying that today's autonomous processing results from conscious processing of the past. This unconscious audience includes unconscious memory archives and automatic routines triggered by their "calling conditions", causing them to appear in the working memory stage. This audience comprises functional networks and routines that perform specific tasks within the brain. Memory systems such as lexicons, semantic networks and beliefs are among the audience members. They are also interpreters of conscious contents, specializing in recognizing spatial relationships to identify objects, faces, shapes and even events. They are also crucial in giving meaning to social inferences. They are involved not only in autonomous routines but also in motivational management systems of the self.

It is important to remember that, despite all of the unconscious processing in the brain, it is only when a thought or experience comes to the forefront of consciousness that the spotlight illuminates it. Consciousness is the portal to our global workspace (theatre) and it is this consciousness that allows various cognitive mechanisms to cooperate and compete in problem-solving. One of the most severe problems with the workspace model is that we are not conscious of things or qualia but only of data encoded as information (Dehaene 2014). Furthermore, Baars makes no explicit attempt to justify whether the mere presence of information in the theatre workspace contributes to the emergence of consciousness or whether the broadcasting phenomenon is consciousness in and of itself. Though this theory appears to be firmly in favour of emergence, i.e. consciousness is an emergent product of the global workspace, it also hints at identity theory by claiming that consciousness is the workspace at the time of information dissemination.

The entire workspace is a decentralized brain system dealing with various chunks of information from various inputs. Another flaw in this theory is how the integration of this information occurs (if it occurs) in such a way as to produce a unified and integrated consciousness. Furthermore, this theory is very suggestive of functionalism. The task assigned to consciousness is to select and integrate relative composites of information by linking various coalitions of neuronal networks to create an integrated whole available for various executive functions such as planning, reasoning and decision making. It is hence subject to the same criticisms as functionalism. A critical take away from this discussion is that this workspace should never be regarded as a physical space in the brain. These are purely functional networks operating in the brain, tasked with various processes such as information collection and integration into a coherent whole. As of now, it is safe to assume that it is a mix of emergentism, functionalism, physicalism and a smidgeon of identity theory, all of which contribute to making this a coherent theory.

Despite of the theory's glaring quibbles, it was one of the first attempts in the neuroscientific domain to develop a unified theory of the brain. As evidenced by significant studies conducted by the younger generation of scientists, this model satisfies the thirst for a theoretical explanation of the brain and has a promising neuroanatomical context in which it should be viewed. The most promising finding is that consciousness requires a vast decentralized network of neuronal cells to be produced and thus activated. Also, keep in mind that the direct impact of a global workspace is to bring various such networks into the loop, whereas a secluded network would have failed to produce the desired effects, i.e. production of consciousness. The final point is how unconscious systems influence our daily conscious experiences. This theory solves a significant portion of the explanatory gap's problem. However, like all current models, this model is beset by the problem of qualia.

Nevertheless, this model indeed accounts for the vast functional specialization of various brain systems and aims to solve the binding problem by pointing out that consciousness emerges when all of the components of the global workspace (as represented by the theatre metaphor) come together and information is integrated. However, one central question remains unanswered: when, where and how do these informational inputs provided by the decentralized neuronal architecture become integrated? This is the issue I believe we are yet to deal with (Moser 2016).

Embodied Mind in Damasio

As we mentioned earlier, there are two approaches in the cognitive neuroscientific domain concerning the study of mind. One goes for what has been called the disembodied mind. This approach tends to study the mind and brain in isolation. The brain is just an information-processing machine that computes data based on a set of laws. The brain does these computations and the mind is an emergent phenomenon arising out of the brain processes that happen in isolation. Then we have a newer faction that argues for the embodied mind. The mind, as we all know, requires a physical body (Varela et al. 2016: 172-79). At the very least, embodied cognition admits that the brain is connected to a body and that we are inextricably linked. Abeba Birhane (2017) meant the same in his article when he said that a person is a person through other persons.

In traditional sciences, there are two concepts of the mind. Following Descartes, one of the disembodied mind's main ideas was that reason is disembodied since the mind is disembodied, and reason is transcendent and universal. The latest cognitive science calls this entire philosophical paradigm into significant denial based on empirical evidence. The nature of our brains, bodies and bodily experiences gives rise to the mind. This is not only the apparent claim that we must be in virtue of a body to reason, it is also the startling contention that the structure of reason itself is derived from the intricacies of our embodiment. To comprehend reason, we must first understand the intricacies of our visual and motor systems and the fundamental mechanism of neuronal binding. Descartes' thought experiment of the evil demon later became the basis for Putnam's brain-in-a-vat thought experiment. This thought experiment later culminated in his famous maxim *Dubito, Ergo Sum; Cogito, Ergo Sum*. In the following philosophical discussion, his mental experiment aimed at envisioning a disembodied mind met with both fierce criticism and appraisal (Kirkeben 2001; Kripke

1980).[10] The criticism, however, is not new and was mentioned by Princess Elizabeth of Bohemia in her letter to Descartes, wherein she says:

> How the mind of a human being can determine the bodily spirits [i.e. the fluids in the nerves, muscles, etc.] in producing voluntary actions, being only a thinking substance. For it appears that all determination of movement is produced by the pushing of the thing being moved, by how it is pushed by that which moves it, or else by the qualification and figure of the surface of the latter. Contact is required for the first two conditions and an extension for the third. [But] you entirely exclude the latter from the notion you have of the body, and the former seems incompatible with an immaterial thing. — Princess Elisabeth of Bohemia 1969: 274-75

Damasio calls this "Descartes' error" and hence the name of one of his famous publications. He says in the same book:

> I had grown up accustomed to thinking that the mechanisms of reason existed in a separate province of the mind, where emotion should not be allowed to intrude, and when I thought of the brain behind that mind, I envisioned separate neural systems for reason and emotion. This was the widely held view of the relation between reason and emotion in mental and neural terms. This is Descartes error, the abyssal separation between body and mind. — Damasio 1994: xii

He argues that this commonly accepted belief is incorrect as shown through many case studies of people with brain damage and neurological explanations. Feelings, memory and perceptual images all play a role in our experience, and because the body and mind are so intertwined, feelings and rationale interact. Feelings are crucial to our minds and our ability to function in society. Feelings and emotions, as Damasio points out, are not acausal. They influence our decision making and thinking in significant

---

10 One can also look at Geir Kirkeben and Damasio's debate in the *Journal of the History of the Neurosciences* (Damasio 2001).

ways. According to Damasio, the brain and its functions, including consciousness, cannot be examined in isolation. The brain's activity and cognitive function should be viewed as part of a complex interaction between the organism and its surroundings. As a direct consequence, mental states appear to be deeply embodied, and they cannot be explained without taking into account the reciprocal influences between the body and its surroundings (Johnson 2006: 51-53). According to Damasio, Descartes' greatest blunder is that he failed to acknowledge that the mind, body and environment all shape each other.

The human brain and the rest of the body are connected by mutually interactive biochemical and neurological regulatory circuits, forming an indivisible organism. The mind exists within and for an integrated organism; our minds would not be what they are today if it were not for the interaction of the body and the brain during evolution, individual development and so on. The mind could not have existed unless it was first connected with the body. Based on the ground reference that the body constantly offers, the mind can be intentional about many other things, both actual and fictitious. The organism, in turn, interacts with the environment as a whole: it is not just the body or the brain that interacts with the environment. Finally, the physiological functions that we term the mind are generated from the structural and functional ensemble rather than the brain alone: mental experiences can only be fully understood in an organism's interaction with its environment (Bondebjerg 2015). Every interaction between the brain and its internal and external sociocultural factors alters how the mind represents the world.

One of Damasio's most significant advancements is to provide a clear distinction between the mind and consciousness. He defines the mind as

> the body, as represented in the brain, may constitute the indispensable form of reference for the neural processes that we experience as the mind. — 1994: xvi

What then is consciousness? Consciousness is the feeling of being aware of a feeling. Damasio, in his recent book *Feeling & Knowing* (2021), defines consciousness as a state of the mind created by a biological process that is influenced by diverse mental experiences. These contributions coalesce in a structured way to produce something rather complex and yet completely natural: an all-encompassing mental experience of a sentient body caught in moments, apprehending the world within itself and the wonder of the world around itself. What precisely is a conscious mind? According to conventional wisdom, it is what we lose when we fall into a deep sleep or undergo anesthesia is what we retrieve when we awaken from the sleep or anesthesia. On the other hand, what it is that we lose when we are sedated or in profound, dreamless sleep? Consciousness appears to be a brain feature that occurs when the interaction of the brain, body and environment achieves sophistication.

Damasio identifies three critical components for achieving a full-fledged state of consciousness: wakefulness, a functional mind and a sense of self. First, for him, being conscious primarily requires a state of wakefulness.[11] Second, consciousness necessitates functional and operational mind — i.e. a mind capable of acting as an efficient interface between the body and the world. Third, the mind should be able to generate a sense of self as the experiences' protagonist. The interplay of these three components, that are the defining traits of consciousness, is your very felt thought. Additionally, the mind is a stream of mental images. Images are of sensory mapping that can become the subject of conscious experience. These images can emanate from any sense modality. They can be sensory patterns, such as the one you have now in

11 As demonstrated by the neurological condition known as vegetative state, wherein patients clearly exhibit alternating patterns of sleep and wakefulness but no symptoms of consciousness. Consciousness and wakefulness are different brain processes. (Also explained in Damasio 2021.)

response to the text you are reading or visual images you see. We are not merely passive recipients of visual or tactile images. We have a self that is always present in our thinking, and we have the impression that this is something that all of us are feeling, not just the individual standing next to us. So, to have a conscious mind, you must have a self within your conscious mind. What distinguishes humans is that we use indispensable phenomena such as emotion and feeling, but integrate them with intellectual processes to build an entirely new world around us.

A conscious mind is a mind that contains a self. The self introduces the subjective perspective into the mind, and we are only entirely conscious when the self enters our consciousness (Damasio 2010). Perspective, ownership, agency and primordial feelings are the four components of self-construction. First, the self, necessitates a vantage point or perspective from which the objects of the mind can be mapped and represented in images. Second, the self is predicated on a sense of ownership or the conviction that the objects represented in the mind are only for the self's use. Third, the self is interwoven with the sense of agency, which is the sensation that activities carried out by the body are controlled by the mind attached to a body. Finally, the self must be anchored in an inner world with emotions that interact with bodily sensations (Damasio 2021: 68-105). These activities are performed in our bodies and include facial expressions, postures and visceral changes.

Primordial feelings are images connected to the organism's internal state and bodily sensations, which are produced by primordial feelings and maps relating to the organism's other features. As a result of their specific relationship to the body, feelings, according to Damasio, constitute a particular sort of representation. Feelings, in his terms, are naturally-sensed images. This structure establishes a clear difference between emotions and feelings. Emotions are simple behavioural reactions that are mostly related to automated action routines.

On the other hand, feelings are composite views of what is going on inside the body when emotions occur. They are pictures of acts rather than actions themselves. In other words, emotions are reactions to ideas and specific patterns of thinking, whereas feelings are perceptions of what the body does while emoting and perceptions of the corresponding state of mind (Damasio 1999). As a result, the process of interoception characterizes the unique interaction between the brain and body. These four components yield a self in its most basic form, which Damasio refers to as a proto-self. The proto-self is an interoceptive integration of neural patterns that serve as a map of the physical state of the current organism.

Different types of dynamic maps are used to encode these changes. Damasio divides maps into three categories: interoceptive, proprioceptive and exteroceptive. Interoceptive maps are representations of the body's internal structure and state. These images represent the functional status of body tissues, such as muscle contraction or dilatation. Joints, viscera and striated muscles are all represented by proprioceptive maps. Finally, the exteroceptive maps are representations of external world states. These representations describe events or objects that excite sensory systems such as the retina, cochlea and skin receptors. Internal maps are integrated with external sensory inputs. Integrations take place at both the brainstem and the cerebral cortex levels. The proto-self serves as the foundation for constructing a core self. A core self is formed when primordial feelings are turned into sensations of knowledge, that the proto-self is engaged in changes caused by objects seen in the exterior world.

Damasio posits one of the most sophisticated neuroscientific theories of consciousness. He asserts that specific brain regions are more significant than others in forming consciousness. This point of view is widely shared among neuroscientists. He believes that the brainstem and cerebral cortex are crucial in constructing the proto-self, which may serve as the foundation for the conscious mind. He also emphasizes how consciousness leads to a progression of sensitivity, allowing it to produce more sophisticated images of the world. Each time the organism comes into contact with an object, its proto-self is altered. Changes in the proto-self result in creating the core self, the protagonist of a narrative in which the organism connects with the events in which it participates. The coupling of the modified proto-self to the object that triggered the modification is required to develop the core self. This process follows a basic cycle: an item engages the body sensorily from a specific perspective, which causes the body to alter and, ultimately, the object's existence is felt, identified and made salient. The narrative of such constant engagements is about how the self manifests itself. This narrative evolves into a series of images, resulting in changes to the proto-self and emotional responses or feelings elicited by the perceived things.

Damasio places what he refers to as the autobiographical self at the zenith of this hierarchy of selves. The autobiographical self is our autobiography comes to life. It comprises personal memories, life experiences and plans — however specific or hazy they may be. It is what makes up a person's autobiographical self and, like the proto-self and core self, is an entity that is constantly being rebuilt via a complex psychophysical process. A set of autobiographical memories represented as images are interacted upon by the proto-self and modified by this interaction. This generates a transiently coherent pattern of core-self states in individual frames of reality due to the interaction between the autobiographical images and the proto-self. The brainstem, thalamus and cerebral cortex are the brain areas involved in generating the autobiographical self.

As a result, consciousness and emotions appear so intertwined that there could be no consciousness without feelings. For him, consciousness arises through the complex interaction of numerous cognitive and emotional processes. The brain processes produce a mash-up of images that represent the contents of consciousness and the feeling of self. These images furnish representations of the world, making it comprehensible and survivable as the body navigates the world via biological intelligence that enables the essential self-care required to maintain homeostasis[12] – preservation that eventually becomes aglow with feeling. Complex animals can change those images, integrating them into knowledge, which the nervous system makes explicit by producing patterns and committing them to memory, allowing the organism to plan, reason and reflect (Damasio 2021).

Integrated Information Theory

What is consciousness? This seems to be the central question and is still being tried to be answered. Giulio Tononi asks us a somewhat different question, one that can be of crucial import if we ever start developing conscious machines as such. Can we measure consciousness? Can we come up with a mathematical quantity that can measure consciousness? Another novel approach to breaking the traditional neuroscientific approach starts with consciousness itself to study consciousness rather than taking the brain to be the physical substrate of consciousness. For Tononi, the "hard problem of consciousness" is accurate because any theory that attempts to reduce consciousness to brain structures and processes will fail as it will eventually land on the hard problem. So, the theory delves into the first-person phenomenology and then tries to supplement it with the third-person empirical objective data to ensure verifiability and falsifiability, which are the supposed rigors of modern scientific theories. To do this, he demarcates a difference between axioms and postulates. Axioms are essential properties of qualitative experiences which are self-evident without proof. Postulates are hypotheses unless proven.

Contrary to the view of NCC, integrated information theory

12 Any self-regulating process by which biological systems tend to preserve stability while adjusting to appropriate survival conditions (*Encyclopedia Britannica*).

(IIT) starts with the experience itself and lays down a few axioms of consciousness. Tononi says:

> My experience seems to be the only proof that consciousness exists. Indeed, as Descartes realized four centuries ago, the only fact I am immediately and absolutely certain of is that my experience here and now exists — that it is real or actual. Furthermore, my experience exists from its unique point of view, unaffected by external observers. — Tononi and Koch 2015

So, consciousness for him exists and is not illusory as Dennett would believe. Second, every conscious experience is structured because there are multiple aspects of an experience, such as the experience of reading this text. It has a specific font, size, colour and indent. Additionally, words are used in a context to convey a specific meaning. All of these coalesce into one single entity in an experience. Third, every experience is unique, or it is the way it is. This text that you are reading has the components above coming together that make it a unique one. If you re-read this text, it would be a new experience, let aside the emotional layering, which is to say that the next time you read this text, it can be dull or can bring some new insight. Because you, the reader, will read it in a different context, perhaps in a new environment with a new mood. He calls the intrinsicality of information, i.e. what the information feels from the inside (Lombardi and López 2018: 5-11). One person can have around fifteen to twenty of these experiences in one second.

Fourth, every experience is unified in the sense that it is integrated. There may be several components to an experience, but they all coalesce into one in the moment of experience. For example, "SLEEPLESSNESS". This word can be divided into three components "SLEEP", "LESS", "NESS". But when you were earlier reading it, all these three words come together to convey a meaning that is not the import of either of these three subcomponents. You know yourself, the object and the knowledge itself in one experience. An experience may not be typical compared to a broader baseline, but it is a unified and an integrated experience. Next is the exclusion principle, which states that each expression is unique concerning both the spatiotemporality and the content. There is just one experience at a given moment. There is no simultaneity of experience. Every experience is a one-off phenomenon. Tononi claims that these axioms follow all experiences. Based on these axioms, he next sets out to find what kind of a physical system would be needed to exhibit such properties of consciousness. This, he thinks, can answer why some and not all processes become conscious (Bayne 2018: 4-6).

In an attempt to explicate these axioms of conscious experience, Tononi comes up with the approach in the discussion: the integrated information theory (IIT). For him, information is meaning (Oizumi et al. 2014). A word at a given instance in time, at that very moment, can have only one meaning. For example, a period can either refer to a given interval of time or it can refer to a woman's menstrual cycle, which occurs after a specific interval of time for all biological implications. Only one meaning will flash in your mind when you read the word, say in a given context or isolation. Either it will refer to the concept of time or the phenomenon of menstruation. As a result what an information for the present context means is that the term has a definite, unique meaning at a given moment by narrowing down all the probable meanings the word could imply. Thus, the information has the uniqueness of data achieved by reducing the probabilities of reference whenever an instantiation of the word occurs. Therefore, a physical system that can differentiate between several instantiations of probable meaning can exhibit more information encoded by the system's syntactic. However, it is not just such instantiation that helps a system exhibit consciousness. It must also be able to integrate information in a spatiotemporal framework to generate a coherent, unitary and irreducible image of reality to be conscious. Now each frame of the conscious state is an integrated whole wherein the amount and degree of information integration are computational features rather than purely physical properties. The same data could be integrated in the same way by a wide range of physical systems. How do we measure this integration of information? What is the relationship between massive volumes of integrated information, measured in whatever way, and the level of consciousness that humans possess?

Tononi, for this purpose, develops a mathematical tool that he calls phi (ϕ) and "Qualia Space (Q)". Let us deal with these terms one by one. Phi is considered to be a consciousness measure. It assesses the quantity of integrated data present in a multi-partite system. This phi, a measure of integrated data that corresponds to consciousness, is derived from maximally irreducible concept structure (MICS).[13] We must understand Tononi's viewpoint that consciousness cannot be for nothing to elucidate the concept. It must exhibit causal powers. Hence, the system exhibiting consciousness should also exhibit causal powers upon itself. This is called a cause–effect repertoire. This repertoire of individual parts of the system forms a cause–effect structure in a specific state at a given point. In complex systems, the possibilities of states are more. Finally, only one MICS is chosen as the final frame among these cause–effect structures and is irreducible because it is the most non-redundant.[14] It is the MICS which is the conscious state (Fallon 2018).

> Consciousness is definite in content and spatiotemporal grain: each experience has the set of phenomenal distinctions it has, neither less (a subset) nor more (a superset), and it flows at the speed it flows, neither faster nor slower. Thus, the experience I am having is of seeing a body on a bed in a bedroom, a bookcase with books, one of which is a blue book, but I am not having an experience with less content — say, one lacking the phenomenal distinction blue/not blue, or coloured/not coloured; nor am I having an experience with more content — say, one endowed with

[13] Also, conceptual structure.

[14] Hence this state is of pure information which is randomness or entropy.

> the additional phenomenal distinction high/low blood pressure. Similarly, my experience flows at a particular speed — each experience encompassing a hundred milliseconds or so — but I do not have an experience that encompasses just a few milliseconds or minutes, or hours.
>
> — Tononi and Koch 2015

A complex is a collection of elements that define a conceptual structure. It is prudent to think of a conceptual structure as a form in cause–effect space, with all the complex's conceivable past and future states. Tononi refers to the unit that successfully integrates information as complex. A complex is a collection of elements that together create a whole that has $\Phi > 0$ and is not part of a bigger group of elements with higher Φ. Complexes correspond to the actual "subjects" of conscious experience since they are areas where information is absorbed. A state's experience is identical to the conceptual structure specified by its complex elements. Several complexes can be combined to form a system, with the main complex being the one with the highest value. Complexes can also be connected to elements that do not strictly belong to them and can act as ports through which information is transferred, as the same element might be a part of more than one complex. As a result, the pieces that make up a complex and underpin consciousness are not static but can be thought of as evolving into a dynamic complex. As information can only be integrated inside its bounds, a complex appears to have a unique and private perspective or point of view. As a result, consciousness appears to have an irreducibly subjective aspect.

All of the internal connections between the system's constituents form a topographic space, which Tononi refers to as qualia space, in which every potential state of the system has a dimension. A specific set of connections inside this space provides a distinctive form or quale, the conscious experience of being in a particular condition. A complex generates qualia, a highly-ordered pattern of integrated information. Every specific quale can thus be a representation of an external object. It is a characteristic of consciousness as integrated information to demonstrate complexes' ability to derive order and meaning from a chaotic reality. An experience is a specific shape in the qualia space, and it is this shape or quale that characterizes the quality of conscious content wholly and unambiguously. Because each experience is defined by a specific shape and not by others, conscious experiences among individuals can be similar or dissimilar to the extent that their shapes are similar or dissimilar.

Q is a measure for all of the qualitative spaces of the various human sensory modalities, including all kinds of dedicated cells for things like facial or pattern recognition. With a high *Q*-value, selecting a point or area in the space excludes many possible positions in the space and other information, thereby reducing uncertainty by a significant amount. The significance of a possible state is associated with an increase in consciousness and is determined by the number of discriminations that the system is capable of performing. It implies that the greater the number of possible states for a system, the more critical it is for the system to be in a specific state. Meaning appears to emerge spontaneously from the repertoire of possible states that a system is capable of generating. As a result, the value of being in a particular state is strictly associated with the range of possibilities the system can select to create an experience (Balduzzi and Tononi 2009).

Considering the complexity and mathematical jargon behind this theory, I am sure it is not easy to digest. One can understand it with the analogy that Tononi uses: the analogy of the camera. Consider a camera with many pixels whose data is not integrated. Each pixel's information has a distinct ontological existence, separate from the whole picture. The information at each point in the imaged is independent of the information at the other points. It is atomic. The camera is not conscious. A single photodiode in the camera representing the presence or absence of light is also unconscious because it does not register the absence of the alternatives, such as colour or shape. It does not represent light as light, as opposed to colour or shape. Why is a single photodiode receiving a single type of information not conscious? What if, unlike the diode, every pixel could register information in multiple possible dimensions and continuously pass information to every other pixel so that the state of each pixel became responsive to the state of every other? Tononi believes that with this type of reception and integration of multidimensional information, we are on the verge of reaching, if not already in, the conscious state. Consciousness, for him, seems to be a specific process that integrates information encoded in differentiated and distinguishable states (Tononi 2008). Now, if consciousness is defined as an integrated information, then by definition, every system with the ability to integrate information to create a qualia-space is also conscious.

According to IIT, consciousness does not necessitate many characteristics that we naturally associate with being humans, such as emotions, memory, language, self-reflection and a sense of agency. These abilities should not be required for a system to integrate information. This leaves the essential features of a conscious experience, most importantly, emotional layering. Though the theory starts with novel phenomenological considerations, it becomes a theory of information and less about consciousness. Consciousness herein does not appear to be a one-size-fits-all phenomenon. Because consciousness is an inherent property of integrated information, any system capable of elaborating information in this manner has some level of conscious experience. As a result, the integrated information model raises the intriguing question of at what level information integration becomes relevant to have full-fledged consciousness. Indeed, if the model is correct, it should be possible to precisely measure the level of consciousness of any system, regardless of its ability to account for it.

The integrated information model defends identity not between conscious experiences and brain processes, but between conscious experiences and shapes of informational relationships, making

Tononi a functionalist rather than a straightforward physicalist since it is not just brains. However, other systems too can generate such informational relationships. This viewpoint is opposed to the claim that meaning and subjective experience are mutually exclusive properties of biological matter. IIT takes a clear stance on whether AI can be conscious: AI will necessarily be conscious if it can generate a critical amount of integrated information. This has significant philosophical implications. In essence, philosophical zombies or creatures that are exact replicas of other people but are not conscious are not conceivable within the framework of IIT. While it is true that consciousness is more or less integrated in the sense that it is not entirely disjointed, the converse is not valid. It does not follow that if the information is integrated, it must manifest consciousness. It is not easy to understand why information, or bits — 1s and 0s — flying around in whatever structure should be the same thing as consciousness. It is not very easy to see the connection between large amounts of integrated information, by any measure, and the level of consciousness that humans exhibit.

IIT does not shed much light on the issues of epistemology; for example, do we cognize concepts, or do we cognize their instantiation? Other criticisms question the theory's scientific verifiability and what the theory entails.[15] The string theory is the most precise mathematical theory of consciousness that we have today, but as we all know, it is not testable under the current scientific establishment. On the other hand, IIT does postulate a theoretical structure that can affect the easy problem, viz. what kind of complex system would exhibit which kind of consciousness. Ones with maximally irreducible conceptual structure (MICS) and having high Φ value. It does take into account the mathematical syntax of information processing. It lays down its elaborate structure, which may or may not be accurate, but how does this

15 One such criticism considering the structure of the theory is levied by Scott Aaronson on his blog *Shteti-Optimized.*

information differentiation and integration come together to create the inner theatre of qualia or subjective consciousness? How can the information of differentiating the taste of many chocolates like Perk and KitKat make one like the taste of a rather not so costly eclairs more? To me, IIT provides no insights on this account. Despite all this said, IIT is perhaps the only leading theory that implicates panpsychism since phi, a measure of integrated information that is a measure of consciousness, can never have a value less than or equal to zero.

Orch-OR Theory

We have hitherto seen two approaches from the physical sciences. Both of them catered to the recent developments in cognitive sciences. Their approach is different in that the NCC approach by Crick and Koch focused mainly on reducing consciousness to brain processes and deriving a correlate of consciousness. The next advancement came from psychology in the form of Global Workspace theory which harnesses the tremendous success of cognitive computation and psychology and tries to explain consciousness at that level while finding the biological underpinnings of it as well. We also saw a novel approach, IIT, which caters to the brain's mathematical and logical computation and structures. For the IIT theorists, consciousness is information processed in the brain via complex mathematical processes. The problem for them is the dichotomy of syntax and semantics. Like Shannon and Minsky, you start from syntactics, but how does semantics step in is the question. This is to state the point that though brain if it were a computing machine, computes based on an algorithm, how is it that it gets imbued with meaning. Alternatively, you follow an approach like Tononi and go for a top-down theory starting with consciousness itself, which is laden with semantics at any given frame of experience. Now the problem for them is that if you consider such a subjective approach to consciousness, how do you define semantics from the perspective of consciousness. There is no clear definition of semantics in this account and approach.[16] This forms what we can call the disembodied mind approach. They are diverse in their treatment, but they allude consciousness to in the brain. We also saw the embodied approach of Damasio, which is better and take the complexity of the problem of consciousness into account. We are bodies with a mind. Our minds are somehow situated in our minds, and our bodies are situated in an environment with a sociocultural and economic context. Our minds interact or act through our bodies, and our body and mind, in turn, act in the world. This, however, is not the end of it all.

The sheer translational problem, i.e. the problem of making sense of the empirical data from a neuroscientific perspective, too many correlates of consciousness, the localization and the globalization problem in the brain, the discovery of the gut-brain (Ambrosini 2019) and its link to neurodegenerative disorders stand in front of neuroscientists. Also, if one were to observe every theory about consciousness, no matter from which angle it is approached, it ends up explaining the angle more than consciousness itself. We explain cognition, psychology and information, but just as we feel we are approaching the problem of qualia, the answer seems to slip out of our hands like water. The explanatory gap in the sciences is that some experts feel that we need something extra to explain consciousness — that extra for some delves deep down into the quantum realm (Atmanspacher 2004: 51-53).

It is imperative to talk about why some of the most highly respected individuals in physics think that perhaps we need consciousness to explain quantum mechanics and vice versa. Why did some of the theories' founders believe that consciousness and quantum mechanics were inexorably linked? First, the quantum universe's behaviour is out of this classical world. Objects existing in numerous locations simultaneously, communicating faster than

[16] This problem was very well explained to me in my interaction with Sisir Roy at our departmental lecture series (Roy and Nath 2022). I would also like to thank Alok Bajpai for the same.

light or experiencing multiple timelines communicate with one another.[17] The principles that govern the microscopic quantum world of atoms and photons appear foreign. The wave–particle duality principle asserts that any quantum of energy can have the attributes of both a particle and a wave. Finally, the uncertainty principle stipulates that a particle's momentum (i.e. the quantity of motion measured as a product of its mass and velocity) and location cannot be precisely determined simultaneously. If the momentum is known, the location is unknown and vice versa.

Nonetheless, we have rules that allow us to simulate and model quantum systems — principles encoded in quantum mechanical mathematics. In spite of its remarkable success, we are now over a century past the founding of quantum mechanics and scientists are still discussing how to understand its equations and the strangeness they reflect. Moreover, the belief that consciousness may directly alter quantum systems — and thus reality — is ubiquitous. First, we must return to one of the early interpretations of quantum physics, the Copenhagen interpretation, which is typically associated with Niels Bohr and Werner Heisenberg.

It teaches us that measuring or observing causes an experiment to determine an outcome and that discussing a well-defined objective reality before that measurement is done is useless. Let us look at where this strange idea originated, using the classic example of the double-slit experiment, in which a single electron is blasted through a pair of slits. It goes through and is registered on the other side's detection screen. A series of bands is formed when several electrons are blasted one after the other. An interference pattern is the same pattern formed by a wave travelling through both slits. That is peculiar because this interference pattern directs each electron's route independently of the others. Each electron must be somehow conscious of the full-wave pattern, which implies that it must pass through both slits somehow. The Copenhagen interpretation explains the experiment's results by stating that the

[17] The phenomenon of quantum entanglement.

electron does NOT travel as a particle or a physical wave down one of these paths. Instead, consider it an abstract "probability wave" — sometimes known as a wave function. If you try to measure it, that probability wave defines the electron's location at any moment (Rovelli 2014).

According to the Copenhagen interpretation, discussing the actual physical condition of the electron before a measurement is pointless. It only exists as a possible outcome of a future measurement. It "IS" its wave function before measurement. Going by the Copenhagen interpretation, when we make that measurement, the wave function "collapses" or transitions from a cloud of conceivable final destinations for the electron to a more or less definite point on the detector screen. Because our large-scale classical world is not formed of probability clouds but of objects with clearly characterized attributes, wave function collapse appears to be crucial. So, when does the quantum-to-classical transition occur? In the procedure and the context of the double-slit experiment. The electron wave function travels through both slits to the electronic detector and triggers a second electron anywhere on the detection screen. That second electron starts a cascade, an electrical impulse that passes through circuits and is processed by a computer, which changes an image on a computer screen to show where the electron landed. Photons carry that information to light-sensitive molecules in our retinas, which commence electrical signals to our visual cortex. More electrical signals in other brain regions result in a subjective perception of the initial electron's chosen destination on the screen (Penrose 2004).

This information chain between the detector and the mind is known as the von Neumann chain, named after the Hungarian-American scientist John von Neumann. He wrote that wave function collapse must occur between the measuring instrument and the conscious perception of the measurement's result. But where exactly? Probably not until our electron wave function arrives at the detector. The initial electron to be stimulated in the detector is also a quantum entity. The wave function of the moving electron will simply become mixed with the wave functions of all electrons that it may stimulate. We should get what is known as a superposition of states: a wave function in which an electron at every spot on the detector screen is both excited and not excited at the same time. So, the wave function transition may occur somewhere in the circuitry, the computer or the retina. Everything is formed of atoms and the "von Neumann chain" from the detector to consciousness is a chain of quantum objects. Where does the wave function collapse occur when there is no apparent boundary between the quantum and the classical? This unanswered question is known as the measurement problem. According to von Neumann, the wave function collapse must occur at the moment of conscious awareness of the outcome of an experiment (von Neumann 1955, 2012).

Eugene Wigner agreed with him. The von Neumann–Wigner interpretation, a subset of the Copenhagen interpretation, holds that consciousness collapses the wave function. Wigner devised a thought experiment in 1961 to argue for the role of consciousness. The Wigner's friend experiment goes like this: imagine you do not perform the double-slit experiment, but your friend does. You know the experiment was successful because only one photon reached the detector and your friend is aware of the outcome, but you are not. So, we have an extra step in our von Neumann chain: before the information about this quantum experiment reaches your conscious awareness, it must first pass through the conscious awareness of your friend. So now we are, midway between the landing of that electron on the screen and your friend informing you of the outcome. From your viewpoint, your friend's entire brain exists in a quantum superposition of all potential outcomes. Only after your friend informs you of the experiment's findings does their brain–wave function collapse to a single experimental outcome. You inquire of a friend, "How does it feel to have your entire brain in a superposition of states?" They claim that the wave function collapsed once the physical experiment was completed. But, from your viewpoint, there was no way for that collapse to have occurred because no information had reached you. Consequently, various observers claim that the wave function collapses at different times (Wigner and Margenau 1967; Wigner et al. 1995).

Wigner felt that this conflict meant that it was impossible for entire brains-or-conscious experiences generated by those brains — to be in a superposition of states. He concluded that conscious experience must play a role in generating wave function collapse. Wigner and von Neumann were not the only ones who questioned the relationship between the mind and the measurement problem. Wolfgang Pauli was perhaps the first to assert the connection (Primas and Atmanspacher 2009: 171-210) and his influence may have started the development of the Copenhagen interpretation — later mainly attributed to Bohr and Heisenberg. Bohr himself was careful about claiming any direct role of the conscious mind and vigorously defended himself after Einstein accused him of introducing mysticism into physics. Heisenberg, on the other hand, was more open to mystical interpretations and the direct effect of consciousness.[18] He asserts that the wave function collapse must be a continual process between the measuring apparatus and the conscious mind rather than a one-time occurrence induced by the latter. Wigner, too, shifted sides and argued against the essential function of consciousness. He rejected the solipsistic approach, which holds that the mind is first and foremost, and that consciousness creates the cosmos (Wigner et al. 1995: 139-43).

There is a notion that external reality does not exist objectively — that our ideas create the cosmos. Furthermore, as Richard Feynman on wikiquote puts it, "If you think you understand quantum

---

[18] One can also look at the Einstein and Tagore dialogue which talks about the mysticism and mind. On similar lines is Schrödinger's book *Mind and Matter*.

mechanics, you do not".[19] In a similar tone, Bohr says, "Anyone who is not shocked by quantum theory has not understood it". The more you learn about this theory, the less likely you are to claim to comprehend its ramifications completely. Notwithstanding this, the founders of the theory were correct in examining the function of consciousness and the relationship between the subjective and objective reality. Although the measurement problem has yet to be fully resolved, current quantum theory has gone a long way since its inception. There are several particular reasons why the wave function tends to collapse. We must first comprehend what happens to these various events when the electron wave function reaches the detector — and why these histories cease to communicate with one another. We must educate ourselves on quantum physics. These very pertinent issues are the foundational basis of quantum approaches to consciousness. If one glances at it, just as there is no single voice from physics neither is there a single theory for the consciousness problem. Therefore, I would like to discuss one currently prevalent theory of consciousness that attempts to solve the problem using this approach: Penrose–Hameroff's Orchestrated Objective Reduction (Orch-OR) Theory.

In his interview with Robert Kuhn, Sir Penrose (2019) presents three theoretical alternatives that comprise most options given to explain conscious occurrences:

- The first hypothesis regards consciousness as a quality based on natural physical processes, a natural evolutionary outcome of the nervous system's biological growth. The dominant view in cognitive neuroscience is that consciousness arises from complicated biological computing

---

[19] They are frequently produced by those who have never studied the theory in depth, but feel confident in misinterpreting some of its early musings. I do not want to mention names, but it is a massive market that any genuine academic scholar should avoid. Also, I too do not claim to be an expert in quantum mechanics and hence have tried to show the current context from what I could gather.

mechanisms. However, there are different ideas on when, where and how consciousness first arose in natural history. Did it first emerge in humans or earlier in lesser creatures? Consciousness here is an epiphenomenon, a by-product of the brain incapable of causally influencing behaviour or playing an influential role in creating human activities; it does not appear to be a fundamental component of nature.

- The second approach regards consciousness as a separate entity with distinct qualities irreducible to physical processes and unregulated by physical laws. Consciousness has always been in the universe, but scientific explanations are unattainable due to its non-physical nature. Descartes' attitude and idealism, stating that consciousness is all that exists and that the material world is an illusion typified this viewpoint. The pervasive presence of consciousness in the matter is also at the foundation of panpsychism, which assigns consciousness to objects regardless of their material make-up.
- Penrose's third possibility for consciousness results from discrete physical processes that have always been in nature as non-cognitive and proto-conscious phenomena. According to this point of view, living creatures evolved complex machines capable of orchestrating (organizing and isolating from random external interferences) these different physical events so that they might be linked to specific brain activity. This linkage is natural in human brains and results in significant conscious states that impact and affect behaviour. As a result, consciousness appears to be a characteristic of a specific quantum mechanical interaction in nature's fabric.

The Penrose–Hameroff theory has a tripartite structure and I shall try to discuss the theory while elaborating on these three components:

- The first is the Gödelian component,[20] which uses Gödel's Incompleteness Theorem to demonstrate that humans possess the cognitive capacity they would not have if they operated according to classical physics principles. Penrose contends that because classical physics' laws are mathematically deterministic, the output of any computer behaving under the classical laws should be deductible, to arbitrarily good accuracy, from a finite-step procedure based on a finite set of mutually consistent rules that encompass the laws of arithmetic. Humans can be appropriately defined as classical computers, capable of knowing the truth of just those propositions based on a finite-step calculation based on a certain set of rules that controls the computer at any given finite time. Gödelian arguments allow mathematicians to prove the validity of mathematical propositions that cannot be determined by any finite-step demonstration based on those rules, given any finite set of consistent logical rules containing arithmetical principles (Gödel 1992).[21] This appears to imply that a good mathematician may be conscious of things that no classical physics model of himself could ever be aware of, such as the truth of statements that his classical computer simulation could not verify in a finite time (Penrose 2005: 64-116; 2016: 129-80).
- Second, the gravity component of the Penrose–Hameroff technique asks when a quantum system transit from one energy state to the other?[22] As per general relativity, space–time is not a solid flat structure but rather a flexible medium. The twisted way is related to how matter is dispersed inside it. This concept was conceived within classical physics and most

---

20 A short discussion regarding the same can be found in Searle et al. 1997.

21 A lucid explanation can be found in Bragg 2008.

22 The idea of quantum jump.

applications are made inside a classical framework. When the quantum nature of matter is taken into account, issues occur. As per the conventional quantum theory, a particle, such as an electron, is non-local: its position is determined by a "probability cloud". If the positions of the particles are not clearly defined, then, according to general relativity, neither is the shape of the space–time structure in which the particle structures are embedded. Penrose conceived that the wave function collapse was the sole physical basis for a non-computable process (Penrose 2016: 538-40). It included providing a mathematical mechanism that accounts for the collapse in cases when we predict only one result, in contrast to the probability cloud obeying the Schrödinger equation. In the two-slit experiment, we may argue that the electron is a wave defined by the wave function as it travels, but when it interacts with matter in the photographic plate, the wave collapses into a narrow region with a probability following precise criteria and we observe a clear result. Discontented with its unpredictability, he developed objective reduction, a new type of the wave function collapse that happens in isolation.

- Nature, according to Penrose, abhors uncertainty in the fabric of space–time. When there is too much ambiguity in the space–time structure, a quantum leap to a less ambiguous structure occurs. This principle enables him to link quantum leaps to the uncertainty in space–time structure. Penrose suggests a definite rule concerning when quantum leaps occur by adopting the principle that nature finds excessive ambiguity intolerable in the structure of space–time. Penrose's hypothesized principle is based on two properties of nature: Planck's constant that links energy and time[23] and Einstein's law of gravity. A time interval associated with

[23] This constant divided by any amount of energy yields a corresponding timespan.

that jump may be defined if the energy associated with a possible quantum jump can be defined. He proposed that each quantum superposition has its piece of space–time curvature and that when they are separated by more than one Planck length, they become unstable and collapse. Objective reduction denotes neither randomness nor algorithmic processing but rather a non-computable impact on space–time geometry from which mathematical knowledge and, by extension, consciousness arises (Penrose and Hameroff 2011). Consider a small object represents quantum mechanically by a small cloud that separates itself into two equal portions. The matter is dispersed differently in the two parts and each part generates a distinct distortion of space–time. It is possible to compute the energy required to bifurcate two copies of the item against their gravitational attraction, assuming each copy is located at the position specified by one of the two clouds. A timespan linked with this distortion of space–time into these two separate structures is determined when Planck's constant is divided by this "gravitational energy". Penrose claims that this timespan is when nature would endure the bifurcation of space–time into two incompatible parts before transitioning to one of these two forms (Penrose 2004: 782-815).

- The third component comes from Hameroff's belief, which relates Penrose's principle and consciousness to the neuronal substructure called microtubules. Microtubules are automata that can encode and process information using calculations based on tubulin[24] dipole states. This processing capability

---

24 A protein that is the main component of microtubules. Tubulin dipoles have a huge potential for information integration since they may combine in a variety of states. During the integration phases of neuronal firing patterns, microtubules may be maintained and modulated via quantum dipoles. This orchestration would lead to tubulin superposition and quantum integrated computing (Bajpai 2018).

is based on quantum mechanical rules, which indicate that quantum-superposed states can run concurrently until an objective reduction or "choice" happens. The most logical location for microtubule Orch-OR and the emergence of consciousness would be in the cellular body of neurons' post-synaptic dendrites. Hameroff observed a close correlation between the effect of various anesthetics on consciousness and the ability of these anesthetics to mitigate the ability of the electron to move from one stable location to the other, implying a possible link between consciousness and microtubule configurational activity. This allowed an empirical test of Penrose's OR to be done, implying that consciousness may be linked to tubulin configurational activity via gravity (Hameroff and Penrose 2014). Hameroff and Penrose have published calculations that can be used to estimate when the state-reduction process will begin.

Furthermore, the "decision" involved in the objective reduction process would be accompanied by a proto-element of experience known as proto-consciousness. Consciousness would seem like a specific series of space–time geometry configurations chosen from superpositions of earlier quantum state (Hameroff 2006). The brain would use the property of quantum physical systems to be in several superposition states to investigate various possibilities in a short period. Before Orch-OR, the brain would be able to create several scenarios simultaneously by superimposing different quantum states of the universe. A quantum mechanical approach to consciousness may account for all manifestations of human activity, including mind-body aspects that defy traditional computational explanations, such as the faculty of understanding, intuition, creativity and free will (Hameroff 2012).

We have hitherto had a brief overview of what incites the quantum mechanical approach towards the problem of consciousness, particularly the measurement problem, the lacuna in explaining the collapse of the wave function, the wave-particle duality exposed by the famous double-slit experiment, the supposed emergence of space–time (Hoffman 2016) and the EPR paradox. The gaps in explaining particles and their behaviour at the quantum level make the theory exotic rather than mystical. Sir Penrose, who won the Nobel Prize in 2020, while arguing for the quantum theory of consciousness also points out the need for expanding the realm of known physics as of today to address the problem while simultaneously insinuating that perhaps consciousness too needs to be put into the current perspective of physics to enlarge the broader spectrum of academic debate (Penrose 2022; Schafer 2022). No matter how nuanced or in good faith Orch-OR maybe, it too is not far from criticism.

In his book *Our Mathematical Universe*, Max Tegmark (2014) levies two fundamental criticisms. First, the brain is too warm and quantum states cannot survive in such an environment since the wave function collapse would happen quite early before it even gets to influence any neural processes. Second, there is a big-time gap from quantum processes to classical manifestation. The quantum processes happen in the order of 10^{-15} to 10^{-12} (in femtosecond to the picosecond range), while the neurophysiological processes occur at milliseconds, which is in the order of 10^{-3} (Tegmark 2014). Also, there are objections to the Gödelian component. To be precise, Gödel's Incompleteness Theorem has its fair share of criticism (Raatikainen 2022). Nirmalya Guha (2016), in his succinct paper on "Mahāvidyānumāna", criticizes Cantor's Diagonal Argument, which Gödel used to make a case for Incompleteness Theorems. As for the gravity part, it too has its fair share of criticism. Quantum gravity has not yet been proved. So, basing a theory on such a paradigm is not justified (Paulson 2017). It is quite a concern in the academic realms about linking gravity to quantum mechanics and it was Einstein's unfinished project. In lieu of the criticisms above, Penrose and Hameroff have reasonably responded both in academic circles and otherwise (Hameroff 2015; Satsangi and Hameroff 2016). The truth of the theory, however, remains a matter of contention.

The Need for a Comprehensive Theory

Until now, we have explored some of the most important scientific theories of consciousness and, as is the tendency of our time, the topic of consciousness is investigated mainly from a neuroscientific standpoint. This is primarily owing to the convergence of biology and physics, with physics coming in with tools like EEG and functional magnetic resonance imaging (fMRI). Francis Crick made one of the earliest attempts to examine consciousness scientifically, hypothesizing after his seminal work on DNA that consciousness is a problem that requires attention on a biological level.[25] Ryle and Dennett at Oxford University attempted to disseminate the Cartesian theatre paradigm during this period. This attempt came forward in the form of the "Ghost in the Machine" analogy and later in the form of "Rejection of the Cartesian Theatre". In 1974, Nagel published the famous article "What Is It Like to Be a Bat?", which really turned things around and is ground-breaking in terms of succinctly expressing the problem of consciousness. In 1988, about 150 years after psychology separated from philosophy, the Global Workspace Theory emerged, which, in my opinion, is one of the most complete models of consciousness from a cognitive psychology perspective. By this time, silicon integrated circuitry chips had significantly decreased the size of computers and the concept of investigating consciousness in terms of a functional information-processing machine had gained traction. It was not until 2004 that IIT was initially proposed. If we go back a little before 2004, two revolutionary ideas that have completely transformed the discourse on consciousness came up. The first was that we need quantum mechanics to explain the problem of consciousness and the second was Damasio's idea that minds do not work in isolation; one has mind in his body that is situated in an environment that has a sociocultural context driven by various factors such as geography and history.[26]

---

25 As Alok Bajpai notes it.

26 The thesis of embodied cognition.

What is the purpose of reiterating the same remarks I have previously made? Primarily to illustrate the diversity of discourse on consciousness. It is fascinating to witness this period in history when consciousness is being taken seriously from a multidisciplinary standpoint. Biology, computational sciences, mathematics, psychology and physics are all converging on the topic of consciousness. Consciousness is no longer regarded as a philosophical whimsy after the Dark Ages and the time of Enlightenment. Second, one critical question at this point in consciousness research is, "What is the right level to investigate and explain consciousness?" To me, the solution is unambiguous. All of those above. Consciousness is a multidisciplinary research topic and should be handled as such. This simple response has a critical and nuanced significance that I want to direct your attention to examination. All of the disciplines mentioned above examine numerous aspects of nature differently. In my perspective, all sciences are poetically inspired by nature.

Consequently, all of the different biological, physical and psychological levels are imbued with consciousness in terms of the subject matter they address. Finally, this shows the urgent and overwhelming need for a comprehensive theory of consciousness that approaches the problem at all levels. It is an arduous endeavour that requires our utmost effort. One such remarkable attempt is made by Alok Bajpai, a neuropsychiatrist who appreciates the intricacy of the challenge exceptionally well. His book *Maya Is Reality and Brain Creates It* and his abridged online MOOC course titled "Psychiatry: An Overview and How Brain Creates Mind" on SWAYAM-NPTEL, Bajpai first provides a succinct account of the dimensions and the complexity concerning the problem of mind and consciousness. Then he provides a brief account of his theory regarding consciousness. Hence, it is prudent to explain things in the same sequence.

When we consider the brain, several levels of complexity are involved (Table 3.1). It may begin with microtubules at the subcellular level, which the Orch-OR Theory attempts to address. It is most likely here that the realm of quantum mechanics exhibits its influence. During our chat, he expressed his belief that quantum effects occur in the brain. This viewpoint is gaining traction,

Table 3.1: Levels of Complexity at the Level of Brain

Structures	*Observations*	*Realm of Inquiry*
	Quantum Mechanics	
Molecular and Synaptic Level		
Physics of ion channels	Membrane properties	Neurochemistry, psychopharmacology
Single Neuron Level		
Electric compartment Models	LTP, LDP	Biophysics, neurophysiology
Neural Assemblies		
Spiking neurons, cell assemblies	Single and multi-electrode recordings	Neurophysiology and computational neuroscience
Small Networks		
Recurrent networks	Memory effects, EEG, MEG	Computational neuroscience, neuropsychology
Transcortical Networks		
Platonic model feature spaces	Mind, intuition, categorization	Psychology, history, biology
Functional Broadman Areas		
Probabilistic Finite State Automata (PFA)	Behaviour, immediate reaction	Behaviouristic and cognitive psychology
Brain with a Rational Mind		
Knowledge-based systems and symbolic processing	Reasoning, problem-solving	Artificial Intelligence and psychology of thinking

Source: How Brain Creates Mind?

particularly after Anirban Bandopadhyaya (2010) effectively replicated quantum effects in microtubules. He, on the other hand, is sceptical.

> Unlikely, because microtubules are extensively scattered and regulate neurotransmitter release at the micro-level, whereas real processes are electromagnetic in nature, spreading far and consolidating through excitation and inhibition to translate into behaviour, with several systems involved. — Bajpai 2018

Synaptic transmission occurs at a time scale of 10^{-4} (at least 0.5 milliseconds). As we can see, there is a difference in temporal magnitude (from 10^{-14} to 10^{-4}). The synaptic transmission then disperses into Hebbian neuronal cell assemblies, which operate between 10 and 100 ms (milliseconds). This Hebbian assembly embeds learning and memory at the neuronal level via its pre-synaptic and post-synaptic firing patterns. From here, Donald Hebb coined the famous phrase, "Neurons that fire together, wire together". Artificial neural-network training works at this level.

Together with neurotransmitters like dopamine and serotonin, these cell assemblies establish reward centres or specialized brain pathways. It is at this level that psychiatric pharmacology exhibits its effects. It is also here that neuropsychology steps in. These cell assemblies come together to form mini and microcolumns. Here due to dipoles, we have a voltage difference that causes oscillations. Crick's NCC Theory talks about this level. Next, we move to particular functional Brodman areas of the brain. The thalamus integrates and accepts all differentiation and integration of information. The thalamo-cortical loops create this isolation, as we saw in Tononi's IIT, which keeps you awake and leads you to sleep. The firing of the amygdala, on the other hand, adds its emotional input. The cerebellum, which has extra cells for fine-tuning movement, and the basal ganglia, which determines choices, are also present. Next, we have two hemispheres joined by a corpus callosum to create the whole brain. The question that Alok Bajpai asks is "How are we going to put it all together?".

Alok Bajpai is also critical of the whole NCC approach and refrains from delving into the functional localization of consciousness approach. He recognizes the challenge of definition, viz. that NCC does not define consciousness. To be crystal clear, the whole localized approach to finding the seat of the soul/ consciousness has failed. Consciousness is a global property of the brain. From a philosophical perspective of inquiry, it is a reasonably prudent modern-day question that needs to be asked why consciousness exhibits neural correlates. Why should neural activity accompany any conscious experience and why does brain damage alter the human experience. For some, like Donald Hoffman, it is not the brain playing the trick. The consciousness, in conjunction with the mind, is playing the trick (Hoffman 2019: 1-21).

Synaptic transmission is an electrical activity, yet every activity contains a magnetic component. So, what role does it play? Is it only an electromagnetic activity or is there anything else at work? It appears to be quantum gravity for Penrose. What aspects of these firing patterns contribute to the perception of a unitary self, i.e. "I"? What causes the experience to be integrated? In all species, the input stimuli contributing to the unitary sense of self and the integrity of experience are comparable. What, therefore, distinguishes us as humans?

Given that a dog has a prominent nose, bats have Bio-SONAR and certain animals can hear sounds up to 10 km away, human multi-modal stimuli are pretty constrained in all modalities. The present nomenclatures of "access consciousness" and "phenomenal consciousness" are modern usages of the term's unconscious and consciousness wherein consciousness's easy and hard difficulties pour their secrets upon. These are the pertinent questions that, in my opinion, all theories partly address in their respective frameworks but not in their entirety. I would state here that it is not the case in any bad faith but the enormous complexity of the problem.

Māyā Is Reality Model of Consciousness

It all begins with the various sensory modalities that bring in external stimuli. The eyes capture electromagnetic waves. The ears pick up pressure waves. The nose and mouth catch molecules. The skin has temperature and pressure sensitivity. Sensory modalities, such as the eyes, convert sensory impulses to electrical activity patterns so that specialized brain areas can work on them. The brain incorporates all processed information from each sensory modality. It is vital to note that only at a threshold of 30 ms does one begin to differentiate the stimulus' modality. If two or more stimuli arrive simultaneously in less than 10 ms, there is no differentiation. If a car comes hurtling at you, you just move without thinking. This action is carried out via a particular system of biological circuitry. The instruction for a reflex action is sent via the autonomic nervous system from the thalamus to the amygdala to the hippocampus and hypothalamus (the limbic system). There is no cognitive appraisal by the cortex in such a circumstance. This technique is rapid and effective, but it is employed only in times of distress. This ingestion of information is not solely the function of the brain. While doing so, the brain creates a memory bank based on the physical attributes of the information, which is then stored and mediated by the brain, while also altering the .1 per cent diversity in genetic code. This is done to help people survive daily by regulating bodily processes. To accomplish all of this, it collects data, encodes it into electrochemical signals and stores it for later retrieval. In a typical gestalt fashion, this entire information process is an act of synergy wherein an interaction between the individual components gives rise to a whole that is greater than the simple sum of its parts.

It should be noted that separate data are ineffective. Before reaching the specialized primary sensory cortex, the general-purpose weighted (based on multiple varied inputs) signal interfaces with non-deterministic quantum states in deeper centres such as the thalamus, which is the coordination centre for sensory inputs and the amygdala (which is a part of the emotional hub also known as the limbic system). The basal ganglia, located deep within the brain, is the decision-making centre for the movement. The cerebellum (which contains 50 per cent of cortical neurons and has massive connections to emotional areas and the cortex) fine-tunes balance and movement, influencing the emotional-cognitive phase space[27] through predominantly inhibitory control. The composite signal continues to fire as a mirror wave and is sent to the primary cortex for detailed image reconstruction. Due to inputs from memory, emotions, different senses and firing from the stable pattern constituting self, the signal wave is converted to a complex wave function. These patterns may represent multiple states representing different dimensions of a single bound "I", but they are more than just thought and abstract cognition. This data is differentiated and integrated into 10 ms to 500 ms out of consciousness processes, possibly in a quantum to classical decoherence[28] process to create a frame of reality that adheres to the external world for survival. Damage to any of these changes the wave function in its entirety, as do drugs that alter chemical switches and subsequent excitatory/inhibitory control. Things enter the framework of conscious cognitive affairs once a threshold of 200 ms is met. Nothing is consciously experienced, or, to put it another way, nothing enters your conscious brain until 200 to 500 ms have elapsed. What emerges as the ultimate frame of reality is what the access consciousness or unconscious has previously

---

[27] A phase space is a space that represents all possible states of a system, with each possible state corresponding to one unique point in the phase space. In mechanical systems, the phase space typically includes all possible values of position and momentum variable (Nolte 2010: 33-38).

[28] Superposition is a quantum property that allows a physical system to exist in two or more states until it is measured. This relationship of states in a superposition is quantified by quantum coherence. Decoherence describes the loss of such quantum effects whereby the particles and its states cannot be fully explained by quantum laws but classical laws (Adams 2021; Zyga 2015).

hammered out. This data differentiation and integration happen 10 ms to 500 ms out of the unconscious processes, possibly in a quantum to classical decoherence process or classical non-linear processes, to create a frame of reality that adheres to the external world for survival. The mind must be aware of the unconscious pressure concerning reality, as well as have the ability to provide feedback to change the next 500 ms of the frame which is something that requires being aware every second.

Consciousness arises from the integration or synergy of all the individual components of information processing. This implies that there must be some synergy at the baseline in neural network systems and encoded as well as differentiated information. After that, it is further integrated to achieve a different state of synergy, which means that this synergy and the individual association among components change with each instance. Every second, the brain evolves. Then no two brain states can be the same. If it is about information inflow and encoding of information, and there is an association between, say *x*, *y*, *z* and new things are being added all the time, then the whole thing is evolving, and this is what we call emergent consciousness. So, despite all of the imaging, we have not been able to locate the seat of consciousness; there are areas where, if damage occurs, there will be a loss of consciousness; however, these areas do not prove to be the seat of consciousness. With the whole process of information processing, consciousness appears to be a global property of the brain.

For continuity and meaning, the creation of reality/perception in a 500 ms bracket must be similar in subsequent brackets. Now Alok Bajpai asks the question: Is it possible that one such frame of reality influences the firing of the next bracket to produce similar frames until the stimulus disappears? If that is the case, how does it happen? While integrating memory, an internally-triggered reality is compared to the externally-oriented reality. The cortical centres correspond to the two versions and inhibit the internal frame while awake unless it corresponds to the other. Internal frames roam freely in dreams. This serves as a survival process for orienting oneself in a given external space–time in which individual subjective experiences occur.

These structures make decisions and fine-tune movements, while the motor cortex controls gross movement. This would not be possible without feedback from the body, which is processed by the thalamus. If the brain achieves the desired state both externally and internally, feedback loops complete the cycle and return to the Default Mode Network; however, if a gap remains, a new phase space is created and the gap is conveyed back to the Central Executive Network and Salience Network, and a reattempt is initiated, with the entire cycle repeating but with a lower degree of freedom to maintain certainty. Each successive attempt and gap between the desired phase space and the attained phase space widens the gap, with each successive phase space having a decreasing degree of freedom.

The fundamental dynamics are critical because many of these states are transitory and are experienced by most people. A mental health patient's cognitive structure causes them to magnify the discomfort in varying degrees of intensity. This could be a feedback loop pointing to the gap between desired and attained phase space, with higher centres perceiving it as a threat, the inability of will to create a comforting alternative model of reality allowing expression of amygdala firing and subsequent expression in behaviour.[29] Unable to control the strange attractors,[30] CEN allows the vector to move in an entirely different direction as the emotional centres clamour for its attention. The feedback loops formed due to the

---

29 Cognitive Behaviour Therapy aims to correct the trigger of threat perception and magnification, but fails to recognize that it may be the will's decision or CEN's decision to reduce the burden of repeated feedback information on the mismatch.

30 An attractor is a set of states towards which a system tends to evolve for a wide range of starting conditions in the mathematical field of dynamical systems (Otto 2008).

environment's reaction to our actions amplify these feelings. This establishes a new level of subjective reality – conscious thoughts. Morality, justice, empathy and even destructive concepts are intertwined with this subjective feeling. They arose due to external feedback and their ability to change the self-phase. The repeated loops and iterative firing change the geometry of synaptic connectivity or neuronal connections, resulting in reinforcement and, eventually, self-organization as memory. The words we throw out into the world are inputs and feedback through our senses that activate our aural, visual sketchpad, forming new word images in our minds that symbolically represent the external world.

The brain is particularly adept to handle these associations between the pattern known as a word and the object or phenomenon it represents. Thoughts are created by the flow of words in some sequence in time and their correlation with the existing external reality, however fleeting it is. The image and sound are constantly playing in the patterns and fields of the brain, but they are never detached from the context. Because the metaphor and meaning must be woven into the self, the thought appears to emerge from interactions. Even the words are derived from cultural and linguistic inputs that the brain acquires during development. In the context, the signifier and the signified, the structure of word and concept, and the creator and the created are all intertwined. The spoken language must adapt to external feedback systems more quickly so that the tongue says what the social neurons push.[31]

The error's feedback mechanisms may misfire under the false sense of comfort or reward. The rewards sustain the lie, and acceptance externally alters the narrative to fit in these rewarding

[31] This gap may be the basis of double talk or lying, the gap between faster social language and the inner slower belief, the story of self. The small window of 200-500 ms is the short gap between unconscious and conscious, as well as the repetitive feedback may hold the key to mind training as in techniques used by mystics (Bajpai 2017: 47).

acts, resulting in further feed-forward loops and the extinction of other people's uncomfortable not-so-rewarding firing patterns. Fragmented self, visible in the world, is a result of smeared INNER VOICE or the distorted story of self, and many people realize that their true self is different from the one they live in. The projected selves collide in the world, creating multiple levels of needs and desires, a second lot camouflaging the original one. Multiple such versions exist in each head and multiple selves in turn. The unconscious process' suggestion is used in a feed-forward loop to change behaviour and then act on the small window to prevent any other behaviour or thought from being triggered.

Over time and space, the feed-forward and feedback loops extinguish the "pathological" firing patterns. In my discussion on the issue with Alok Bajpai, he succinctly reiterates the same. Nothing in firing patterns is pathological; the relevant context determines it. Every 400 ms, an individual frame of reality emerges as a representation of deeper unconscious processing in the conscious brain. This unconscious is shaped by the sociocultural and economic contexts, their spatio-temporal history and geography. What is right and wrong when a thought first appears? An emotional and moral overlay occurs only after a series of feedback loops are created, and a specific meaning is assigned to the conscious thought. However, it is essential to remember that these thoughts are individual frames of reality that occur in continuous succession and are guided by a series of feedback loops. As a result, the initial feelings and thoughts are never the same.

Anger and its control are two common examples. A student who is angry in front of his seniors is considered ill-mannered; however, if that student tames his anger and becomes a so-called successful person according to societal standards, that anger is cherished as his will and determination. Assume the student joins the army and goes to war. He is not expected to be calm as part of his job description as a mercenary. Killing a man in a warzone, be it a terrorist, is not something one does calmly. On the other hand, having a calm attitude can help a soldier deal with terrible situations, such as the Kargil War, in which our soldiers waited three days without water during the fight over capturing a certain peak to make the enemy presume they were dead. Finally, the summit was captured. Consider a road rage incident. We can watch videos of road rage on the Internet. If you have a big car, the first thing you do in road rage is stepping out and abuse the person in the smaller or similar vehicle. There are also instances of people attempting to be considerate. For example, while travelling in a metro, an elderly stranger began abusing me because I had my bag on my back and it touched his stomach. A fellow traveller attempted to defuse the situation by saying, "Do not worry, it is hot outside, and everyone is tired and wants to go home".

The repertoire of activity expands in the first 3-6 months after conception, adding adaptive, social and motor behaviour. The cue-related and spontaneous activity through a feedback system related to pleasure and pain assessment within the limbic system consolidates the pre-existing networks. This means that after the first neuron is formed in the mother's womb, it begins to learn from its surroundings. Therefore, asking a question like "Is an individual neuron conscious in some way?" is not such an absurd exercise in faith. Alok Bajpai believes that the brain is not an equation-bound dynamics, but is a comparator process in which each of these phase spaces is compared and integrated with the phase space called the self.

However, I am afraid I have to disagree with him. I agree with him till he says that there are significant gaps in our understanding. From the McCulloch–Pitts model to modern neuroscience, we have learned a lot. However, I understand the gestalt issue of synergy. That is why philosophy, in collaboration with the sciences, must make a concerted effort to incorporate the abstract, subjective component into the scheme of things. The most difficult challenge in scientific methodology is the demand for objectivity that the sciences themselves cannot meet. Sciences dismiss the philosophical approach as a futile exercise, forgetting that their methodology is based on strict correlations, and as we have discussed, correlations are not identity. I may be a naive optimist, but I believe we can have an equation for qualia.

The self has both internal embodied inputs and external, contextual inputs in memory, and through feedback loops, each subsequent input is modified to provide the best harmonious fit. Is all of this, from neurons to environment, really a field that gives the illusion of an independently existing mind? This is the billion-dollar question for both science and philosophy, in my opinion. A relevant debate in Indian philosophy in a similar vein is the debate between Buddhists and the Advaita Vedāntins. Buddhists believe that reality is a transitory flux, while the Advaita Vedāntins take a tripartite conception of reality. This world on an empirical level is undoubtedly in a state of transitory flux, but there is an immutable entity beyond this level that governs this empirical world from a transcendent standpoint. Though Buddhists may disagree on this, they too within the Mādhyamika framework came up with the conception of *śūnya* and bifurcating the reality between *saṁvr̥ti* and *paramārtha*.

The basic survival needs that emerge from the brain following finely tuned feedback from the body regarding glucose levels, electrolyte levels, blood flow, respiration and cardiac rhythms are primarily controlled by the hypothalamus and limbic structures of the autonomic nervous system. Hunger, thirst, sex and sleep-related emotions and thoughts create a different phase space that involves the body and frequently overrides the primary states. The sense of agency, or the will of this self, may not be the primary vector; rather, feedback from the environment to the action (generated in the unconscious brain) creates the perception of whether or not it is appropriate. Subsequent corrections in the same phase space for the best fit generate a sense of right — these societal reactions have evolved over millions of years through the same process and form the basis of morality. There is a desynchrony between motor execution and feedback from limbs (proprioception) during sleep paralysis. There will be no sense of right or wrong if there are no dynamic relationships or feedback loops.

How does the will component fit into the scheme of things? Libet's experiment shows that the decision to act is taken by the brain at least 200 ms before the action itself. Unconsciously, the brain process involved in preparing the voluntary action, begins at least 350-400 ms before the conscious will to move. Perhaps the brain need to organize the movement before the person can consciously recognize the desire to act. After that, Libet inquired whether the conscious will could still play a role in performing a voluntary act. His response was in affirmation. Even though the readiness potential[32] comes before W (Will), the 150-200 ms interval between W and muscular activation provides enough time to decide whether to complete or abort the movement consciously. As a result, even though the onset of the voluntary action is initiated unconsciously in the brain, consciousness does influence the outcome of the volitional process by either approving or halting it. Libet dubbed this as the essential function of awareness, conscious veto. Did the conscious veto have an unconscious origin? In other words, do we become aware of the option to veto while we become conscious of the desire to act? (Libet 2004).

According to Libet, the veto decision would be an unconscious causal event, and thus consciousness would be completely powerless. His solution was based on a subtle distinction between consciousness and its contents. He admitted that full consciousness of the decision to veto an action might necessitate prior unconscious processes, but he contended that the contents of that consciousness would also necessitate such processes. The process of consciousness and its contents should be considered two distinct aspects of consciousness so that the neurophysiological time delay that characterizes the former does not affect the latter. According to

[32] The readiness potential is a brain signal associated with voluntary movement (Aaron Schurger 2021).

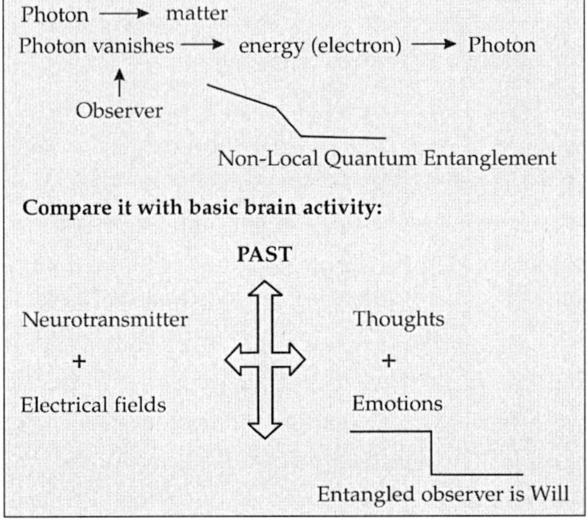

fig. 3.4: Quantum processes and dimension (Bajpai 2018: 54)

Libet, the essential nature of the conscious veto is to exert a control function on action planning, and this control can only occur at the moment of one's consciousness of the desire to move. Unconscious brain processes do not always underpin the function of conscious content control. However, there are movements that people are aware of in the real world but cannot stop. For example, patients with Tourette syndrome may exhibit involuntary tics. Alok Bajpai raises these free will questions because the mechanism by which physical activity in the brain generates an emergent non-physical property like the conscious mental field (which, in turn, can have a re-entrant effect on cerebral processes) is unknown. He attempts to explain this phenomenon by bridging the quantum–classical gap (*fig.* 3.4).

He invites us to consider: What if we assume that all physics occurs in the brain and is carried from there? In terms of behaviour, our experiential world is a classical one within a deterministic cause–effect framework operating in the temporal order of seconds to hours. Let us assume that Penrose is correct in orchestrated objective reduction and that quantum tunnelling[33] occurs at the subcellular and synaptic levels. Perhaps our free-floating thoughts in random probability states are embedded in these quantum processes. These states are constantly becoming more reductionist until the final 500 ms frame of reality brings one probability state to fecundify after much unconscious processing. Now, the question is how quantum tunnelling and Orch-OR manifest into electrical activity. When sensory inputs perturb these quantum states, they decohere and the non-linearity is caused by neuronal connections. Neurons that fire simultaneously may wire together, but they are not spatially bundled. It is a valuable connection. Each neuron in the cortex is linked to 10-1,000 others, forming an intertwined connection. One neuron can contribute to multiple assemblies or one assembly can receive input from others. This causes synaptic transmission and the sensitivity to the initial condition causes a non-linear trajectory. The information associated with the presenting stimulus is thus briefly reactivated in less than 200 ms, resulting in a new attractor dimension.

Whether this is the desired dimension or an actual dimension will determine what kind of feedback is sent to the higher centres of the brain, specifically the pre-frontal cortex. If there is a gap between what is desired and what occurs, that gap will generate feedback. The mind decides to try once more. This results in creating a new will W2 that is not free. It is tethered to the first will W1. There may also be a W3 that is linked to W2. W1 + W2 add up to W3, which is greater than the sum of these individual wills. The feedback system and the gaps mentioned above are what cause the emergence of a new will by combining the previous ones. Will

---

33 Quantum tunnelling is the passage of a particle through an energy barrier in spite of the lack of energy required to overcome the barrier, as defined by classical physics. Although the phenomenon is not fully understood theoretically, it underpins a variety of practical technologies ranging from scanning tunnelling microscopy to flash memories (Adams 2021; Zyga 2015).

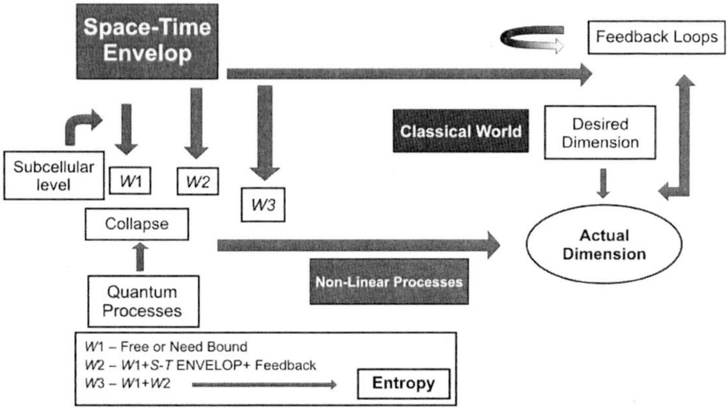

fig. 3.5: *Māyā* is reality model

is not found to be free because, as previously stated, this process begins at birth and includes a person's genetics. Every ostensible will is constrained by necessity. My following sentence states that W4 is bound to what I am doing now. Every time I decide and do something, there is a gap between the desired and actual dimensions (*fig.* 3.5). This is why, according to the Buddha and Indian systems, *tṛṣṇā* is the cause of a person's entanglement in this world. Every desire or *tṛṣṇā* is clinging because, with every will, new intentionality is established, that is not the sum of previous wills. Maybe, this is the material root of *māyā*.

This gap, however, is fed back to the higher cortical centres via a feedback loop. Perhaps it is this chasm that causes frustration. The deeper centres of the brain do the emotional lacing in this gap. The feeling or internal sense of not achieving the desired goal causes frustration. It is here that mental training takes place. Now, the brain is only aware of a small portion of the story, from the entire quantum process to the electrochemical firing pattern to the 400 ms frame of reality. These contexts, and thus the frames of reality, are constantly changing. The environment's demands and context dictate their movement.

Concluding Observations

I want to summarize what we have covered so far in this chapter. We began with a quick survey of modern scientific research into the subject of consciousness, demonstrating that the scientific study of consciousness is not a recent development. Such research can be traced back to Greek and Indian physiologists. This research has been ongoing and Descartes explicitly mentions it in his attempt to pin the seat of consciousness to the pineal gland. Phineas Gage and current psychophysical research and physics-based technologies like EEG and fMRI were significant breakthroughs. Then we looked at essential theories of consciousness from other fields of study and we concluded that consciousness is far too complicated a subject to be studied in isolation from the perspective of a single discipline. It necessitates a multidisciplinary approach and a thorough model of consciousness. In my opinion, Alok Bajpai's "*māyā* is reality model" appears to answer this need. This model not only tries to bridge the gap between the other theories discussed, starting with quantum mechanics and progressing through neuronal firing patterns to behaviour and mind in a sociocultural and economic context, but it also considers the feedback loop system involved in each level of complexity. This happens simultaneously, resulting in a 400 ms flash of a frame of reality, which governs higher functions like free will. Significant advances in this theory will be described in detail in the conclusion, but I would like to highlight a few of them here:

- Rather than seeking a neural correlate of consciousness, the theory recognizes that the majority of the brain is active at all times, creating a composite image that gives us a sense of typical integrative daily life experience. It is because of this that scientists had to depart from the NCC approach to locating the soul's seat after a long time.
- The theory also accepts that consciousness is both transcendental and immanent because it is permeated with consciousness at every degree of complexity we have seen.

- Though consciousness manifests only after observation and the wave functions steadily collapse from random probability states to definite ones, there must be an ever-present consciousness even before an observation is made at the quantum level.
- It recognizes the abstract component of synergy and keeps the door open for philosophy to contribute since, as previously noted, emergence is very Gestalt in scope.
- Though our conscious experience is always loaded with emotions primarily motivated by socio-moral conceptions of right and wrong, there is no such thing as right and wrong at the level of reality's 400-500 ms flashing frame.
- The feedback loop determines morality, and it can never truly end, even if a person is isolated or in coma, because feedback loops are embedded in the fundamental fabric of reality, spanning from quantum to gross cellular and even DNA levels.
- He acknowledges and succinctly points out the deficits in our understanding of the problem.

In the last section of his book, he quotes the Indian conception of *māyā*, which I would like to reiterate here as the concluding remark of the chapter:

> So, change at a deep level is permanent within a finite frame, but the variation it creates in the human spectrum of behaviour is complex and amazing. Each individual has a unique meaning-making capability. This interface of meaning-making and its components of emotion, cognition, and conation is the real fleeting cloud. Buddha realized it when he said *sabbam aniccam* and *sabbam anittam* — all is uncertain and transitory, the fleeting reality and the Vedānta mentioned it as *māyā* (illusion). The world is a creation of *māyā* probably means that this interface between mind and external world, the meaning that the mind makes of the world, is *māyā* ... we live in it. *Māyā* is Real. — Bajpai 2018: 174-75

4

Conclusion

THE mind-body problem is one of modern philosophy's most fundamental and profoundly tricky conundrums. The issue is the link between cognition and consciousness in the human mind and the brain as a physical body component. We began by challenging the cosmos, the subject matter of metaphysics and identifying the place of the human and his experiences in this world surrounded by cosmos in the realm of ontology. Philosophers have examined a range of theoretical positions to uncover and untangle the conceptual intricacy of consciousness. The investigation and study of consciousness as the underlying base of all human experiences and information or knowledge is now a topic of academic conscience. However, dismissing philosophy as purely conceptual and science as entirely factual would be a mistake.

A Statement of Academic Deficits

Before proceeding further, I believe it is vital to review the academic deficits that the book aims to address.

- First, it seeks to identify various "mind-body problems".
- Second, it investigates various philosophical and scientific theories addressing the mind-body problem.
- Third, it seeks to identify the flaws in those theories.
- Fourth, it proposes that emerging neuro-philosophy dominates the Western understanding of the issue and thus seeks to develop a concise Indian model.
- Fifth, it attempts to argue for an integrated, unified theory of consciousness by mapping the Indian model with the scientific model.

- Finally, it seeks to identify additional research questions to improve the model.

A Statement of Academic Deficits

We began with Descartes and asked: "What exactly is the mind-body problem?" Then, in the Keith Campbell format, we proposed a logical formulation of the problem. Next, we saw the distinction between spatiality and non-spatiality,[1] intentionality and phenomenological properties known as qualia. Finally, we distinguished the immediacy of mental knowledge instead of the illusory nature of supposed physical objects. One never doubts their existence in all states of being, including waking, dreaming and sleeping. Despite "nulla cogitatio", we do not doubt that I slept well. The book raises three questions: the ontological question of mind over matter, matter over mind, or having both in different domains, and the causal question of interaction leading to the problem of phenomenal consciousness (qualia).

Western Philosophical Theories

We investigated two kinds of mind-body theories: monism and dualism, and discussed their flaws. A list of the problems involved is given below. The book probes brief accounts of naturalism advanced by various philosophers, namely Chalmers, Dennett and Searle. As a deflationist materialist, Dennett explains away the mental. Material reductionism is an ontologically flawed theory because it violates the fundamental concept of the mind's independence by reducing it to the body. Chalmers believes that phenomenal consciousness is irreducible and involves subjective, first-person and phenomenality. The scientific third-person solution replaces consciousness with something else, leading to the hard problem of consciousness. So, how does a phenomenal experience emerge? Even if we can objectively and scientifically explain psychological

---

1 Amputees feel phantom pain which is V.S. Ramachandran's line of work.

states, we do not understand how phenomenal experiences arise. The dual-aspect theory of consciousness solves the "hard problem" by recognizing two sides of reality: its physical and functional organization and its experiential aspect. This solves the problem on an ontological level by removing the subjective first-person experience. Intentionality is a normative feature of consciousness that cannot be explained within a strict naturalist framework.

To account for intentionality, we must go beyond reductive naturalism. Searle's non-reductive naturalism contradicts the notion of consciousness' irreducibility, which is ontologically required if we move away from reductionism. It is not irreducible if conscious states exist independently and assert autonomy from brain states. How does consciousness gain subjectivity when caused by the brain, a material entity in and of itself? This question remains unanswered in Searle's biological naturalism. There is a logical possibility of a universe with physical reality but no qualitative

Table 4.1: Hitherto Approaches and Issues Involved

Anti-Materialism	*Materialism*	*Dualism*
• The hedonist problem (solipsism)	• Qualia: "The hard problem"	• What is the causal mechanism?
• The problem of other minds	• Inverted spectrum	• Causal closure of the physical
• Science and its predictive power	• Multiple realizability	• Locus of interaction
• Mind-independent material objects	• The zombie argument	• Simplicity. If two, why not three or more?
• Why patterns in thought?	• The knowledge argument	• Two problems of the self (identity)
• Dissimilar emergence (How *P* from not-*P*?)	• Nagel's bat argument	
	• The Chinese room argument	

experience. Such a scenario may give rise to the notion that every piece of materiality is endowed with experientiality so that no part of the universe is devoid of mental elements.

Scientific Theories of Consciousness

We analysed some scientific theories of consciousness in the third chapter, most of which face similar philosophical challenges. Consciousness appears as a single experience or thought. On the other hand, the mind is not remarkably unified because one thing happens in it entirely independently of another. A stream of disconnected thoughts, some unconscious, can be interrupted by a memory, or the results of an unconscious calculation can appear suddenly for no apparent reason. So, why would the presence of information in different locations within the global network count as integrated enough to be consciousness?

Let us look at an example to demonstrate the point. Take a step back and survey your department's structure. One can notice trees, cars, a tin shed, bicycles, people making noises, a library, a water cooler with cold water and various other objects as one walks around it. These objects and people have distinct shapes, sizes, colours, textures and solidity. Various objects coalesce into one unified experience as one walks through the department, a fascinating experiential phenomenon. From a third-person perspective, no matter how many objects are there when you experience the same, it all appears to be one unified experience. It is important to note that different parts of the brain process different aspects of experience.

For example, various features are extracted by different parts of the visual cortex. The auditory component is processed in the temporal lobes. One does not need to learn about one's affiliation with one department, its history or the reason for going to the department every day. Every time a person visits the department, he/she has the same emotional experience. If one visits the department for the first time, one may be pleased to study in one of the largest departments at the nation's third best university. The experience is influenced by the individual's cultural and socio-economic background and personal interactions with others. Someone from a remote location may be humbled by the opportunity, whereas someone from a metropolitan area may dislike it. A person's experience may improve if he/she makes good friends and spends quality time with them. Nonetheless, it is a unified experience for which we do not need to think much about the fact that, "Oh! I shall have this experience today". The unconscious layering of memory governs that experience without being too explicit in the experience itself, such as what one ate for breakfast or whether one fought with his parents.

Francis Crick's 40 Hz hypothesis does not tell us why any rhythm at any frequency should be associated with consciousness. Where does the binding of individual components of an experience happen? The Global Workspace Theory addresses this issue by bringing in the theatre analogy, but does not tell us when the unconscious processing turns conscious and where does that happen? It is a defect in Bernie Baars's view that what we are conscious of is neither things nor qualia but information. It is not clear whether the mere presence of information in the global workspace constitutes or provokes consciousness or whether it is the broadcasting itself that is the consciousness. Baars seems to favour a kind of emergentism in which consciousness emerges from the global workspace, when strictly what his theory entails is the identity theory: consciousness is the global workspace at the broadcast. The significant advantage of this theory is in explaining cognitive aspects of consciousness and settling the local–global brain processing debate. Just as the 40 Hz hypothesis, it does not provide much insight into where the different components of experience, say visual experience, get integrated. However, there are fair insinuations that it might be the thalamus. Integrated Information Theory (IIT) is a significant theory of consciousness that follows a top-down approach and gives a theory that describes consciousness in terms of mathematical structures and information theory. As with any top-down theory, the problem is that it starts with the experience itself, and that experience is subjective. In the context of IIT, Tononi tries to measure that in terms of information, but the problem is that the concept of information shifts from C.E. Shannon's information theory, and then we have a definition that information is a cutback of certainty, which in my opinion is not a vague definition. Also, defining it as a maximally irreducible conceptual structure is like bringing an abstract component to explain a subjective experience to explain intentionality. This is a good approach, but it fails to address Western conceptions of empirical rigour like verifiability, the primary criticism against the theory. Also, it suggests that the thalamocortical re-entry loop might be the Neural Correlates of Consciousness (NCC) which is a point of neuroscientific debates since there is no single consensus on a particular NCC. It helps us bring home a crucial point: phenomenal consciousness is a process and not a single voila moment.

Antonio Damasio, in his theory, introduced some brilliant new advancements. First, he acknowledges that any experience has emotional layering embedded in it. This is a significant advancement, particularly in deconstructing the whole experience into various components like intelligence, emotion and consciousness. He also acknowledges that we are situated in a world that shapes our experiences. Finally, the most significant advancement is acknowledging that we have an embodied brain rather than a disembodied one. The whole bodily set-up with basic input features like temperature, sensation and blood cell count is stored in maps in the brainstem daily to regulate homeostasis. This slowly changing embedded map of regulating homeostasis gives one a sense of the self. The problem, however, is that it still bifurcates the self and consciousness, and hence resorts to maps of bodily activity, which again is a slowly fleeting one but fleeting all the more. He also brilliantly points out the distinction between intelligence, which even organisms like bacteria exhibit in the sense that they can have a sense of their surroundings and showcase the faculty of will, like deciding to move left or right for survival needs like food. We differ because we can represent what we detect from our surroundings in mental images, and we can know that all those representations relate to our body and its organs via a self that is the brain maps of our bodily interior created for homeostasis.

Finally, we explore the Orch-OR theory, which is brilliant in its approach because it begins with our most fundamental current understanding of matter, the murky quantum world. It is not the first theory to suggest a quantum approach to consciousness. Previous attempts include the Pribram–Bohm Hypothesis. For Roger Penrose, some problems, such as Penrose's tiling problem, are non-computable, as are self-referential paradoxes. However, we can use self-referential paradoxes to demonstrate that our mathematics lacks such explanations.[2] First, he illustrates the point of non-computability and highlights that such philosophical or academic problems do not trouble the human mind. "A barber only shaves those who do not shave themselves." Does the barber shave himself? Though the paradox may be a mathematician's nightmare, a loving barber would shave himself instantly, even at night, if his wife commands it before dinner. He explains that this scenario could exist in our physical world.

Next, he is deterministic and caters to the collapse of the wave function computed by Schrödinger's equation. In contrast, the measurement problem is probabilistic. For Penrose, this is a flaw in current physics and he uses it to argue that the correct theory (perhaps his theory of quantum gravity) will deviate from Schrödinger's equation and shift the cat from being "both dead and alive" to being "dead or alive".[3] Now such macroscopic phenomena

---

[2] Gödel's incompleteness theorems.

[3] Famous Schrödinger's cat thought experiment.

for him happen in the microtubules in the brains. Their problem lies in accepting unproven premises to build their argument. Though much experimental work from people like Anirban Bandopadhyaya may seem promising, there is a large gap to fill.

Towards an Integrated Theory of Consciousness

An overview of these deficits led us to acknowledge the need for a unified theory of consciousness that starts from our most basic understanding of matter and moves up to the mesoscopic human level and perhaps further. Alok Bajpai's "*māyā* is reality" model endeavours to address this deficit. The book opines on the lucrative approach he takes to solve the easy problems first and tries to deconstruct the phenomenal experience into its major components, saving him from the fallacious neural correlations theory because the brain is locally global. He shows that the individual brain regions perform individual information processing via the thalamocortical loops and become an integrated whole that gets acted upon in the external world by the parietal relay, thereby engendering a larger feedback loop on the feedback loops at the individual processing hierarchies. Wave functions become reductionist by the feedback loops and the successive layer of will or intent over the original one. Thereby he integrates the quantum level without commitments to quantum gravity or microtubules.[4]

Indian Model of Consciousness

The book voluntarily keeps the orthodox Indian theories of consciousness at the beginning itself so that while reading the other accounts, one gets a gist of the problems with contemporary philosophical and scientific theories. Then, it tries to build up an integrated model of consciousness based on the significant points of agreement among various philosophical schools. What we have in the end is an Advaitin model that acknowledges consciousness as being both transcendent and immanent.

---

4 He is sceptical about it.

Phenomenological experience is a conceptually distinct and mutually irreducible dynamic of Mind–Body and Consciousness (MBC). The body, which includes the nervous system, sense organs and brain structures, is a gross matter subject to disintegration. The mind is a cognitive instrument connected to the body on the one end and consciousness on the other. Consciousness is not the same as the body or mind. It is temporally linked to the mind but not spatially. Spatio-temporality does not bind the mind, a more subtle form of matter than the gross body. There are three distinct levels of experience:

- The observational level is the sensory information processing through the body's instrumentalities.
- The mind acts on informational processing, facilitating the second level of comprehension.
- Transcognitive realization of truth by removing sensory and informational conditioning is the third level.

The three stages of experience represent the notions of *śravaṇa* (literally hearing, but can be equated with observation), *manana* (comprehension) and *nididhyāsana* (realization). There is subject–object differentiation during observation and comprehension, and thus between thought and action. Knowing and being are two different things. Even if one knows something is illusory, one can still act on it. In the contemplative mode of *nididhyāsana*, the distinction between subject and object, thought and action, and knowing and being merges so that one becomes/does what he knows to be true. The person (*jīva*) is the knower (*jñātā*), enjoyer (*bhoktā*) and agent (*kartā*). Thinking, feeling and doing constitute mundanity, are cognitively biased and do not accurately reflect the state of affairs. The ego-principle brings in intentionality via the pleasure–pain principle.

Thoughts, emotions and actions condition the being acting via the mind mediated by the physical apparatus, and the state of the body cognitively biases the being. The presence/reflection of *ātman* determines the person's unity in the midst of changing images of the self (transcendental consciousness). Transcendental consciousness[5] known as *Brahman*, *ātman* or *puruṣa* pervades the person and the universe, manifesting as unity in diversity found in the universe and the shifting the spectrum of events in one's life. It is not localizable because it illuminates the form the mind takes in its connection with the environment via sensory gateways. Phenomenal consciousness entails one's knowledge, affections and volitions because the person is a reflection of consciousness and illumined mental states.

The Integrity of the Approach

What is reality? External worldly perceptual reality is representational. Like bees and dogs, the bat sees the world differently than we do. Different sensory-motor apparatuses work differently, resulting in different representations and radically modifying knowledge of the environment. Herein truth relates to external objects and occurrences seeking inter- and intra-subjective confirmation. Noumena is astoundingly unknown. Our knowledge of the world is valid only in our mutual agreement. Anil Seth refers to this as a collective hallucination of reality. The reality, both phenomenologically and absolutistically, is consciousness itself. As equated with consciousness, reality is more than representational experience; it is non-representational and non-intentional consciousness. The book underlines that this notion is superior to Western panpsychism since it advocates non-dualism or non-difference and acknowledges that reality has three levels: absolute, empirical and illusory. Every level of reality, thinking, being, action, event and object is permeated with consciousness, yet pure consciousness remains transcendent. Absolute consciousness can be experienced while on the empirical plane. Even hallucinations

---

[5] It has several negative connotations such as unchangeable, undefined, unqualified, formless and non-intentionality.

and psychotropic medicines induce altered states of consciousness, which are visible alterations of the same continuous self.

A Comparative Estimate

- In contemporary times, the working definition of the mind is "whatever the brain does". As a result of the brain's operation, the mind develops phenomenal consciousness.
- The mind has undergone a conceptual upheaval in the last century due to attempts to reduce it to just brain structures. However, such a reduction is now widely viewed as unattainable. From Ivan Pavlov's behaviourism through Giulio Tononi's information theory to Max Tegmark's mathematical structure theories to Penrose's quantum computation, the concept of the mind has become subtle.
- The brain as the seat of consciousness debate has failed because the brain has a comprehensive structure with individual specialized structures performing varied specialized activities, making it both locally global and globally local. The integration of these individual processes is greater than the sum of their parts.
- Recent research on the gut–brain axis considerably undermines the disembodied approach. The disembodied brain debate must be replaced with the embodied brain discussion.
- The contemporary view bifurcates the self and consciousness, which makes explaining the continuity of experience problematic. The concepts "self" and "consciousness" in the Indian model refer to an undivided, non-dual reality with no internal or external divisions.
- There are two integrated levels of consciousness: empirical and transcendental.
- Empirical consciousness is tied to limiting adjuncts such as

the body and thinking, an empirical impact of *māyā* or *avidyā*. It is perceiving "worldly consciousness" personified.

- The Indian model also distinguishes between concepts used interchangeably in common parlance. *Citta*'s supposed locus is the limbic system, and it defines consciousness as a mental quality that includes unconscious processing at the level of memory. This level is responsible for the illusion of duality. *Sākṣī*'s level of witnessing is where concepts like metacognition come into play. Mindfulness, attention and the supposed distancing of the self from immediate response all work at this level. The final level is awareness, also known as transcendental consciousness, in which dualities of subjectivity and objectivity cease to exist. One is simply aware of the entirety of one's being.
- The dynamic interplay of the mind and matter results in a finite and limited field of existence in phenomenal consciousness.
- *Māyā*'s limiting adjuncts do not influence consciousness transcendentally.
- Everything that is created exists within spatiotemporal confines, but nothing created exists beyond.
- *Antaḥkaraṇa* (mind) is created and exists within space–time boundaries.
- Although the mind is created by matter, it cannot exist without matter. This mentality is fundamental.
- Deflationary reductionists analyse every experience, will, intent and intelligence in the light of evolutionary survival needs. What determines survival needs in the brain? The brain is not a conscious, decision-making entity. How can the brain, a complex material structure, develop anything non-material like consciousness if it is not already conscious?
- An evolutionary theorist may claim that Deoxyribonucleic Acid (DNA) stores memories, but what causes DNA to do so?

What motivates survival? Dopamine and reward circuits take us back to the level we are explicating, trapping us in a vicious circle.

- This is a pessimistic stance that leaves little room for benevolence. Human history has not been kind, yet we had Buddha, Kṛṣṇa and Christ. We have mothers who refuse to eat until the baby is fed. Why would a mother do that daily if it is all evolution? The healing of a shattered femur is thought to be the first sign of civilization, which would not have been possible without acts of kindness. The problem lies not in pessimism but in rejecting data of benevolence.
- Sāṁkhya's evolution model prioritizes the cognitive components of evolution and accounts for the current predicament better than the Darwinian model.[6] It similarly solves the dilemma of identity and combination edging over the Darwinian model.
- The mind is the internal cognitive instrument that exhibits consciousness in various ways, cogitates and produces the embodied self through ego overlaid on top of cognition because of its link with consciousness.
- Its primary feature is cognition, making it an instrument for cogitation, volition and emotion. It is the seat of emotions and will, and it interacts with the body to mediate its external manifestation.
- The West is beginning to understand that perhaps everything is consciousness pertinently with the extended mind debate.
- Brain-oriented functionalism suffers from the problem of intentionality. Nevertheless, according to the Indian model, consciousness can be non-intentional, achieving the true goal of life.

---

6 The *buddhi* develops initially. The *ahaṅkāra* came next, followed by the *manas*.

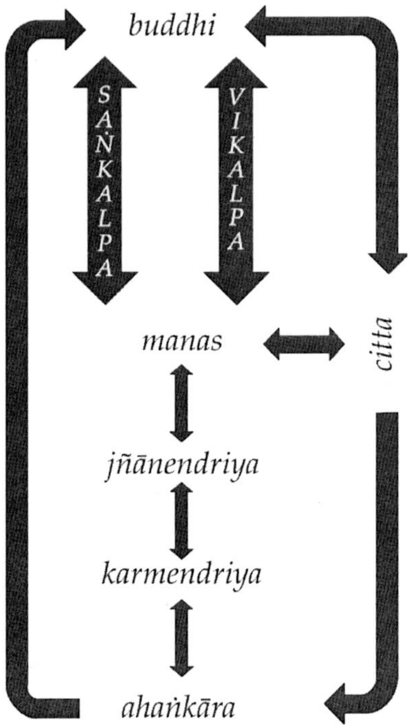

fig. 4.1: Advaita feedback loop-based model:

Levels of Investigation

Experience can be investigated on several levels as:

- The "psychophysical level" is where the mind engages in transcendental consciousness and self-realization. Understanding the connection between physical and mental states requires that body, mind and consciousness be investigated ontologically and physiologically.
- From a "psychiatric level", an experience can also be researched from the mind's perspective to learn how it works, how it is influenced and how it can be regulated to improve the current challenge of mental health.
- From a "computational level", human functioning can be investigated from the standpoint of consciousness

to comprehend and utilize non-physical resources of human functioning made available by the mind's link with consciousness.

- Understanding sensory processing as a mode of information acquisition via informational differentiation, integration and relay determining the nature and content of cogitation necessitates a systematic epistemology and is the first stage of developing a "multidisciplinary Indian cognitive sciences framework".
- The phenomenological attitude emphasizes the primacy of consciousness in its distinct epistemological views, which are phenomenologically provided facts, based on psychological assumptions. This prepares the ground for the "psychotherapeutic level".
- The Indian approach looks inward to discover the individual components of cognitive biases due to inherent and situational constraints such as presuppositions, attitudes and motivations, which limit peer pressure, conditioning and other similar variables in order to investigate methodologies and develop procedures and strategies for controlling them at "psycho-spiritual level of meditation research".

Predictability: A Brief Case Study

Now that we have a comparative estimate of different P-consciousness models, I believe, it is prudent to put the integrated Indian model to test and see what it can predict about a real-world situation.

We frequently see adults, especially those between 18 and 28, become incredibly violent, whether verbally or non-verbally. This behaviour appears seemingly out of nowhere, with individuals saying or doing things that are usually unrelated to the situational context. So why does it happen and what can our model say about it?

Insights — What we ordinarily call the self is not just our beliefs, predispositions and cognitive conditioning. It is a tripartite structure involving what we think of myself, what we think people think of us and what is presented to me in the individual frame of reality. These components work at three levels, particularly ego, which has to do with intentionality. The second has to do with the representational level, where we represent the world outside us. Third, it is concerned with memory. The final part is concerned with the information processing brought about by the mind as a whole and witnessed by *sākṣī*. The self of mundanity takes final shape by the age of 28.

During this age, we get transition from teenage to adulthood. Herein three factors are involved. First is the final definition of puberty features governed by hormonal changes. Second is the transition of personality from an introvert to an extrovert or vice versa. The third is the situational context wherein children complete their studies and step into the definitional phase of their career. Finally, adults begin to acknowledge that the world portrayed in books is not the same as what they witness.

At this age, the metacognitive component is not fully developed. What is metacognition? There are times when we become sad by an unpleasant situation and happy by a cheerful situation. Then there is knowing that I am sad or happy. This is the level of metacognition. Since it is undeveloped in the above age bracket, what happens is that one cannot recognize one's feelings and stays in a state of ambiguity, which the mind cannot accept since it needs to be sure in its being to enhance the chances of survival. To suffice for this unpredictability, one looks at the situational components, i.e. morals, books and people. The situational component brings in too much conditioning in the form of morals, which often teaches nonsense like always being vital for the family, having toxic feminity or masculinity or that one should always be mannered. This leads to the lack of manifestational expression of the internal state of mind generated by such dialectics.

The non-recognition of one's own mental state due to undeveloped metacognition and the dichotomy between morals and the actual world create a split. This split deepens as time passes. The inner voice of conscience dictates the manifestation of these states of reality which are internalized as such since they are not expressed in the actual world. This leads to a lack of feedback loop, which can improve or contradict these internal frames of reality. Over time, these internalized states of reality are representationally attributed to people concerned and the sense of self which involves what one thinks others think about him. All this gets compounded and when the sense of self starts to split beyond a critical point, we see such behaviour. Even Lord Śiva fainted after drinking the poison. We are humans and should behave as such, i.e. express our feelings more openly, learn from our mistakes and modify our beliefs.

Lacunae and Further Research

1. To explain the phenomenal reality of the universe and being, the Advaitins created the principle of illusion (*māyā* or *avidyā*). It differentiates the transcendental consciousness (*Brahman*) from *jīva*. Despite its bewildering nature, a mechanical component must explain the apparent unity of the environment and experiences. That mechanical component must be deciphered in computable terms while taking subjectivity into account. Previously, techniques were excessively philosophical or too logical, making the principle challenging to understand. A phenomenological approach is required to address the problem and establish an appropriate framework for understanding *māyā* while keeping the subjective aspect in mind. My recommendation is to start with temporality, self-referential paradoxes and the simulation theory, following the different definitions in Gupta (1966).

2. There are two problems of other minds as I foresee one on the human level and elsewise.

    i. Humans have been shown to create a "theory of mind", in which we assign mental states to people we see or think of. When we consider that humans express emotions in similar ways, this has a psycho-empirical basis. For example, our lips rise upward when we laugh, droop down when sad and shrink when we are angry. In psychosis, this ability to build a mental model is impaired. How do we go about doing that? Although some studies suggest that specialized mirror neurons (Gallese 1998) may be the underlying structure, the book discovered no reliable epistemological study on the faculty of the theory of mind. An epistemological investigation into "how humans build a theory of mind" is crucial.

    ii. The "problem of other minds" is all about how we know that other minds are conscious. According to extensive studies, many species, such as *Trichoplax adhaerens* (Cepelewicz 2022), exhibit sophisticated behaviours and mushrooms communicate with one another about weather and temperature. Even the most basic organisms require sleep. Before J.C. Bose showed that plants have life, it was widely believed to be non-living beings (Tandon 2019). Plants' leaves have been shown to do mind-boggling computations (Peak et al. 2004). Tononi's theory implies that the Internet may be sentient as well. How can we say that such beings or things are not conscious when we have access to the Internet?

3. There is a pertinent dispute regarding the different Advaitin models like Pratibimbavāda and Avacchedavāda. Though most Indian psychologists like K.R. Rao and linguist philosophers like D.N. Tiwari favour the Avacchedavāda model, I think a relook at other models can provide a better

outlook on the current discussion like insights into the above problem of other minds.

4. "Conservation of mass and energy" has been very problematic an account for the dualist model, even for those that adopt an evolutionary perspective about the non-material faculties of beings. Philosophers like Dasgupta (2018) and Schweizer (2019) try to give probable solutions to the law of conservation of mass and energy in their accounts of the Sāṁkhya model. However, the problem is that although the mind can be physical, consciousness as-such is immaterial, how does that interact with material *prakṛti* to account for the principle.
5. How do we make sense of space and time?
6. *Antaḥkaraṇa*, the conceptual equivalent of mind in the Indian model, is conceived as going out towards the object, modifying into its shape, taking the form of a *vṛtti*, following which knowledge occurs. Is this going out figurative or literal? There are two factions about this among scholars like D.M. Dutta and T.M.P. Mahadevan. Kaplan (1983) acknowledges this dichotomy in Indian academia about the issue. In my age, philosophers like Sacchidanand Mishra and Nirmalya Guha accept the literal going out while other philosophical theorists like D.N. Tiwari point out the deficits in the literal sense and argue for a figurative sense of the term. This "Debate Needs of Antaḥkaraṇa Going Out" needs to be discussed in the light of quantum mechanical approaches. Perhaps it can help us integrate the Indian model with the quantum realm.
7. Lastly, we need to "map the integrated Indian model with neurobiological perspective" to provide a better account of the theory.

Bibliography

Aaron Schurger, Pengbo 'Ben' Hu, Joanna Pak and Adina L. Rōskies, 2021, "What Is the Readiness Potential?", *Trends in Cognitive Sciences,* 25(7): 558-70 (doi:https://doi.org/10.1016/j.tics.2021.04.001).

Aaronson, Scott, n.d., "Why I Am Not An Integrated Information Theorist (or, The Unconscious Expander)", *Shteti-Optimized* (accessed on 28 April 2022) (https://scottaaronson.blog/?p=1799#comment-107443).

Adam, Alonzi and Bernard J. Baars, 2018, "The Global Workspace Theory", in *The Routledge Handbook of Consciousness*, ed. Rocco J. Gennaro, pp. 122-36, New York: Taylor & Francis.

Adams, Betony, 2021, "Do Quantum Effects Play a Role in Consciousness?", *Physics World*, 26 January (https://physicsworld.com/a/do-quantum-effects-play-a- role-in-consciousness/).

Adhvarindra, Dharmarāja, 1983, *Vedānta Paribhāṣā of Dharmarāja Adhvarīndra*, tr. Swami Madhavananda, Calcutta: Advaita Ashrama.

Ambrosini, Yoko M. et al., 2019, "The Gut-Brain Axis in Neurodegenerative Diseases and Relevance of the Canine Model: A Review", *Frontiers in Aging Neuroscience*, 11: 130 (doi:10.3389/fnagi.2019.00130).

Appayadīkṣita, 2011, *Siddhāntaleśasaṁgraha*, Varanasi: Chowkhambha Vidyabhavan.

Ariew, Roger and Donald Cress, 2006, *René Descartes: Meditations, Objections, and Replies*, Indianapolis/Cambridge: Hackett Publishing Company.

Aristotle, 2017, *Oxford Essential Quotations*, ed. Susan Ratcliffe, Oxford University Press (https://www.oxfordreference.com/view/10.1093/acref/9780191843730.001.0001/q-oro-ed5-00000434) (accessed on 11 July 2020).

Atmanspacher, Harald, 2004, "Quantum Theory and Consciousness: An Overview with Selected Examples", *Discrete Dynamics in Nature and*

Society (Hindawi Publishing Corporation) 1: 51-73 (doi:10.1155/S102602260440106X).

Avramides, Anita, 2020, "Other Minds", *The Stanford Encyclopedia of Philosophy* (https://plato.stanford.edu/archives/win2020/entries/other-minds/) (accessed on 21 December 2020).

Ayer, A.J., 1951, *The Physical Basis of Mind: A Sequence of Broadcast Talks*, ed. Peter Laslett, Oxford: Blackwell.

Baars, Bernard J., 1997, *In the Theater of Consciousness: The Workspace of the Mind*, New York: Oxford University Press (https://doi.org/10.1093/acprof:oso/9780195102659.001.1).

———, 1998, *A Cognitive Theory of Consciousness*, New York: Cambridge University Press (first edn 1993).

Bajpai, Alok, 2016, *Psychiatry: An Overview and How Brain Creates Mind?*, Prod. IIT-Kanpur, Kanpur: YouTube via Nptel.

——, 2017, *Cognition, Transformation and Lives*, online course IIT-Kanpur, Comp. Youtube. Prod. IIT-Kanpur, Kanpur, 8 June.

——, 2018, *Maya Is Reality & Brain Creates It*, New Delhi: Kautilya Books.

——, 2021, "Psychiatry: An Overview and How the Brain Creates Mind", Online Video Lectures and Books, Kanpur: Prod. IIT-Kanpur.

Balduzzi, David and Guilio Tononi, 2009, "Qualia: The Geometry of Integrated Information", *PLOS Computational Biology*, 5(8): e1000402.

Bandyopadhyay, Anirban, 2010, *Experimental Studies on a Single Microtubule* (Google Workshop on *Quantum Biology*). VIDEO. Comp. Google TechTalks. YouTube, 22 October (https://youtu.be/VQngptkPYE8).

Barrs, Bernard J., and Adam Alanzi, 2018, "The Global Warkspace Theory", in *The Routledge handbook of Consciousness* ed. Rocco J. Gennaro, new York: Routledge.

Bayne, Tim, 2018, "On the Axiomatic Foundations of the Integrated Information Theory of Consciousness", *Neuroscience of Consciousness* 1: niy007 (doi:https://doi.org/10.1093/nc/niy007).

Berkeley, George, 1948-57, *The Works of George Berkeley*, ed. A.A. Luce and T.E. Jessop, 9 vols, London and Edinburgh: Thomas Nelson and Sons.

Bhatt, S.R., 2002, "Plotinus and Vedanta", *Neoplatonism and Indian Philosophy*, Albany, NY: State University of New York Press.

Bhatta, Jayanta, 1936, *Nyāyamañjarī*, ed. Suryanarayan Shukla, Benares: Chowkhamba.

Bhushan, Braj, 2017, *A Brief Introduction to Psychology*, Prod. IIT-KANPUR, Kanpur, 14 August.

———, 2021, *A Brief Introduction to Psychology*. Comp. IIT Kanpur.Swayam-Nptel, Kanpur (https://nptel.ac.in/courses/109104093).

Bilimoria, Purusottama, 1985, " 'Jñāna' and 'Ramā': The Logic of Knowing — A Critical Appraisal", *Journal of Indian Philosophy*, 13(2): 73-102 (https://www.jstor.org/stable/23444229).

Birhane, Abeba, 2017, "Descartes Was Wrong: 'A Person Is a Person Through Other Persons'", *Aeon*, ed. Sally Davies, 7 April (https://aeon.co/ideas/descartes-was-wrong-a-person-is-a-person-through-other-persons).

Bondebjerg, I.B., 2015, "The Embodied Mind: When Biology Meets Culture and Society", *Palgrave Communications*, 1: 1-15 (https://doi.org/10.1057/palcomms.2015.15).

Bragg, Melvyn, 2008, "Godel's Incompleteness Theorems", *In Our Time*, MP3 (accessed on 19 July 2021) (https://www.bbc.co.uk/programmes/b00dshx3).

Braine, David, 1998, "Negative Theology", in *Routledge Encyclopedia of Philosophy*, ed. Edward Craig (doi:10.4324/9780415249126-K053-1).

Brooks, Samantha, 2016, "A Debate on Working Memory and Cognitive Control: Can We Learn about the Treatment of Substance Use Disorders from the Neural Correlates of Anorexia Nervosa?", *BMC Psychiatry*, 16 January (https://doi.org/10.1186/s12888-016-0714-z).

Brown, W. Norman, 1961, "Some Ethical Concepts for the Modern World from Hindu and Indian Buddhist Tradition", in *Rabindranath Tagore: A Centenary*, ed. S. Radhakrishnan, New Delhi: Sahitya Akademi.

Carabotti, Marilia et al., 2015, "The Gut-rain Axis: Interactions between Enteric Microbiota, Central and Enteric Nervous Systems", *Annals of Gastroenterology*, 28(2): 203-09.

Carruthers, P., 1996, *Language, Thought, and Consciousness: An Essay in Philosophical Psychology*, Cambridge: Cambridge University Press.

Cavanna, Andrea Eugeni and Andrea Nani, 2014, *Consciousness*, Heidelberg: Springer.

Cepelewicz, Jordana, 2022, "This Animal's Behavior Is Mechanically Programmed", *Quanta Magazine*, 16 March.

Chakrabarti, Kisor Kumar, 2001, *Classical Indian Philosophy of Mind*, Delhi: Motilal Banarsidass.

Chakravarthy, V. Srinivasa, 2019, *Demystifying the Brain*, Singapore: Springer Nature Singapore Pte Ltd.

Chalmers, D.J., 1995, "Facing up to the Problem of Consciousness", *Journal of Consciousness Studies*, 2(3): 200-219.

———, 1996, *The Conscious Mind: In Search of a Fundamental Theory*, New York: Oxford University Press.

———, 2000, "What is a Neural Correlate of Consciousness?", in *Neural Correlates of Consciousness: Empirical and Conceptual Questions*, ed. Thomas Metzinger, pp. 17-41, Cambridge, MA: MIT Press.

———, 2003, "The Matrix as Metaphysics", in *Philosophers Explore the Matrix*, ed. Christopher Grau, Oxford: Oxford University Press.

———, 2003a, "Consciousness and Its Place in Nature", *The Blackwell Guide to Philosophy of Mind*: 102-42.

——, 2017, "Naturalistic Dualism", in *The Blackwell Companion to Consciousness*, ed. Susan Schneider and Max Velmans, pp. 363-73, London: Wiley-Blackwell.

Churchland, P.M., 1981, "Eliminative Materialism and the Propositional Attitudes", *Journal of Philosophy*, 78: 75.

Clifford Morgan, Richard King, John Weisz and John Schopler, 2017, *Introduction to Psychology*, New Delhi: McGraw Hill Education.

Copi, Irving M., Carl Cohen, and Kenneth McMahon, 2014, *Introduction to Logic*, Essex: Pearson Education.

Crick, Francis, 1995, *The Astonishing Hypothesis: The Scientific Search for the Soul*, 1st repr., New York: Simon and Schuster.

Crick, Francis and Christof Koch, 1990, "Towards a Neurobiological Theory of Consciousness", *Seminars in the Neurosciences*, 2: 263-75.

———, 1998, "Consciousness and Neuroscience", *Cerebral Cortex*, 375: 121-23.

———, 2003, "A Framework for Consciousness", *Nature Neuroscience*, 6: 119-26.

———, 2005, "What Is the Function of the Claustrum?", *Philosophical Transactions*, 360(1458): 1271-79.

Cummins, Philip Damien, 2008, "Berkeley's Likeness Principle", *Journal of the History of Philosophy* (Project MUSE), 4(1): 63-69 (doi:10.1353/hph.2008.1363).

Damasio, Antonio, 1994, *Descartes' Error: Emotion, Reason, and the Human Brain*, New York: Putnam's Sons.

———, 1999, *The Feeling of What Happens: Body and Emotion in the Making of Consciousness*, New York: Harcourt College Publishers and Orlando: Harcourt Brace.

———, 2001, "Descartes' Error Revisited", *Journal of the History of the Neurosciences*, 10(2): 192-94. doi:10.1076/jhin. 10.2.192.7250.

——, 2010, *Self Comes to Mind: Constructing the Conscious Brain*, New York: Pantheon.

——, 2021, *Feeling & Knowing: Making Minds Conscious*, New York: Pantheon.

Dasgupta, Surendranath, 2018, *A History of Indian Philosophy*, vols 1 and 3, New Delhi: Rupa Publications.

David, Balduzzi, Giulio Tononi, 2009, "Qualia: The Geometry of Integrated Information", *PLOS Computational Biology*, 5(8) (journal.pcbi.1000462. doi:10.1371/).

Davidson, Donald, 1970, "Mental Events", in *Experience and Theory*, ed. L. Foster and J.W. Swanson, pp. 79-101, Amherst, MA: University of Massachusetts Press.

——, 1993, "Thinking Causes", in *Mental Causation*, ed. John Heil and Alfred Mele, pp. 3-18, Oxford: Clarendon Press.

Dehaene, Stanislas, 2014, *Consciousness and the Brain: Deciphering How the Brain Codes Our Thoughts*, New York, NY: Penguin Publishing Group.

Dennett, Daniel C., 1988, "Quining Qualia", in *Consciousness in Modern Science*, ed. A. Bisiach and E. Marcel, New York: Oxford University Press.

——, 1991, *Consciousness Explained*, London: Penguin Press.

Descartes, Renè, 2019, *The Principles of Philosophy*, Munich: BookRix.

Dubray, Charles Albert, 1911, "Naturalism", in *The Catholic Encyclopedia*, vol. 10, ed. Charles Herbermann, New York: Robert Appleton Company. (https://en.wikisource.org/wiki/Catholic_Encyclopedia_(1913)/Naturalism).

Edelman, Gerald, 2007, *Second Nature: Brain Science and Human Knowledge*, New Haven, Connecticut: Yale University Press.

Emm, Quigley, 2017, "Microbiota–Brain-Gut Axis and Neurodegenerative Diseases", *Current Neurology and Neuroscience Reports*, 17 (doi:10.1007/s11910-017-0802-6).

Encyclopedia (ed.), 2022, "Homeostasis", *Encyclopedia Britannica*, 8 April (https://www.britannica.com/science/homeostasis).

Fallon, Francis, 2018, "Integrated Information Theory", in *The Routledge Handbook of Consciousness*, ed. Rocco J. Gennaro, pp. 137-48, New York: Taylor & Francis.

Feynman, Richard, 1970, "The Feynman Lectures on Physics" (https://www.feynmanlectures.caltech.edu/I_04.html).

Feynman, R., R. Leighton, and M. Sands, 2013, "Quantum Mechanics: The Feynman Lectures on Physics, Volume III", *California Institute of Technology* (accessed on 9 March 2021) (https://www.feynmanlectures.caltech.edu/III_toc.html).

Francisco, J. Varela, Evan Thompson and Eleanor Rosch, 2016, *The Embodied Mind: Cognitive Science and Human Experience*, Cambridge, Massachusetts: The MIT Press.

Gallese, Vittorio and Alvin Goldman, 1998, "Mirror Neurons and the Simulation Theory of Mind-reading", *Trends in Cognitive Sciences*, 2(12): 493-501 (doi:https://doi.org/10.1016/S1364-6613(98)01262-5).

Ganeri, Jonardon, 2012, *The Self-Naturalism, Consciousness, and the First-Person Stance*, Oxford: Oxford University Press.

Garber, Daniel, 2001, *Descartes Embodied*, Cambridge: Cambridge University Press.

Gauḍapāda, Śaṅkara, 1949, *Māṇḍūkya Upaniṣad* (*Gauḍapāda Kārikā and Śāṅkarabhāṣya*), tr. Swami Nikhilananda (https://www.wisdomlib.

org/hinduism/book/mandukya-upanishad-karika-bhashya/d/doc143605.html).

Gibbs, Phil, 1996, http://math.ucr.edu/home/baez/physics/General/occam.html.

Gödel, Kurt, 1992, *On Formally Undecidable Propositions of Principia Mathematica and Related Systems*, New York: Dover Publications.

Gohn, R. Scarle, 1997, *The Mystery of Consciousness*, New York: New York Review of Books.

Graham, George, 2019, "The Stanford Encyclopedia of Philosophy", in *Behaviorism*, ed. Edward N. Zalta, March (accessed on 3 April 2022) (https://plato.stanford.edu/archives/spr2019/entries/behaviorism/).

Guha, Nirmalya, 2016, "A Monstrous Inference called Mahāvidyānumāna", *Journal of Indian Philosophy* (Springer Verlag), 44(3): 557-79.

Guitchounts, Grigori, 2017, "A Brainless Breakthrough in Neuroscience", *Nautilus*, 30 November.

Gupta, Bina, 2003, *CIT Consciousness*, New Delhi: Oxford University Press.

Gupta, Sanjukta, 1966, *Studies in the Philosophy of Madhusudan Saraswati*, Calcutta: Sanskrit Pustak Bhandar.

Gutfreund, Yoram, Framework, 2018, *The Mind-Evolution Problem: The Difficulty of Fitting Consciousness in an Evolutionary, Frontiers in Psychology* (doi:10.3389/fpsyg.2018.01537).

Hacker, Paul, 1995, *Philology and Confrontation: Paul Hacker on Traditional and Modern Vedanta*, Albany, NY: State University New York Press.

Hameroff, Stuart, 2006, "Consciousness, the Brain, and Spacetime Geometry", *Annals of the New York Academy of Sciences* (New York Academy of Sciences), 929(1): 74-104. (https://doi.org/10.1111/j.1749-6632.2001.tb05709.x).

———, 2012, "How Quantum Brain Biology Can Rescue Conscious Free Will", *Frontiers in Integrative Neuroscience*, 6 (doi:10.3389/fnint.2012.00093).

Hameroff, Stuart and Roger Penrose, 2014, "Consciousness in the Universe: A Review of the 'Orch OR Theory' ", *Physics of Life Reviews* (Elsevier) 11 (1): 39-78 (doi:https://doi.org/10.1016/j.plrev.2013.08.002).

Hebb, Donald, 1949, *The Organization of Behavior*, New York: Wiley & Sons.

Hegde, Shantala, 2017, "Music Therapy for Mental Disorder and Mental Health: The Untapped Potential of Indian Classical Music", *BJPsych International*, 14(2): 31-33.

Hoffman, Donald, 2016, "Does Consciousness Cause the Cosmos?", interview by Robert Lawrence Kuhn, Youtube. July 5 (https://youtu.be/Jv25EcaUQBo).

———, 2019, *The Case Against Reality: How Evolution Hid the Truth from Our Eyes*, London, UK: Penguin Books Limited.

Horgan, John, 2015, "Can Integrated Information Theory Explain Consciousness?", *Scientific American* (1 December). (http://blogs.scientificamerican.com/cross-check/can-integrated-information-theory-explain-consciousness/).

Huxley, T.H., 1874, "On the Hypothesis that Animals Are Automata and Its History", *The Fortnightly Review*, 95: 240.

Jackson, F., 1982, "Epiphenomenal Qualia", *Philosophical Quarterly*, 32: 126-36.

Johnson, Mark, 2006, "Mind Incarnate: From Deuey to Damasio", *Daedalus*, 135(3): 46-54.

Kak, Subhash, 2000, "The Gods Within: On the Vedic Understanding of Mind and Neuroscience", *Adyar Library Bulletin*, 64: 7-55.

Kaplan, Stephen, 1983, "Mind, Māyā, and Holography: A Phenomenology of Projection", *Philosophy East and West* (University of Hawai'i Press), 33(4): 367-78 (https://www.jstor.org/stable/1398595).

Kemmerer, David, 2015, "Are We Ever Aware of Concepts?: A Critical Question for the Global Neuronal Workspace, Integrated Information, and Attended Intermediate-Level Representation Theories of Consciousness", *Neuroscience of Consciousness*, 1 (doi:https://doi.org/10.1093/nc/niv006).

Kim, Jaegwon, 2008, *Physicalism, or Something Near Enough*, Princeton, NJ: Princeton University Press.

——, 2011, *Philosophy of Mind*, Boulder, CO: Westview Press.

Kirkeben, Geir, 2001, "Descartes Embodied Psychology: Descartes or Damasio's Error?", *Journal of the History of the Neurosciences*, 10(2): 173-91 (doi:10.1076/jhin.10.2.173.7255).

Kissin, Benjamin, 2011, *Conscious and Unconscious Programs in the Brain*, New York, NY: Springer.

Kleisiaris, Christos F. et al., 2014, "Health Care Practices in Ancient Greece: The Hippocratic Ideal", *Journal of Medical Ethics and History of Medicine*, 7(1): 6.

Kripke, Saul, 1980, *Naming and Necessity*, Cambridge, MA: Harvard University Press.

Kuppuswamy, B., 1993, *Sourcebook of Indian Psychology*, Delhi: Konark Publishers.

——, 2001, *Elements of Ancient Indian Psychology*, Delhi: Konark Publishers.

Larson, Gerald James, 2011, *Classical Samkhya: An Interpretation of Its History and Meaning*, Delhi: Motilal Banarsidass.

Levine, Joseph, 1983, "Materialism and Qualia: The Explan for Gap Pacific", *Philosophical Quarterly*, 64(4): 354-61.

Libet, Benjamin, 2004, *Mind Time: The Temporal Factor in Consciousness*, Cambridge, MA: Harvard University Press.

Locke, J., 1689/1975, *Essay Concerning Human Understanding*, Oxford: Oxford University Press.

Lokhorst, Gert-Jan, 2021, "Descartes and the Pineal Gland", in *The Stanford Encyclopedia of Philosophy*, ed. Edward N. Zalta, Metaphysics Research Lab, Stanford University (https://plato.stanford.edu/archives/win2021/entries/pineal-gland/).

Lombardi, Olimpia, and Cristian López, 2018, "What Does 'Information' Mean in Integrated Information Theory?", *Entropy (Basel)*, 20(12): 894 (doi: 10.3390/e20120894).

Luce, Arthur, 1968, *Berkeley's Immaterialism: A Commentary on His "A Treatise Concerning the Principles of Human Knowledge"*, New York: Russell and Russell.

Lycan, William, 1996, "The Blackwell Companion to Philosophy", in *Philosophy of Mind*, ed. Nicholas Bunnin and Eric Tsui-James, pp. 173-201, Oxford: Blackwell Publishers.

Maurer, Walter H., 1975, "A Re-examination of Rigveda", *The Journal of Indo-European Studies*, 3(3): 217-38.

Mayeda, Sengaku, 1979, *A Thousand Teachings: The Upadeśasāhasrī of Śaṅkara*, Stony Brook, NY: State University of New York Press.

Metzinger, T. (ed.), 2000, *Neural Correlates of Consciousness: Empirical and Conceptual Questions*, Massachusetts: MIT Press.

———, 2006, "Mind Incarnate: From Dewey to Damasio", *Daedalus* 135(3): 46-54 (http://www.jstor.org/stable/20028051).

Mill, John Stuart, 2002, *A System of Logic*, Honolulu: University Press of the Pacific.

Misra, Vācaspati Īśvarakṛṣṇa, 1995, *Sāṁkhyakārikā of Īśvarakṛṣṇa with the Tattva-Kaumudī*, tr. Swami Virupakshanand, Madras: Sri Ramakrishna Math.

Morgan, Clifford, Richard King, John Weisz and John Schopler, 2017, *Introduction to Psychology*, New Delhi: McGraw Hill Education.

Moser, Edvard I., 2016, *The Future of the Brain: Essays by the World's Leading Neuroscientists*, ed. Jeremy Freeman Gary Marcus, Princeton, NJ: Princeton University Press.

Muni, Vidyaranya, 2018, *Vivarana Prameya Sangraha*, Varanasi: Sampurnanand Sanskrit University.

Nagel, Thomas, 1974, "What Is It Like to Be a Bat?", *Philosophical Review*, 83(4): 439.

von Neumann, John, 1955, *Mathematical Foundations of Quantum Mechanics*, ed. and tr. Robert Thomas Beyer, Princeton, NJ: Princeton University Press.

——, 2012, *The Computer and the Brain*, ed. Ray Kurzweil, New Haven and London: Yale University Press.

Newell, A., 1990, *Unified Theories of Cognition*, Cambridge: Harvard University Press.

Nolte, D.D., 2010, "The Tangled Tale of Phase Space", *Physics Today*, 63(4): 33-38 (doi:10.1063/1.3397041).

Norelius, Per-Johan, 2016, "The Honey-Eating Birds and the Tree of Life: Notes on Ṛgveda 1.164.20-22", *Acta Orientalia*, 3-70.

O'Flaherty, Wendy Doniger, 1981, *The Rig Veda: An Anthology*, New York: Penguin Books.

Oizumi, M., L. Albantakis and G. Tononi, 2014, "From the Phenomenology to the Mechanisms of Consciousness: Integrated Information Theory 3.0", *PLOS Computational Biology*, 10(5) (doi:10.1371/journal.pcbi.1003588).

Otto, Edward, 2008, "Attractor Dimensions", *Scholarpedia*, 3(3): 2110 (doi:10.4249/scholarpedia.2110).

Pais, Abraham, 2005, *Subtle Is the Lord*, Oxford: Oxford University Press.

Paulson, Steve, 2017, "Roger Penrose on Why Consciousness Does Not Compute", 27 April (accessed on 14 January 2022) (https://nautil.us/roger- penrose-on-why-consciousness-does-not-compute-6127/#!).

Patañjali, 1988, *Patañjali's Yogasūtras with the Commentary of Vyasa and the Gloss of Vachaspati Misra*, tr. Rama Prasad, New Delhi: Munshiram Manoharlal.

Peak, David, Jevin D. West, Susanna M. Messinger, and Keith A. Mott, 2004, "Evidence for Complex, Collective Dynamics and Emergent, Distributed Computation in Plants", *Proceedings of the National Academy of Sciences*, 101(4): 918-22 (doi:10.1073/pnas.0307811100).

Penrose, Roger, 2004, *The Road to Reality: A Complete Guide to the Laws of the Universe*, London: Jonathan Cape.

——, 2005, *Shadows of the Mind*, London: Vintage Books.

——, 2016, *The Emperor's New Mind*, Oxford: Oxford University Press.

———, 2019, Interview by Robert Lawrence Kuhn, "Why Explore Cosmos and Consciousness?", *Closer to Truth*, 15 July (accessed on 21 March 2021).

———, 2022, Interview by Jordan Peterson, "Asking A Theoretical Physicist About The Physics of Consciousness", Youtube, 14 April (https://youtu.be/Qi9ys2j1ncg).

Penrose, Roger and Stuart Hameroff, 2011, "Consciousness in the Universe: Neuroscience, Quantum Space-Time Geometry, and Orch OR Theory", *Journal of Cosmology*, 14.

Pepperell, R., 2018, "Consciousness as a Physical Process Caused by the Organization of Energy in the Brain", *Frontiers in Psychology* (doi:10.3389/fpsyg.2018.02091).

Place, U.T., 1956, "Is Consciousness a Brain Process?", *British Journal of Psychology*, 47: 44-50.

Popova, Maria, Albert Einstein and Rabindranath Tagore, 2012, "When Einstein Met Tagore: A Remarkable Meeting of Minds on the Edge of Science and Spirituality", *The Marginalian*, 27 April (accessed on 23 March 2022) (https://www.themarginalian.org/2012/04/27/when-einstein-met-tagore/).

Praśastapādācārya, Śrīdhara Bhaṭṭa, 1982, *Padārthadharmasaṁgraha of Praśastapāda: With the Nyāyakandalī of Śrīdhara*, tr. Ganganatha Jha, Varanasi: Chaukhambha Orientalia.

Primas, Hans, 2005, "Complementarity of Mind and Matter", in *Recasting Reality: Wolfgang Paulis's Philosophical Ideas and Contemporary Science*, pp. 171-209, Berlin and Heidelberg: Springer.

Primas, Hans and Harald Atmanspacher (eds), 2009, *Recasting Reality*, Heidelberg/Berlin: Springer-Verlag.

Princess Elisabeth of Bohemia, 1969, "Letter to Descartes, May 6-16, 1643", in *Descartes: Philosophical Writings*, tr. Elizabeth Anscombe and Peter Thomas Geach, pp. 274-75, London: Nelson.

Puccetti, Roland, 1977, "The Great C-fiber Myth: A Critical Note", *Philosophy of Science*, 44(2): 303-05.

Putnam, Hilary, 1967, "Art, Mind, and Religion", in *The Nature of Mental States*, ed. W.H. Capitan and D.D. Merrill, Pittsburgh: Pittsburgh University Press.

——, 1988, *Representation and Reality*, Cambridge, MA: MIT Press.

Raatikainen, Panu, 2022, "Gödel's Incompleteness Theorems", in *The Stanford Encyclopedia of Philosophy*, ed. Edward N. Zalta, Metaphysics Research Lab, Stanford University (https://plato.stanford.edu/archives/spr2022/entries/goedel-incompleteness).

Radhakrishnan, Sarvepalli, 1947, *Religion and Society*, London: George Allen and Unwin.

——, 2008, *Indian Philosophy*, 2 vols, New Delhi: Oxford University Press.

——, 2019 (1994), *The Principal Upanishads*, New Delhi: HarperCollins.

Rao, K. Ramakrishna and Anand C. Paranjpe, 2017, *Psychology in the Indian Tradition*, New Delhi: D.K. Printworld.

Rao, S.K. Ramachandra, 1960, *Shankar: A Psychological Study*, Mysore: Kavyalaya Publishers.

——, 1962, *Development of Psychological Thought in India*, Mysore: Kavyalaya Publishers.

Robb, David and John Heil, 2021, *Mental Causation*, ed. Edward N. Zalta (https://plato.stanford.edu/archives/spr2021/entries/mental-causation).

Rovelli, Carlo, 2014, *Seven Brief Lessons on Physics*, tr. Simon Carnell and Erica Segre, New Delhi: Penguin Random House UK.

Roy, Sisir and Rajakishore Nath, 2022, *Understanding Mind through the Lens of Artificial Intelligence*, Department of Philosophy and Religion, BHU, Varanasi, 26 March (https://youtu.be/0FJSb5Jfa14).

Ryle, Gilbert, 2002, *The Concept of Mind*, Chicago: University of Chicago Press.

Sahni, Vishal, 2015, "Consciousness in the Universe: Review of the 'Orch or' Theory_176 Prof Stuart Hameroff", *Workshop by Quantum and Nano Computing Virtual Center*. Video. Comp. Vidya-Mitra. Prod. Quantum and Nano Computing Virtual center. Youtube 20 May (https://youtu.be/nxECZwhXSt8).

Saksena, Shri Krishna, 1944, *Nature of Consciousness in Hindu Philosophy*, Benares: Nand Kishore & Bros.

Śaṅkara, 1931, *Dr̥g-Dr̥śya-Viveka: An Inquiry into the Nature of the Seer and the Seen*, ed. Swami Nikhilananda, Calcutta: Advaita Ashrama.

Śaṅkarācārya, 1932, *Vivekacūḍāmaṇi*, Kolkata: Advaita Ashrama.

Śaṅkarācārya 1979, *A Thousand Teachings: The Upadeśasāhasrī of Śaṅkara*, by Sengaku Mayeda, Stony Brook, NY: State University of New York Press.

——, 2000, *Brahmasūtra Bhāṣya*, tr. Swami Gambhirananda, Kolkata: Advaita Ashrama.

Satsangi, Prem Saran and Stuart Hameroff (eds), 2016, *Consciousness: Integrating Eastern and Western Perspectives*, New Delhi: New Age Books.

Schafer, Lothar, Interview by Robert Lawrence Kuhn, 2022, *Quantum Physics of Consciousness*. Youtube, 28 April (https://youtu.be/YvphbU2qRA0).

Schneider, Susan, 2017, "Daniel Dennett on the Nature of Consciousness", in *The Blackwell Companion to Consciousness*, ed. Max Velmans and

Susan Schneider, John Wiley & Sons Ltd. (https://doi.org/10.1002/9781119132363.ch22).

Schrödinger, Erwin, 2012, *What is Life*?, Cambridge: Cambridge University Press.

Schweizer, Paul, 2019, "Sāṁkhya-Yoga Philosophy and the Mind-Body Problem", *Prabuddha Bharata*, 124(1): 232-42.s

Searle, J., 1980, "Minds, Brains and Programs", *Behavioral and Brain Sciences*, 3: 417-57.

——, 1992, "Interview by Robert Lawrence Kuhn", *The Rediscovery of Mind*, Massachusetts: MIT Press.

——, 2016, Interview by Robert Lawrence Kuhn, "John Searle: Solutions to the Mind–Body Problem?". (YouTube 29 February) https://youtu.be/IgWbExnceHE (accessed on 3 April 2022).

Searle, John R., Daniel Clement Dennett, and David John Chalmers, 1997, *The Mystery of Consciousness*, New York: New York Review of Books.

Seife, Charles, 2006, *Decoding the Universe*, New York: Viking.

Seth, A.K., 2004a, "Evoluting Action Selection and Selective Attention Without Action, Attention or Selection", in *Synergistics and Psychology*, vol. 3, ed. V. Shendyapin, I. Trotimoua, and V. Arshinou, pp. 225-43, Moslow Logi to Press.

Seth, Anil K. and Bernard J. Baars, 2004, "Neural Darwinism and Consciousness", *Consciousness and Cognition* (Elsevier Inc.), 14: 140-68 (doi:10.1016/j.concog. 2004.08.008).

Smith, L., 1986, *Behaviorism and Logical Positivism: A Reassessment of Their Alliance*, Stanford, CA: Stanford University Press.

Spencer, Caleb D. and Matthew J. Smith (eds), 2022, *Literature and Religious Experience: Beyond Belief and Unbelief*, London: Bloomsbury Publishing.

Sreekantan, B.V. and Sisir Roy, 2020, *Understanding Space, Time and Causality*, New York: Routledge.

Steven, Pollock, Oliver DeWolfe, and Steve Goldhaber, n.d., "Quotes about Quantum Mechanics", *University of Colorado* (accessed on 21 March 2022) (https://physicscourses.colorado.edu/phys3220/phys3220_fa08/quotes.html).

Stich, Stephen, 1983, *From Folk Psychology to Cognitive Science: The Case Against Belief*, Cambridge, MA: MIT Press.

Stuart, Michael T., Yiftach Fehige, and James R. Brown (eds), 2017, *The Routledge Companion to Thought Experiments*, New York: Taylor & Francis.

Sutton, Nicholas, 2019, *The Yoga Sutras*, San Rafael, CA: Mandala Publishing.

Tandon, Prakash Narain, 2019, "Jagdish Chandra Bose & Plant Neurobiology", *The Indian Journal of Medical Research*, 149: 593-99 (doi:10.4103/ijmr.IJMR_392_19).

Tanney, Julia, 2021, "Gilbert Ryle", in *The Stanford Encyclopedia of Philosophy*, ed. Edward N. Zalta, June (https://plato.stanford.edu/archives/sum2021/entries/ryle/) (accessed on 3 April 2022).

Tegmark, Max, 2014, *Our Mathematical Universe*, New York: Knopt Doubleday and Penguin.

Tejomayananda, Swami, 2018, *Divinising the Mind: Siva-Sankalpa Suktam*, Mumbai: Central Chinmaya Mission Trust.

Tononi, Giulio, 2008, "Consciousness as Integrated Information: A Provisional", *Biological Bulletin*, 215(3).

Tononi, Giulio and Christof Koch, 2015, "Consciousness: Here, There and Everywhere?", *Philosophical Transactions of the Royal Society B: Biological Sciences* 370 (1668): 20140167 (https://doi.org/10.1098/rstb.2014.0167).

Tripathi, K.M., 2014, "Concept and Scope of Pratyāhāra in Management of Mental Health", in *Foundations and Applications of Indian Psychology*, ed. R.M. Matthijs Cornelissen, Girishwar Misra, and Suneet Varma, Noida: Dorling Kindersley (India).

Turing, A.M., 1950, "Computing Machinery and Intelligence", *Mind*, 49(236): 433-60 (doi:https://doi.org/10.1093/mind/LIX.236.433).

Tuszynski, Jack A. (ed.), 2006, *The Emerging Physics of Consciousness*, Berlin/Heidelberg: Springer.

Tye, Michael, 1997, *Ten Problems of Consciousness: A Representational Theory of Phenomenal Mind*, Cambridge, MA: MIT Press.

———, 2006, "Absent Qualia and the Mind–Body Problem", *Philosophical Review*, 115(2): 140.

Vaihinger, H., 1924/1935, *The Philosophy of "As if": A System of the Theoretical, Practical and Religious Fictions of Mankind*, tr. C.K. Ogden, London: Routledge & Kegan Paul (https://en.wikipedia.org/w/index.php?title= Hans_Vaihinger&oldid=1022668612).

Varela, Francisco J., Evan Thompson and Eleanor Rosch, 2016, *The Embodied Mind: Cognitive Science and Human Experience*, Cambridge, MA: MIT Press.

Vatsyayana, 1939, *Nyāyasūtras of Gautama with Vātsyāyana Bhāṣya*, tr. Ganganatha Jha, Poona: Oriental Book Agency.

Vidyabhaskar, Ramavatar, 2012, *Pañcadaśī*, Varanasi: Chowkhambha Sanskrit Pratishthan.

Walther, Eric, 2001, "Damasio on Consciousness", *Iyyun: The Jerusalem Philosophical Quarterly* (S.H. Bergman Center for Philosophical Studies): 63-72 (https://www.jstor.org/stable/23352803).

Werner, Karel, 1977, "Symbolism in the Vedas and Its Conceptualisation", *Numen* (Brill), 24: 223-40.

Westphal, Jonathan, 2016, *The Mind–Body Problem*, Cambridge, MA: MIT Press.

Whicher, Ian, 2000, *The Integrity of the Yoga Darśana: A Reconsideration of Classical Yoga*, New Delhi: D.K. Printworld (first published by State University of New York Press, Albany in 1998).

Wigner, Eugene and Henry Margenau, 1967, "Remarks on the Mind–Body Question, in Symmetries and Reflections, Scientific Essays", *American Journal of Physics*, 35(12): 1169-70 (doi:10.1119/1.1973829).

Wigner, Eugene Paul, Jagdish Mehra, and A.S. Wightman, 1995, *The Collected Works of Eugene Paul Wigner*, vol. 6, ed. Jagdish Mehra, Berlin: Springer.

Wigner, Eugene P., 1995/1997, "Remarks on the Mind-body Question", in *Philosophical Reflection and Syntheses*, pp. 247-60, Berlin/Heidelberg: Springer.

Wikipedia Contributors, 2020, "Ahimsa in Jainism", *Wikipedia: The Free Encyclopedia*, 11 July (accessed on 19 July 2020).

——, 2022a, "Cortical Homunculus", 5 February (https://en.wikipedia.org/w/index.php?title=Cortical_homunculus&oldid=1070134249) (accessed on 4 April 2022).

———, 2022b, "Phineas Gage", *Wikipedia: The Free Encyclopedia*, (https://en.wikipedia.org/w/index.php?title=Phineas_Gage&oldid=1079986785) (accessed on 29 March).

———, 2022c, "Phrenology", 7 March (https://en.wikipedia.org/w/index.php?title=Phrenology&oldid=1075762591) (accessed on 3 April).

———, 2022d, "Supervenience", 27 March (https://en.wikipedia.org/w/index.php?title=Supervenience&oldid=1079475515) (accessed on 3 April 2022).

———, 2022e, "Cartesian Theater", (https://en.wikipedia.org/w/index.php?title=Cartesian_theater&oldid=1061417920) (accessed on 9 June 2022).

Wikisource, 2021, "The Rig Veda/Mandala 1/Hymn 164" (https://en.wikisource.org/w/index.php?title=The_Rig_Veda/Mandala_1/Hymn_164&oldid=11721526) (accessed on 3 January 2022).

Wills, Peter R., 2016, "DNA as Information", The Royal Society Publishing, (https://royalsocietypublishing.org/doi/10.1098/rsta.2015.0417) (accessed on 13 March).

Wittgenstein, Ludwig, 1953, *Philosophical Investigations*, tr. G.E.M. Anscombe, New York: Macmillan.

Zeki, S.M., 1978, "Functional Specialization in the Visual Cortex of the Rhesus Monkey", *Nature*, 274: 423-28 (doi: https://doi.org/10.1038/274423a0).

Zimmer, Carl, 2013, "The Virus That Learns", *National Geographic*, 27 February (https://www.nationalgeographic.com/science/phenomena/2013/02/27/the-virus-that-learns/).

Zyga, Lisa, 2015, "Physicists Find Quantum Coherence and Quantum Entanglement are Two Sides of the Same Coin", *Phys.org* (25 June). (https://phys.org/news/2015-06-physicists-quantum-coherence-entanglement-sides.html).

Subject Index

Name and Title Index